The Law/Politics Distinction in Contemporary Public Law Adjudication

THE LAW/POLITICS DISTINCTION IN CONTEMPORARY PUBLIC LAW ADJUDICATION

Edited by

BOGDAN IANCU

eleven international publishing

Published, sold and distributed by Eleven International Publishing
P.O. Box 358
3500 AJ Utrecht, The Netherlands
Tel.: +31 30 231 0545
Fax: +31 30 225 8045
info@elevenpub.com
www.elevenpub.com

Sold and distributed in USA and Canada
International Specialized Book Services
920 NE 58th Avenue, Suite 300
Portland, OR 97213-3786, USA
Tel.: +1 800 944 6190 (toll-free)
Fax: +1 503 280 8832
orders@isbs.com
www.isbs.com

Printed on acid-free paper.

ISBN: 978-90-77596-65-4

Printed in The Netherlands

Table of Contents

List of Contributors

Adam Czarnota
Associate Professor of Law and Director, European Law Centre, University of New South Wales, Sydney, Australia

Dieter Grimm
Former Justice of the German Constitutional Court, Professor Dr. Dr. h. c. (Emeritus) Humboldt University of Berlin, and Permanent Fellow, Wissenschaftskolleg zu Berlin-Institute for Advanced Study

Bogdan Iancu
Lecturer in Public Law, University of Bucharest, Faculty of Political Science

Christian Joerges
Research Professor of Law, University of Bremen, Law Department

Roderick A. Macdonald
F. R. Scott Professor of Constitutional and Public Law, McGill University, Faculty of Law

Thomas McMorrow
Doctoral Candidate, McGill University, Faculty of Law

Armand de Mestral
Jean Monnet Professor in the Law of International Economic Integration at McGill University, Faculty of Law and Co-Director of the Institute of European Studies (McGill-Université de Montréal)

Alexander Somek
Charles E. Floete Chair in Law, University of Iowa College of Law

Bernd Rüthers
Professor Dr. iur. dres h.c. (Emeritus) of Law, University of Constanz

András Sajó
University Professor of Law (on leave), Central European University, Budapest, Law Department; Judge, European Court of Human Rights

Jan A. Winter
Professor of European Community Law, Free University of Amsterdam

Acknowledgements

Earlier versions of most papers collected in this volume were presented in Bucharest, in 2007 and 2008, at the conferences "The Law/Politics Distinction in Contemporary Public Law Adjudication" and "The Role of Law in Periods of System Transformation."

Both conferences were hosted by the New Europe College-Institute for Advanced Study and generously funded by the Hertie-Stiftung, Frankfurt/Main, within the Program *Exzellenznetzwerk Deutschland-Südosteuropa*/Networks of Excellence Germany – South-Eastern Europe.

I chose the general themes and conceptual breakdowns of these conferences in consultation with Professor Dieter Grimm, to whom thanks are due for advice and support. I owe a debt of gratitude and affection to Dr. Katharina Biegger, Mrs. Marina Hasnaş, Professor Anca Oroveanu, and Professor Andrei Pleşu, all associated with (and, indeed, constituting) the New Europe College. I thank Ms. Marianne Ojo and the Center for European Law and Politics at the University of Bremen for editorial assistance. Special thanks are due to Professor Corina Petrescu, whose friendship and graceful nature I kept exploiting for editorial and style support, and who elegantly pretended to be always happy to help.

Bogdan Iancu

Law/Politics Distinctions – The Elusive Reference Points

The law is reason unaffected by desire.

Aristotle, Politics [Bk. III, 16, 5] (Jowett)

1.

Public (administrative and constitutional) law is sometimes referred to as "political law," especially when juxtaposed and contrasted with its traditional private counterpart. By the same token, public lawyers in academia (save perhaps for the various "legal realist" schools) seek to drive a wedge between politics and public law proper. The academic preoccupation with the law-politics distinction mirrors a practical necessity in public law adjudication. Public law, albeit "political," must not be politics.

The essential conceptual and practical problems entailed by the need to separate law from politics in adjudication are clearly illustrated by a *dictum* in one of the first administrative law decisions, which dealt with an action in replevin brought in 1598 before the Court of Common Pleas by one Rooke against the Commissioners of Sewers. The Commissioners, Rooke argued, had unlawfully assessed only his property, a long stretch of land adjacent to the bank of the river Thames, even though owners of inland properties also profited from the public works that had secured the banks against flooding; when he refused to pay, his property was taken to satisfy the assessment. The Commissioners responded in court that their governing statute gave them unfettered discretion with regard to apportionments of property assessments.

In the concluding its ruling for the plaintiff, the court replied to this bold assertion of discretionary authority as follows: "And notwithstanding the said words of the said Commission give authority to the Commissioners to

Bogdan Iancu (Ed.), The Law/Politics Distinction in Contemporary Public Law Adjudication, 1-17.

doe according to their discretions, yet their proceedings ought to be limited and bound with the rule of reason and Law. For discretion is a science or understanding to discern between falsity and truth, between right and wrong, and between shadows and substance, between equity and colorable glosses and pretenses, *and not to doe according to their wills and private affections*; for as one saith, *Talis discretio discretionem confundit*."[1]

An accusation of political abuse may have descriptive and rhetorical usefulness; we all (or perhaps each of us) have the capacity to recognize mistreatment. However, it does not have any legal-methodological value. The essential juridical problem resides in determining the ways in which a court can control an abuse of political discretion normatively. Otherwise, if arbitrariness cannot be prescriptively reduced, the decision of the judge would itself be the result of "will and private affection," the only difference being not the exercise of arbitrary power as such but its decision-making institutional venue. The crucial question is: how can adjudication and politics be legally protected from mutual abuse?

2.

The first and most evident answer to this question (conceptually as well as historically) is the institutional one. In order to ensure judicial impartiality with respect to the political branches and hence to fend off political justice, the judiciary has to be independent. Early attempts to give judges a measure of insulation from direct political influence are said to date back to the XV century, when Henry VI began to appoint Barons of the Exchequer *quamdiu se bene gesserint*, during good behavior, rather than at will, *durante bene placito*, as the practice had been.[2] The problem of judicial tenures was settled with finality in the wake of the great seventeenth-century conflicts between Parliament and the Stuarts. In 1701, the Act of Settlement entrenched the principles that future judicial commissions would only be granted *quamdiu se bene gesserint* and that removals could be effected by way of joint addresses of both Houses of Parliament to the King.[3] In 1761, George III introduced legislation to the effect that judicial commissions, unlike those of all other officers, would continue indefinitely after the demise of a sovereign, and stated publicly in the corresponding parliamentary address: "I look upon the independency and uprightness of the Judges of the land as essential to the

[1] Rooke's Case, 5 Co. Rep. 99b (1598) [first emphasis supplied]. Louis Jaffe believed that this last paragraph was most likely written by the reporter, Justice Coke. *See* L. Jaffe, *Suits Against Governments and Officers: Sovereign Immunity*, 77 Harv. L. Rev. 1 (1963-1964).

[2] *See* C. H. McIlwain, *The Tenure of English Judges*, *in* Constitutionalism and the Changing World (1939).

[3] 12 & 13 Will 3, c.2, § 3 (1701). The only judge to be removed until today was Sir Jonah Barrington of the Irish Admiralty Court, in 1830, on accusations of embezzlement.

impartial administration of justice, as one of the best securities to the rights and liberties of my loving subjects, and as most conducive to the honor of the Crown."[4] Once the new idea that judgeships constituted an independent office subordinated to the law only had been clearly affirmed, it would be further embraced and developed with almost lighting speed. On the eve of the Revolutionary war, American colonists assumed the principle of an independent judiciary to have been their common law birthright.[5] Indeed, as Benjamin Franklin pointed out in his Causes of the American Discontent before 1768, one of the main revolutionary points of contention in the American colonies was that the 1767 Townshend Acts taxed the colonists in order to raise revenues for the maintenance of a judicial system subject to whimsical at-will removals of judges by the colonial governors.[6] The long-term result of those debates would be the constitutional provision in Article III of the 1787 Constitution, to the effect that not only tenure during good behavior became a constitutionally protected value but the financial security of federal judges was also entrenched in the fundamental law, through the clause prohibiting reductions in judicial salaries. Parallel contemporaneous developments can be identified on the Continent, albeit in the guise of Enlightened despotism self-limitation rather than as claims of right. Thus, Frederick William I of Prussia officially rebuked judges who would have treated him, in a private litigation, better than the other party in dispute, as acting thus "in forgetfulness of God and their duty and lacking in conscience."[7] His son, Frederick the Great, gave a yet clearer recognition of the autonomy of courts, when he declared himself "determined never to interfere in the course of justice: in tribunals, the laws must speak and the sovereign keep silent."[8]

The converse is however also true: the sovereign (politics) must "keep silent" in judicial matters on the assumption that and inasmuch as the law and not the judge "speaks." The judge is still presupposed to be, ideal-typically at least, "only the mouthpiece of the law" (thus famously Montesquieu). Actual or perceived departures from this ideal-type are constitutionally and politically censored. This tension can be found in the institutional structure of post-war constitutional courts in Europe: the appointments of constitutional judges are expressly politicized, on the explicit recognition that their task is more

[4] 1 Geo. 3, c. 23 (1761). 15 Parl. Hist. Eng. 1007 (1761). This sentence – in republican paraphrase – would be reproduced almost verbatim in the Maryland Declaration of Rights of 1776, Art. XXX.

[5] J. H. Smith, *An Independent Judiciary: The Colonial Background*, 124 U. Pa. L. Rev. 1104 (1975-1976).

[6] *Id.*, at 1125.

[7] O. Mayer, Le droit administratif allemand [German Administrative Law] 54, n. 15 (1903).

[8] "[J]e me suis résolu à ne jamais troubler le cours de la procedure: c'est dans les tribunaux où les lois doivent parler et où le souverain doit se taire," *in* C. Schmitt, La Dictature [The Dictatorship] 303 n. 43 (2000).

political in nature.[9] The same assumption served as an impetus for the creation in France of a separate administrative justice system under the Conseil d'État. But even with respect to the independence of the "ordinary" judiciary there are numerous ambivalences and wide variations across systems. To wit, the independence of the individual judge is not coextensive with the independence of the judiciary.[10] Moreover, judiciaries which, by institutional design, are shielded from political control may well become irresponsible, self-governing, rent-seeking corporations[11] and develop pathologies, including political ones, of their own.[12]

The second level at which the law/politics question can be answered is procedural. Jurisdictional design influences judicialization trends[13] and so too does the willingness or reluctance of courts to assume jurisdiction over particular matters: extraterritorial jurisdiction is the obvious case in point.[14] Courts have also developed procedural limitations in order to avoid *ex ante*

[9] *See generally* C. Guarnieri & P. Pederzoli, The Power of Judges – A Comparative Study of Courts and Democracy (2002).

[10] *See* J. Bell, Judiciaries within Europe – A Comparative Review 26 (2006).

[11] *Cf.* M. Cappelletti, in the context of discussing judicial liability, *"Who Watches the Watchmen?" – A Comparative Study on Judicial Responsibility*, 31 Am. J. Comp. L. 1, at 48 (1983):

> Modern systems have fought against two possible, and in some ways opposite, kinds of degeneration of disciplinary liability: first, its becoming the instrument for judicial subservience to the political branches, especially the executive – hence, ultimately, its becoming just one more forms of 'political' responsibility; and, second, its being monopolized by the judiciary itself as a pure instrument of political control.

[12] This appears to be the case with the Italian High Council of the Judiciary, the most autonomous of its kind in Europe, which has developed within itself ideological (political) factions – *correnti* – competing for control of the Council and thus of the judiciary (*cf.* Guarnieri & Pederzoli, *supra* note 9, *passim*). A similar case can be made based on post-communist developments in Eastern Europe (*see* infra, my chapter on Romania). *But cf.* Bell, *supra* note 10, who sees the matter in a more benign light, as an expression of the judges' desire to air their different views about the character of justice and making themselves heard by politicians (at 25-26).

[13] *Cf.* A. Stone Sweet, Governing with Judges-Constitutional Politics in Europe (2000), arguing that, given the European context of centralized majoritarian parliamentarism, relatively difficult constitutional amendment processes, and open-ended constitutional rights provisions, the existence of abstract review referrals by parliamentarians will continuously reinforce the judicialization of politics, connecting parliamentary opposition and constitutional courts "by a kind of judicializing transmission belt" (at 55) and conditioning the political process through an ever more dense normative argumentative structure, so that the constitutional court becomes a kind of third chamber of parliament and the parliament, correspondingly, a sort of first-instance constitutional court.

[14] *See* for instance In re Yamashita, 327 U.S. 1 (1946), holding that jury trial protections do not apply to a prisoner of war tried by a military tribunal outside the United States, Johnson v. Eisentrager, 339 U.S. 763 (1950), similar, and United States v. Verdugo-Urquidez 494 U.S. 259 (1990), holding that the Fourth Amendment guarantees against "unreasonable searches and

a direct confrontation with politics. The most representative example is the vast body of "justiciability" doctrines developed by the Supreme Court of the United States around the "Case or Controversy" requirement of Article III, understood to bar the solution of constitutional and administrative issues which do not arise out of a concrete and actual controversy between litigants: standing, mootness, ripeness, the refusal to answer "political questions" or to deliver advisory opinions to the other branches of government. Last but not least, it is often argued that the intrinsic features of the judicial process constrain politicization. The fundamental characteristics of adjudication, namely, the fact that a court proceeding is not self-activating (*nemo judex sine actore*) and that courts are subject to impartiality (*nemo judex in causa propria*) and fair hearing (*audiatur et altera pars*) requirements would, according to this line of argument, function as structural rationalizing elements.[15]

But procedure is, as Bentham puts it, "adjective law" and thus, like all adjectives, it only qualifies. For instance, it can be noticed that the application of very restrictive standing limitations would have nowadays deleterious systemic consequences. The appearance of the "non-Hohfeldian" or "ideological plaintiff" is the result of non- or no longer-"Hohfeldian" legislation and legal systems.[16] But it can also be doubted that the procedural structure of adjudication can function for too long as a barrier against judicialization outside the paradigmatic decision-making setting which this procedure was essentially meant to serve. As Lon Fuller argued in his classic article on adjudication, the high demands of rationality embedded in judicial decision-making may be inextricably linked to a model of judicial decision centered on countervailing individual claims of right and duty. The rationalizing effect of the procedural structure would therefore be contingent on this more focused and limited kind of dispute resolution. Hence, the more judges are called to solve "polycentric" issues, namely matters whose consideration ricochets into a multitude of subsequent systemic factors and consequences that have to be taken into account by the decision-maker, the less useful the rationality and principled character of adjudication would be to decision-making. According to Fuller, one should always bear in mind that "[the] higher responsibility toward rationality is at once the strength *and the weakness* of adjudication as a form of social ordering."[17]

seizures" do not apply to a search conducted in Mexico, without a US court warrant, by DEA agents acting in cooperation with Mexican federal police.

[15] This is a common contemporary line of argument. *See, e.g.*, M. Cappelletti, *The Law-Making Power of the Judge and Its Limits: A Comparative Analysis*, 8 Monash U. L. Rev. 15 (1981-1982), A. Chayes, *The Role of the Judge in Public Law Litigation*, 89 Harv. L. Rev. 1281 (1975-1976) and W. Hassemer, *Politik aus Karlsruhe? [Politics from Karlsruhe?]*, 1(63) Juristen Zeitung 1 (2008).

[16] L. Jaffe, *The Citizen as Litigant in Public Actions: The Non-Hohfeldian or Ideological Plaintiff*, 116 U. Pa. L. Rev. 1033 (1967-1968).

[17] L. Fuller, *The Forms and Limits of Adjudication*, 92 Harv. L. Rev. 353, at 367 (1978) [emphasis

3.

The answer to the judicialization/politicization dilemma must consequently be sought at a third, substantive level, to which institutional and procedural safeguards are conceptually subordinated. In this respect, it has been observed that the classical constitutional state presupposed, perhaps as a condition of its possibility, the existence of foundational distinctions between private and public, internal and external.[18] Such systemic demarcations also made the distinction between law and politics clearer, by allowing the judge to relate in categorically different ways to the exercise of various types and domains of state action.

The conceptual justification is apparent in Locke's normative theory of separation of powers. In his argument, from the limitation of legislation to the enactment of "settled standing laws … stated rules of right and property,"[19] derives as a consequence the "ministerial" nature of the "executive" power (by executive Locke understands the application – enforcement and interpretation- of a legislative norm).[20] Namely, when the jurisdiction of the legislature is normatively limited to rules of just conduct, the application of the rule, its enforcement and interpretation, will be unproblematic, more or less a subsumption of rules to facts. Yet, from this limitation, itself a corollary of the limited trust that government is, further derive two kinds of state functions, called in the *Second Treatise* the "federative" and the "prerogative" power,[21] which are characterized as discretionary in essence. Their exercise cannot be predetermined, conditioned, by an "antecendent, promulgated, standing rule." True, Locke does not want to equate discretion with arbitrariness and repeatedly asserts that these powers should be carried out "in the public good."

in original]. Similar argument in a more polemical key, P. Devlin, *Judges and Lawmakers*, 39 Mod. L. Rev. 1 (1976).

[18] *Cf.* D. Grimm, *The Constitution in the Process of Denationalization*, 12 Constellations 447 (2005).

[19] J. Locke, Second Treatise on Civil Government § 137 (1690).

[20] His theory of separation of powers is "normative" in the sense that Locke analyzes the exercise of state powers starting from the premise of a legal-constitutional limitation, which is his definition of the legislative function, on which all other functions conceptually depend. The question that he asks with respect to the exercise of a state function is always the question of jurisdiction and justiciability: "Who will be the judge?" This is precisely why Locke is considered the theoretical father of modern constitutionalism. *See*, for similar observations on Locke's separation of powers theory, R. Carré de Malberg, Contributions à la Théorie générale de l`État [Contributions to the General Theory of State] (1922), vol. II, at 3 ff. and Sir Ernest Barker' Introduction to O. von Gierke, Natural Law and the Theory of Society [Das Deutsche Genossenschaftsrecht], Sir E. Barker (Ed.) (1934).

[21] The names are irrelevant, as Locke himself strove to underline: "So be the thing understood I am indifferent as to the name." (§ 146). The federative is the power which concerns what we would now call foreign affairs, the prerogative, the power "of doing public good without a rule," a mixture of equity-related and emergency attributions.

But it is clear from the argument that the essential Lockean (and constitutional) question ("Who will be the judge?") can only be answered, with respect to such exercises of state power, politically ("The people will be judges"). What is in the public good, unless a normative principle guides and constrains the evaluation itself, cannot be rationally and therefore judicially determined. Likewise, in terms of actual legal practices, classical constitutional doctrine presupposed bright-line adjudicatory dichotomies, along right/privilege and external/internal normative baselines, in terms of how the judge would interpret the governing legal provisions, what procedural safeguards had to be secured, and how intensively the factual accuracy and consistency of a political – legislative, executive, or administrative – determination would be judicially probed.[22]

The rise of the welfare and regulatory state has changed the normative character of both legislative and constitutional structure. Insofar as modern statutes are more "promotional" and tentative in nature and create rights that are themselves "promotional" or "social" rather than individual,[23] the judicial posture has also become more prospective, tentative, policy-driven, acquiring political features. Similar transformations can be observed at the constitutional level. Partly as a result of foundational irresolution or dilatory compromises with respect to conflicting value-systems,[24] partly also in response to this unprecedented extension of the state, the new numbers, limitations, and qualifications of fundamental rights render constitutional adjudication much more complex.[25] The transformation as such may well be inevitable: "Like 'Big Government', 'Big Business', 'Big Labor' and 'Big Foundation' demand 'Big Litigation'- and 'Big Judge.'"[26] But no solution to these politicization/ judicialization problems, at least no apparent one, presents itself.

In terms of judicial review of administrative action, where the stakes are usually concentrated on the appropriate methodology of statutory interpretation, none of the classical approaches seems to suffice. For instance, in the case of porous legislation filled with open-ended formulations, literalism, this expression of forlorn "paragraph automaton" expectations, would have

[22] The issue is evident in state and federal American constitutional and adminisitrative law. *See, e.g.*, McAuliffe v. Mayor of City of New Bedford, 29 N.E. 517 (1892) (a public job does not entail a right to free speech), Mahler v. Eby, 264 U.S. 32 (1924) (legislative formula granting the administration power to deport aliens considered "undesirable" not unconstitutional legislative delegation, since the power is an exercise of sovereignty).

[23] *E.g.*, Cappelletti, *supra* note 15, at 26.

[24] Stone Sweet, *supra* note 13, at 197: "Indeed, the rights provisions we find in contemporary Europe reflect, rather than harmonize, the opposed visions of society held by the political parties at the time the constitution was negotiated."

[25] Whereas in newer, e.g., European, constitutions this irresolution is textually apparent, in the United States the transformation took place as a result of the post-New Deal judicial retraction from the field of social and economic legislation review and – correspondingly – the post-Caroline Products Footnote Four "compensation."

[26] *Id.*, at 38.

as a consequence a massive aggrandizement of executive and bureaucratic power (and the consequent potential for abuse). At the same time, purely purposive interpretation cannot be the solution either, be it only because much modern legislation, due sometimes to interest-group politics but often enough to foundational irresolution with respect to the subject matter, proffers a cornucopia of conflicting statutory purposes. How are these purposes to be judicially ranged in order of priority can the interpretation method as such not answer.

In terms of constitutional adjudication, the contemporary doctrinal answer to these transformations – across jurisdictions – has been the emergence of balancing and proportionality review of clashes between countervailing rights or rights and public interests. This seems at first sight to be a line of judicial compromise which could be accepted by all parties, since the purpose-means measurement and attention to context entailed by the balancing methodology appear to leave the playing field open for future encounters. Just like in a legislature, what is lost by an interest or ideological viewpoint today, may be won, within a different dispute constellation, tomorrow. It could however be argued that balancing has already created cause for grievance both in instrumental and overall normative consistency terms.[27] Whereas the methodology as such creates a measure of systemic ad-hocery and unpredictability, the solution given to a certain clash of worldviews – apparent in the case of balancing collisions between rights – will "freeze" that segment of reality, probably for ever. This is due to the fact that amending constitutional rights provisions is often extremely difficult in practice and in some jurisdictions also constitutionally impermissible. A value conflict decided and a segment of reality constitutionally blocked without principled, normative justification, is regarded by many critics as an orthodoxy arbitrarily imposed by judicial fiat.[28] But even staunch advocates of balancing virtues recognize, albeit unwillingly, the normative limitations of the methodology. A prominent contemporary scholar, former Israeli Supreme Court Chief Justice Aharon Barak, for instance, attempts to fill the normative gap with an appeal to justice and the ethical integrity of the judge. But calls to ethical integrity and direct invocations of justice are, from the perspectives of disappointed normative expectations, legal predictability, and doctrinal consistency, of relatively little comfort.[29] If judicial decision-making is characterized in

[27] *See, e.g.*, J. Finnis, *Liberalism and Natural Law Theory*, 45 Mercer L. Rev. 687 (1993-1994) (what Finnis defines as liberalism is arguably the recent transformation of liberal constitutionalism) and T. A. Aleinikoff, *Constitutional Law in the Age of Balancing*, 96(5) Yale L. J. 943 (1987).

[28] This is the common tenor of conservative criticism, *see, e.g.*, R. Bork (Ed.), A Country I Do Not Recognize: The Legal Assault on American Values (2005) and Coercing Virtue: The Worldwide Rule of Judges (2003).

[29] *See* A. Barak, The Judge in a Democracy (2006). Justice Barak defines the role of the judge as being "to bridge the gap between law and society" (sometimes "law and life") (*passim*),

essence as "a subjectivity governed by objective principles" and direct appeals to justice, it could be reasonably replied that hopes and expectations of professional enlightenment and probity could be projected unto the politicians as well.[30] Whether the concerned individuals or professional categories meet these expectations or not will from there onwards be a matter of biographical facts, viewpoints, and opinion polls.

These developments will continue. It is inevitable, in the absence of accepted boundaries, that a decision-making system which operates on a rationalized pattern of justification will progressively "rationalize" systems of decision-making which are, from its perspective, "irrational," i.e., base their decisions on considerations of opportunity or aleatory aggregation of votes.[31] The evolution is further complicated by a measure of cross-jurisdictional overlap, as different judicatures lay conflicting claims to finality in the interpretation of conflicts between rights and legitimate public interests. The case of rights-adjudication by the European Court of Justice is a particularly good example, insofar as the Court "borrows" the language of rights from the context of national constitutionalism, elevates it to a level of definitional abstraction at which the concerned right ceases to have any operative conceptual meaning ("the common constitutional traditions"), and then "descends" contextually and instrumentally into balancing, potentially against the national constitutional definition.[32] Some decisions of the European Court of Human Rights exhibit similarly expansive characteristics.[33] Since national courts do not fail to respond to such interferences,[34] what results may optimistically be described as an emerging transnational comity or a judicial-dialogical exercise of sorts. It certainly exhibits refreshing checks-and-balances safeguards, since, to paraphrase the Madisonian aphorism, the interests of the men are connected

recognizes that "[i]nterpretation without judicial discretion is a myth" (at 146), arguing at the same time that the balanced "values are not the personal values of a judge" (at 135). The values are objective, meaning for instance, in the context of statutory interpretation, that the judge takes into consideration the "objective purpose" of a statute, which is "to realize the fundamental values of democracy"; the values are sometimes in the constitution, sometimes outside of it, and those that are not in the text "should not be forced into the constitution artificially" (135). However, "these unmentioned values and principles constitute a point of reference for understanding the values and principles that *are* mentioned." (*Id.*, emphasis in original). But who is to find, define, and measure those that *are not*?

30 *Id.*, at 273.

31 *See* Fuller, *supra* note 17.

32 *See* Case C-112/00, Eugen Schmidberger, Internationale Transporte und Planzüge v. Republik Österreich [2003] ECR I-5659, for an unusual definition of free assembly by the ECJ and the general discussion in Alexander Somek, *infra*.

33 *E.g.*, Von Hannover v. Germany (2005) 40 EHRR 1, where the Court imposes a French standard of privacy protection on German law.

34 BVerfG, 14 October 14, 2004, 2 BvR 1481/04 (Görgülü), Official English translation *available at* http://www.bverfg.de/entscheidungen/rs20041014_2bvr148104en.html.

with the transnational-constitutional rights of the place. But the overall picture cannot fail to also convey a certain overall sense of judicial politics.

The underlying general problem seems to be therefore the systemic disappearance of a concept of law and legislation (and of practices generally substantiating this concept) against which claims of right or authority could be measured. In the absence of such a disciplining neutral baseline, the reconciliation of the clashing values takes place without the benefit of a point of reference. Substitute orders of reference, a natural law theory or, in more pedestrian terms, an ideology, would arguably establish a value hierarchy no longer rationally derived from within the legal system.[35]

A general phenomenon of judicialization of politics and politicization of justice can certainly be observed. Courts intervene in fields and processes that had in the past been off-limits to judicial scrutiny. Patterns of intervention can be tabulated, legal-sociological taxonomies tracking fields of intervention can be established.[36] Politics also intervene in processes which were previously relatively neutral. Independence guarantees relating to appointments and irremovability have for instance become political battlegrounds. This is especially the case in the United States. The voting patterns of Supreme Court nominees are now analyzed in terms of ideological orientation and proposals are even made to make these analyses and predictions an explicit factor in the appointment process.[37] Such processes can be expected to further reinforce the judicialization-politicization cycle.[38]

But how can this phenomenon be conceptually-legally assessed? The nowadays ubiquitous accusations of "judicial activism" and recommendations

---

[35] Interestingly, both Kelsen and Schmitt saw this. *See* H. Kelsen, *La garantie juridictionnelle de la constitution [The Jurisdictional Guarantee of the Constitution]*, Revue du droit public et de la science politique en France et à l'Etranger 54 (1928) and C. Schmitt, *Die Tyrannei der Werte [The Tyranny of Values]*, *in* Säkularisation und Utopie: Ebracher Studien. Ernst Forsthoff zum 65. Geburtstag 37 (1967), arguing that in the absence of an external reference point, a "point of attack" has to be posited [*Angriffspunkt*, at 55-57], from the perspective of which the resulting value-hierarchy would be by necessity a form "value-destructive value-realization" [*wertzerstörende wertverwirklichung*, at 57].

[36] *See, e.g.*, cross-jurisdictional general trends indicated in R. Hirschl, *The New Constitutionalism and the Judicialization of Pure Politics Worldwide*, 75 Fordham L. Rev. 721 (2006-2007) and R. A. Miller, *Lords of Democracy: The "Judicialization" of Pure Politics in the United States and Germany*, 61 Wash. & Lee L. Rev. 587 (2004).

[37] *See for instance* the Yale Law School "Alito Project," an informal group of faculty members and students which analyzed Judge (as he then was) Alito's opinions *available at* http://www.campusprogress.org/uploads/YLSAlitoProjectFinalReport.pdf. What is of the essence is the pronounced result- and policy-oriented viewpoint from which the report is written. *See also*, C. Eisgruber, The Next Justice: Repairing the Supreme Court Appointments Process (2007), arguing that ideological orientation should be the primary factor in the appointment.

[38] *Cf.* H. Edwards, *The Judicial Function and the Elusive Goal of Principled Decisionmaking*, 1991 Wis. L. Rev. 837, at 838: "The more that judges are assessed in terms of 'political' (result-oriented) decisionmakig, the more likely it is that this will become a self-fulfilling prophecy."

of "judicial restraint" serve primarily polemical or ideological purposes. The categories as such of "activism" and "restraint" are of limited descriptive use, to indicate broad judicial "moods" and attitudinal predispositions, or serve as mere "code words for criticism and praise," revealing the ideological viewpoints or theoretical predispositions of the observers.[39]

4.

Contributors approach the common subject along lines of concrete inquiry which have been perceived as particularly relevant to the overarching theme.[40] Contributors share (to relative degrees) the common working assumption that a blurring of the classical lines of division between law and politics in paradigmatic constitutional systems (constitutionalism in transformation) also affects systems transitions to liberal democracy (transitional constitutionalism). This appears to impact negatively on the "civilizational capacity" of liberal democratic Western constitutionalism. These common working hypotheses justify the structure of the volume.

The introductory chapter by Dieter Grimm deals primarily with the role of methodology in constraining judicial discretion and thus politicization of adjudication, particularly constitutional adjudication. He regards judicial review of constitutionality, due to the peculiar characteristics of constitutions, as particularly indicative of more general modern developments. Methodology is not approached in a parochially doctrinal fashion. Professor Grimm revisits, builds on, and expands the Luhmannian theory of systemic legal autonomy, namely, the thesis that the legal system constitutes an "operatively closed system" which differentiates itself from its social environment by means of a specialized language and an autonomous operative criterion ("coding").[41] He understands, that if the operative closure and thus systemic integrity is to be preserved, the limitation cannot be purely formal or procedural. Long-term normative limitations cannot be imposed from outside on the legal system either, since, as we now know, all constituent and legislative undertakings to bind judges to words, starting from the *Codex Justiniani* onwards, have been in vain: "All historical attempts by legislators to prohibit interpretations or to prescribe a certain method have proved fruitless. They were themselves subject to interpretation." Conversely, the efforts of legal scholarship to

[39] Barak, *supra* note 29, at 263. *See also* Barak, at 275 ff., for an insightful list of *techniques* for which activist and – respectively – self-restrained judges manifest general predilections (e.g., activist judges prefer balancing over categorization).

[40] Unless otherwise referenced, all following quotes in the text of this Preface come from the respective chapters in this volume.

[41] *See* Dieter Grimm's remarks on this matter and references to Luhmann *in* R. Badinter & S. Breyer (Eds.), Judges in a Democracy – An International Conversation 28-29 (2004).

undermine the autonomy of legal rationality and "unveil" its political undertones (CLS debunking campaigns) are recognized as detrimental self-fulfilling prophecies: "If interpretation and application of the law is regarded as a political operation, then the political preferences and affiliations of the judges are important, whereas they do not matter as much when the neutralizing effect of rationality is recognized." Revising the limitations of all "absolutist" methodological attempts to eliminate judicial discretion (positivism, various kinds originalism), Dieter Grimm proposes a methodological equilibrium. The judge should take into consideration three factors, text, context, and purpose; the purposive inquiry determines the function that a particular constitutional provision is intended to serve in the larger constitutional scheme. Upon the understanding that any methodological combination of this sort is of necessity somewhat unstable, he underlines the need for a measure of flexibility in the constitutional amendment limitations. If amendment requirements are not practically insurmountable, politics can "reprogram" the legal system.

Professors de Mestral and Winter grapple with a related methodological matter, which goes to the root of justiciability self-limitations. They compare two jurisdictions, one relatively recently endowed with constitutional autonomy and a bill of fundamental right and one in search of constitutional legitimacy, one federal, the other quasi-federal. The experiences of the European Court of Justice and the Supreme Court of Canada are compared from the perspective of what in American law is called the "political question" doctrine. Neither of the two concerned jurisdictions expressly recognizes a "political question" doctrine. But such general recognition, as de Mestral and Winter do not fail to note, is of secondary importance insofar as courts can be noticed to defer to the political branches in certain areas, which judicatures perceive as less amenable to judicial determination. David Currie has also pointed out that the existence or unavailability of such doctrines in various constitutional jurisdiction "is a matter more of semantics than of substance."[42] What they observe is on the one hand a practical reluctance to interfere in areas which the judges recognize, lofty judicial self-bootstrapping notwithstanding, as overly sensitive and – as the Canadian Supreme Court puts it- without a "sufficient legal element." In Canada, this concerns issues with onerous fiscal implications (in particular socio-economic rights) and some provincial-federal arrangements, whereas in the case of the ECJ the authors notice a very understandable emphasis on foreign affairs and WTO law. Professors Winter and de Mestral observe on the other hand a counter-current, namely how the relatively recent introduction of fundamental rights review has sensibly and continuously raised the stakes. The

[42] D. P. Currie, The Constitution of the Federal Republic of Germany 170-171 (1994): "It is entirely consistent with a judicial duty to say what the law is to conclude that the law commits a particular issue to the discretion or determination of another branch of government. The German court has done so a number of times, and it is not clear that our political question doctrine means anything more."

paper is in this respect a prophetic "prediction of what the courts will do," since in between one of the developments criticized by the authors, the judgments of the Court of First Instance in *Yusuf* and *Kadi*, has been reversed. The Court of Justice has recently handed an appellate decision in which the judgments of the Court of First Instance were harshly scolded, on the grounds that the Community cannot implement automatically anti-terrorism measures taken by the UN Security Council' Sanctions Committee which infringe on individual rights without providing for individualized procedural safeguards.[43]

Alexander Somek's chapter straddles the thematic line between the role of methodology and the impact of systemic transformations, showing how a system transitions influences and is in turn influenced by constitutional adjudication. The EU system transition is characterized, as Professor Somek persuasively argues, by idealization (a "postmodern" use of constitutional form and language to obscure the substantive lack of constitutionalism) and de-politicization, namely the bureaucratization of political processes and technological stifling of political action: "the European Union is a machine and not a body politic."[44] These processes are reinforced by and fused with the judicial doctrine of economic due process, as Somek calls the recent jurisprudence of the ECJ, evoking the conjoined specters of American pre-New Deal "Lochnerism" and of the related European antebellum fear of "the government of judges."[45] Somek compellingly argues that the economic due process jurisprudential bias of the ECJ is reinforced by the way in which the Court appropriates (and de-politicizes) the major values of nation-state constitutionalism, namely rights, a phenomenon which he expressively calls "the *Schmidberger* trap": "[T]he Court effectively disowned *national* traditions and replaced them with the common constitutional tradition of the Member States. The case was thus transformed into a matter that does not concern the potential collision between national constitutional law and Union law, but rather is presented as fully internal to Union law." This is a very worrisome phenomenon, as Professor Somek also observes in his discussion of *Laval* and *Viking*, since the self-aggrandizement constitutional rhetoric of the Court, indeed an ever more fabulous Münchausen story, reaches the outer limits of plausibility. The problem could be perceived as insoluble if we focused on

[43] Judgment in Joined Cases C-402/05 P and C-415/05 P, Yassin Abdullah Kadi and Al Barakaat International Foundation v. Council and Commission, 3 September 2008.

[44] *Cf.* C. Joerges, *Europe a Großraum? Shifting Legal Conceptualizations of the Integration Concept, in* C. Joerges & N. Singh Ghaleigh (Eds.), Dark Legacies of the Law in Europe: The Shadow of National Socialism and Fascism over Europe and Its Legal Traditions 167 (2003).

[45] The term comes from an influential book by the French comparativist Edouard Lambert, in which Lambert argued against the introduction of judicial review of constitutionality in Europe, pointing out the American decisions invalidating, on economic due process grounds, social legislation: Le gouvernement des juges et la lutte contre la legislation sociale aux États-Unis [The Government of Judges and the Fight Against Social Legislation in the United States] (1921).

the process as such, which has after all its own expansive logic and, looked at from this angle, may escape the will of the European judges, themselves trapped like all other actors in an inevitable systemic logic. Professor Somek believes that the answer could be a re-constitutionalization (or constitutional re-programming as Dieter Grimm would say). And then the constituent question of constituent power, measure of inclusion, homogeneity of values, depth of agreement on them, or indeed lack thereof, would be posed anew.

In their discussion of WTO GMO law, Professor Christian Joerges and his commentator, Professor András Sajó, tackle a transnational judicialization transformation of the highest relevance to the topic. Christian Joerges observes the interconnected way in which the concepts "constitutionalization," "governance," and "judicialization" are circulated nowadays. New vocabularies in public law and legal theory appear for a good practical reason, namely, our incapacity to describe new phenomena in inherited conceptual terminology.[46] Joerges shows how transnational regimes without a political, democratic basis of legitimacy – "governance" – are partially legitimatized by judicialized procedures, which raise afterwards claims of full legitimacy (constitutionalization). The constitutionalization discourse has what Alexander Somek calls "idealization" implications, since it conjures claims of legitimation borrowed (stolen?) from the arsenal of classical nation-state constitutionalism. By the same token, it has also hegemonic implications, insofar as constitutionalization implies finality of decision and hierarchy of norms or legal regimes. This topsy-turvy reversion of the modern logic whereby which a government is bound by a constitution and the supremacy of a constitution is ensured by a final judicature is particularly apparent in value conflicts implicated by the resolution of high-stakes risk-intensive disputes, such as the GMO controversy. Professor Joerges recommends as a solution what he perceives to be the essence of the European legal system, "a conflict of laws of supranational validity." The possibility for such a version of transnational quasi-constitutional comity is also of relevance to the concerns identified in Somek's contribution. However, as András Sajó observes in the closing of his comment, the final direction of this trend of "transnational rule of law without the need or the possibility for substance or democratic decision-making" is almost impossible to define or predict at this stage. This is especially true – we may add – since the clashing judicialized-constitutionalized discourses imply contradictory claims of finality of jurisdiction, which are irreconcilable, since adopted from and within the logics of different systemic ("constitutional") premises (in this case, WTO/EU/national law). This overlap of constitutionalism or claims of constitutional jurisdiction is also relevant to the arguments by Somek and Iancu.

[46] *Cf.* C. Möllers, *European Governance: Meaning and Value of a Concept*, 43(2) CMLR 313 (2006).

The chapter by Professor Macdonald and Mr. McMorrow tackles the issue of constitutional equality and identity, indeed a loud rallying cry for many a politically-charged judicial battle. They start from a new development in Canadian public law, the concept or doctrine of "reasonable accommodation," which is meant to cut little compromises ("accommodations") into various administrative and social practices, insofar as the required changes are exceptional and do not cause "undue burdens"(are, namely, "reasonable"). The doctrine is said to derive from the equality guarantee (Section 15) of the Canadian Charter. The two authors, much to their credit, notice that the new doctrinal invention presupposes rather a condescending assumption of inequality, where the "accommodated" plaintiff seems to be regarded, from the constitutional standpoint, as an eccentric norm-deviant supplicant, whose idiosyncrasies will be, albeit unwillingly, magnanimously permitted. Most of the developments Macdonald and McMorow describe bring freedom of religion into the picture and thus further constitutional complications but the two authors treat the matter from a strictly identity-centered equality perspective. The classical liberal constitutional answer is of course still a neutral concept of equality often associated with itemized grounds of presumptively unconstitutional discrimination. Equality provisions relate at various levels to various degrees of textually – or (the US case) jurisprudentially-defined grounds of constitutionally suspect classification (race, nationality, gender, illegitimacy, etc.). The degree of rationality or permissibility of discrimination is rationally related to the specific characteristics of the ground. But the authors are ambivalent with respect to such general equality guarantees. They are mistrustful of the hegemonic identity-defining tendencies of general equality (at the extreme probably related to the general procrustean character of norms[47]). As they argue, these classical liberal norms are premised on "a standard-instance (a typical citizen) that is naturally given and by reference to which discrimination is to be gauged." Therefore, McMorrow and Macdonald perceive such a position as insufficient to contemporary liberal constitutionalism, which has nowadays to "formulate appropriate legal responses that will facilitate the celebration of social understandings of the complex, fluid, increasingly disaggregated, identities of human beings." The solutions they propose, similar to those adopted by the Quebec Bouchard-Taylor Committee, on which one of them, Professor Roderick Macdonald, sat as a distinguished member, are recognizably legal-pluralist. They are, that is to say, recognizably law-averse, at least in the "monist, centralist, positivist, prescriptivist, chirographic" sense in which Macdonald and McMorrow say non-pluralists understand law to be. Devolution of decision-making, de-judicialization and consensualism, promotion of secularism, and other similar measures are advocated. The reader ponders in closing (this is, needless to say,

[47] Note the demise of the "irrebutable presumptions" doctrine in US constitutional law.

a quality of their contribution) whether the judicialization related to identity-related constitutional trends can be in the end escaped or, indeed, what does a pluralist judge do when identities still clash, claims of discrimination are still raised, and conflict lies once again before a court.

The chapter by Professor Bernd Rüthers treats politicization of law as an inevitable consequence of the interconnection between "*law and metaphysics* or even between *law and ideology.*" Law is, says Rüthers, essentially "normatively coagulated" or "normatively solidified politics." The features of this intrinsic politicization, writes Professor Rüthers, are accentuated and therefore better revealed in the exceptional case of a system transformation: "Such reevaluations take place in periods of normalcy as well but they remain often unnoticed. This holds true, for instance, with respect to the intense bond between the law and extra-juridical variables, such as axiological representations, dogmas, and articles of faith." Proximity to power renders law and lawyers particularly vulnerable to direct and indirect political and ideological manipulation. Conversely, this manipulation of lawyers results in their manipulating the law. In the case of a system transformation, this propensity is reinforced. Viciously self-interested opportunists and enthusiastic new converts can "reorient" the legal system, in times of social and political upheaval, to render it conformant to the needs and commands of the new dominant ideology. They do so by reinterpreting the essential institutions, redefining elastic legislative clauses and general concepts, and indeed, as Professor Rüthers notices, by reinterpreting interpretation itself, i.e., by creating new methodologies: "Questions of juridical methodology are simultaneously constitutional questions. The choice of an interpretive method determines the interpretive results, settling and dislodging the boundary between law-making and adjudication. Therefore, what is at stake is the separation of powers as instituted by the fundamental law." When the transformation is to a dictatorship, the motivational impetuses of the actors (fear, conviction, and interest) often blend into each other, argues Bernd Rüthers. András Sajó's comment elegantly challenges one of the arguments, namely that "the system change affects lawyers as a professional order not only in their existence, but also in their professional reasoning and political-ideological loyalties." Professor Sajó observes that the geography of influence exercised by a regime of unchecked lawlessness varies and is – so to speak – totalitarianism-specific. The National Socialist "dual state" and – respectively – "socialist legality" entailed different demands and implications.

The chapter by Professor Adam Czarnota emphasizes the socio-legal background of post-communist transitions. The argument is directly relevant to matters discussed in the contributions by Somek, Rüthers, Sajó, and Iancu. Adam Czarnota shows how the legacy of the past (its legal legacy as well) and not dealing with it after the regime change is in itself "a constitutional process." Namely, according to Professor Czarnota, the failure to account for the past after the demise of state socialism has led to a "double transformation," in which a veneer of formal reforms ("a façade that is composed of institutions that, from a distance, look like typical institutions of Western free-market liberal democracy") hides actual relations of brutal interest politics. This is a less frightening Doppelstaat but perhaps a very well-entrenched one. Except from advancing the idea of quasi-judicial institutions to bridge the law and politics of the communist past and ostensibly liberal present, Czarnota refrains from providing solutions, perhaps because he believes it is already too late for them. He does indeed observe that in many post-communist countries the structure of the post-post-communist Doppelstaat has achieved a certain degree of refinement and systemic insularity: the parallel logics of post-communist form and substance reproduce themselves. Recent Romanian developments show that the system already has enough resources to neutralize, through the instrumentalization of rule of law ideologies, attempts at substantive change (including quasi-judicial transitional justice mechanisms). Moreover, the EU constitutionalization process seems only to have further legitimatized this cynical type of graft and self-perpetuation politics shielded by manipulative rule of law and human rights formal justifications, a development to which Professor Czarnota alludes.

My own contribution argues that a constitution can only fulfill its integrative function (the root of subsequent law-politics delineations) insofar as the textual provisions and formal mechanisms are underpinned by a deeper sense of the legal concepts and institutions. A substantive criterion is needed in both constitutionalization and constitutional adjudication. Such substantive criterion was presupposed by classical constitutionalism to have implied a measure of universality (my position is therefore moderately "functionalist"). The recent "constitutionalization" process occasioned by the Eastern EU enlargement has failed, I argue, inasmuch as the contradictions of EU constitutionalism have aggravated rather than solved the contradictions of post-communist pre-modern constitutionalism. This failure is not only of parochial interest, since at this point what Dieter Grimm calls the "crude literal understanding" (or "simplistic legal positivism with a thin Marxist sauce," according to Adam Czarnota) characterizing post-communist "positivism" has become, by virtue of formal equality status and due to the consolidation of a system by now impervious to change (*see* related discussion in the Rüthers-Sajó chapter), a European problem. Conversely, the lack of constitutional vision of the Union is emblematic of deeper European constitutional tensions, at both the national and supranational level (a claim also made in this volume by Alexander Somek's contribution).

Part I

Constitutionalism in Transformation

Dieter Grimm

Constitutions, Constitutional Courts and Constitutional Interpretation at the Interface of Law and Politics

1.

1. Before the end of World War II constitutional courts or courts with constitutional jurisdiction were a rarity. Although constitutions had been in place long before, a worldwide demand for constitutional adjudication arose only after the experiences with the many totalitarian systems of the 20th century. The post-totalitarian constitutional assemblies regarded judicial review as the logical consequence of constitutionalism. In a remarkable judgment the Israeli Supreme Court said in 1995: "Judicial review is the soul of the constitution itself. Strip the constitution of judicial review and you have removed its very life … It is therefore no wonder that judicial review is now developing. The majority of enlightened democratic states have judicial review … The Twentieth Century is the century of judicial review."[1] Based on this universal trend the Israeli Court claimed the power of judicial review although it had not been explicitly endowed with it in the constitution.

Yet, just as the transition from absolute rule to constitutionalism had modified the relationship between law and politics, this relationship was now modified by the establishment of constitutional courts. As long as law was regarded as being of divine origin, politics was subordinate to law. Political power derived its authority from the task to maintain and enforce divine law, but this authority did not include the right to make law. When the Reformation

[1] *See* C.A. 6821/93 United Mizrahi Bank Ltd. v. Migdal Village 49(4) PD 221 (1995) (Supreme Court of Israel).

Bogdan Iancu (Ed.), The Law/Politics Distinction in Contemporary Public Law Adjudication, 21-34.

undermined the divine basis of the legal order, and this led to the religious civil wars of the 16th and 17th century, the inversion of the traditional relationship between law and politics was regarded as a precondition for the restoration of social peace. The political ruler acquired the power to make law regardless of the contested religious truth. Law became a product of politics. It derived its binding force no longer from God's will but from the ruler's will. It was henceforth positive law. Eternal or natural law, in spite of its name, was not law, but philosophy.

Constitutionalism, as it emerged in the last quarter of the 18th century, was an attempt to re-establish the supremacy of the law, albeit under the condition that there was no return to divine or eternal law. The solution to the problem consisted in the reflexivity of positive law. The enactment and enforcement of the law was itself subject to legal regulation. To realise this aim, a hierarchy had to be established within the legal system. The law that regulated legislation and law-enforcement had to be superior to the law that emanates from the political process. Yet, since there was no return to divine law, the higher law was itself the product of a political decision. But in order to fulfil its function of submitting politics to law it required a source different from ordinary politics. In accordance with the theory that in the absence of a divine basis of rulership the only possible legitimization of political power is the consent of the governed, this source was found in the people. The people replaced the ruler as sovereign, just as previously the ruler had replaced God. However, the role of the popular sovereign was limited to enacting the constitution, while the exercise of political power was entrusted to representatives of the people who could act only on the basis and within the framework of the constitution.

Hence, one can say that the very essence of constitutionalism is to ensure the submission of politics to law. This function distinguishes constitutional law from ordinary law in various respects. There is, first, a difference in object. The object of constitutional law is politics. Constitutional law regulates the formation and exercise of political power. The power holders are the addressees of constitutional law. Secondly, constitutional and ordinary law have different sources. Since constitutional law brings forth legitimate political power, it cannot emanate from that same power. It is made by or attributed to the people. Consequently and thirdly, the making of constitutional law differs from the making of ordinary law. It is usually a special body that formulates constitutional law and its adoption is subject to a special procedure in which either the people decide or, if a representative body is called upon to decide, a supermajority is required.

Fourthly, constitutional law differs from ordinary law in terms of rank. It is higher law. In cases of conflict between constitutional law and ordinary law or acts of ordinary law application, constitutional law prevails. What has been regulated in the constitution is no longer open to political decision. Insofar, the majority rule does not apply. This does not imply a total juridification of politics. Such a total juridification would mean the end of politics and turn it into mere administration. Constitutional law determines who is entitled to make political decisions and which procedural and substantive rules need to be observed in order to give these decisions binding force. However, the constitution neither predetermines the input into the constitutionally regulated procedures nor their outcome. It regulates the decision-making process but leaves the decisions themselves to the political process. It is a framework, not a substitute for politics.

Finally, constitutional law is characterized by a certain weakness compared to ordinary law. Ordinary law is made by the government and applies to the people. If they do not obey, the government is entitled to use force. Constitutional law, on the contrary, is made by or at least attributed to the people as its ultimate source and applies to the government. If the government does not comply with the requirements of constitutional law, there is no superior power to enforce it. This weakness may differ in degree, depending on the function of the constitution. Regarding the constitutive function, the structure of public power will usually conform to the constitutional arrangement. Regarding its function to regulate the exercise of political power, this cannot be taken for granted. The historical and actual evidence is abundant.

2. It was this weakness that gave rise to constitutional adjudication, in the United States soon after the invention of constitutionalism, in Europe and other parts of the world only after the collapse of the fascist and racist, socialist, and military dictatorships, beginning in the 1950s and culminating in the 1990s. Although many of these systems had constitutions, their impact was minimal and invoking constitutional rights could pose a danger to citizens. In the light of this experience, constitutional courts were generally regarded as a necessary completion of constitutionalism. If the very essence of constitutionalism is the submission of politics to law, then the very essence of constitutional adjudication is to enforce constitutional law vis-à-vis the government. This implies judicial review of political acts – including legislation. However, constitutional courts or courts with constitutional jurisdiction cannot fully compensate for the weakness of constitutional law. Since the power to use physical force remains in the hands of the political branches of government, courts are helpless when politicians refuse to comply with the constitution or disregard court orders.

But apart from this situation, which is exceptional in a well-functioning liberal democracy with a deeply-rooted sense for the rule of law, it makes a difference whether a political system adopts constitutional adjudication or not. Even a government that is generally willing to comply with the constitution will be biased regarding the question as to what exactly the constitution forbids or requires in a certain situation. Politicians tend to interpret the constitution in the light of their political interests and intentions. In a system without constitutional adjudication, the interpretation of the majority usually prevails.

In the long run this will undermine the achievement of constitutionalism. By contrast, in a system with constitutional adjudication, an institution exists that does not pursue political intentions, is not subject to election, and specializes in constitutional interpretation in a professional manner. It is thus less biased and can uphold constitutional requirements vis-à-vis the elected majority. Even more important is the preventive effect of constitutional adjudication. The mere existence of a constitutional court compels the political majority to raise the question of the constitutionality of a political measure quite early in the political process and in a more neutral way. It observes its own political plans through the eyes of the constitutional court.

Kelsen, whom the Israeli Supreme Court quotes approvingly in the *Mizrahi* opinion, may have exaggerated when he said that a constitution without constitutional adjudication is just like having no constitution at all. There are a number of long-established democracies where the constitution matters although no constitutional review exists. Here constitutional values have become part of the legal and political culture so that there is less need for institutionalized safeguards. But for the majority of states, in particular for those who turned toward constitutional democracy only recently, it is true that the constitution would not matter very much in day-to-day politics if it did not enjoy the support of a special agent that enforced the legal constraints imposed by the constitution and to which politics was subject. The small impact of fundamental rights before the establishment of judicial review provides proof of this.

However, the existence of a constitutional court alone is not sufficient to guarantee that politicians respect the constitution. Just as constitutionalism is an endangered achievement, constitutional adjudication is in danger as well. Politicians, even if they originally agreed to establish judicial review, soon find out that its exercise by constitutional courts is often burdensome for them. Constitutions put politics under constraints and constitutional courts exist in order to enforce these constraints. Not everything that politicians find necessary – be it for themselves or their party, be it for what they deem good for the common interest – can be effectuated if the court does not consider it to be in line with the constitution. Politicians therefore have a general interest in a constitutional court that, to put it mildly, is at least not adverse to their objectives and plans. Nonetheless, there is also a specific interest in the outcome of constitutional litigation on which the implementation of a certain policy depends.

Yet, any political interference with the judicial process would undermine the whole system of constitutional democracy. This is why judges must be protected against political influence or pressure. The dividing line drawn by the principle of separation of powers between the various organs of the state is particularly strong where the judiciary is concerned. Independence of the judiciary is indispensable for the functioning of a constitutional system and is therefore itself in need of constitutional protection. If it is true that constitutional courts are helpless when political actors refuse to obey their orders, it is even truer that constitutional courts are useless when they cannot make their decisions independently from politics. The best protection of judicial independence is, of course, a deep-rooted conviction on the side of politicians that any interference with court procedures is unacceptable, supported by a strong backing for the constitution within society. But this cannot be taken for granted. Rather, special safeguards are necessary. Judicial independence must be guaranteed, not only against any attempt to directly influence the outcome of litigation, but also against more subtle ways of putting pressure on the judiciary. This is why constitutions usually guarantee the irremovability of judges and often a sufficient salary, to mention only a few devices.

A special problem in this context is the recruitment of judges of constitutional courts or courts with constitutional jurisdiction. Since these courts have a share in public power the judges need democratic legitimation. If they are not elected directly by the people, a circumstance which presents problems of its own regarding judicial independence, some involvement of the elected branches of government in the recruitment process seems inevitable. Yet, every involvement creates the temptation to elect or appoint deferential judges. The recruitment of judges is the open flank of judicial independence. A constitutional court that simply reflects political interests will hardly be able to keep the necessary distance from politics. Hence, safeguards against the politicization of the court are of vital importance.

Most countries with constitutional adjudication have some special provisions for the election or appointment of constitutional judges. If they are elected by parliament, often a supermajority, like that required for amending the constitution, is prescribed. This means that majority and minority must agree on one candidate, which makes extremely partisan appointments unlikely. Other countries prefer a mixed system of election and appointment by dividing the right to select constitutional judges among different bodies of government. In others, non-political actors are involved in the process, for instance representatives of the legal profession. It may be difficult to determine which system is the best. But it is not difficult to see that some barriers against the threat of a politically docile constitutional court must be erected if constitutionalism is to live up to its aspirations.

3. Judicial independence is the constitutional safeguard against the threat arising from politicians to the judges' proper exercise of their function. It is directed against attempts to induce judges not to apply the law but to bend to political expectations. This is an external threat. Yet it would be naïve to assume that this is the only threat to which the functioning of the constitutional system is exposed. There is an internal threat as well that comes from the judges themselves. It comes in two forms. One is the inclination to voluntarily follow, for whatever reasons, political expectations or even party lines. The other is

the temptation to adjudicate according to one's own political preferences or ideas of what is just and unjust instead of following constitutional standards. The constitutional guarantee of judicial independence protects judges from politics, but it does not protect the constitutional system and society from judges who, for reasons other than direct political pressure, are willing to disobey or distort the law.

Therefore, external independence must be accompanied by internal independence. The constitutional guarantee of judicial independence is not a personal privilege to decide at will, but a functional requirement. It shall enable judges to fulfil their function, namely to apply the law irrespective of the interests and expectations of the parties to the litigation or powerful political or societal forces. It frees judges from extra-legal bonds – not to give them leeway in their decisions, but to enable them to decide according to the law. The reason for the independence from extra-legal bonds is to give full effect to the legal bonds to which judges are subjected. Submission to law is the necessary counterpart of judicial independence. As with external independence, precautions can also be taken for internal independence.

However, since internal independence is largely a matter of professional ethics and individual character, the possibilities of the law are limited. Gross misbehaviour such as corruption can of course be outlawed and made a criminal offence. Experience shows, however, that it is difficult to fight corruption within the judiciary when corruption is habitual among politicians and in the society as well. This seems to be quite a problem in a number of new democracies. It is likewise justified to criminalize perversion of justice. But it is not easy to clearly distinguish perversion of justice from false or questionable interpretation of the law. This is why perversion of justice convictions are rare.[2] Yet, criminalizing corruption and perversion of justice and removing from office judges who committed these crimes is not a violation of the independence of the judiciary.

A more subtle misconduct is the willingness or pre-disposition to interpret the law in a way that is favourable to certain political views or to a party or a candidate running for political office, either in general or in an individual case. This usually appears in the disguise of a legal argumentation that seeks to hide the fact that it is result-driven. This will not always occur intentionally. Self-deception of judges as to the motives of their judicial behaviour is not impossible. The problem is that this type of misconduct does not only appear in a number of new democracies. It can be observed in solid constitutional

[2] The crime of perversion of the course of justice (*Rechtsbeugung*) is defined in the German Criminal Code, par. 339, as follows: "A judge, another public official or an arbitrator, who in conducting or deciding a legal matter makes himself guilty of a perversion of the course of justice for the benefit, or to the detriment, of a party, shall be punished with imprisonment from one year to five years." (Unofficial translation by the German Federal Ministry of Justice). *See, e.g.*, S. Ziemann, *Case Reports-Judge Schill Case (BGHSt 47, 105, 4 Sept. 2001)*, *in* R. A. Miller & P. C. Zumbansen (Eds.), 1 Annual of German & European Law 458 (2003) (Editor's Note).

states as well. The decision of the US Supreme Court in *Bush v. Gore*[3] in the year 2000 may serve as an example. There will hardly be a legal sanction in these cases. But there may be harsh public criticism or even a loss of trust in the judiciary to which no court can remain indifferent.

2.

1. Law owes its existence to a political decision. Political motives are legitimate in the process of law-making. Yet, in a constitutional democracy, politics no longer assumes a role when it comes to applying the law. The application of the law is a matter for the legal system, within which political motives are illegitimate. For this reason, the distinction between law and politics is of crucial importance. But what if law application, and in particular constitutional adjudication, is in itself a political operation, so that all attempts to separate law from politics at the institutional level are thwarted at the level of law application? This is a serious question, and it is a question that should not be confused with the abuse of judicial power which lies in the intentional non-application or misapplication of the law.

Of course, constitutional adjudication is inevitably political in the sense that the object and the effect of constitutional court decisions are political. This follows from the very function of constitutional law, which is to regulate the formation and exercise of political power, and the function of constitutional courts, which consists in enforcing this law vis-à-vis politics. A constitutional court is a branch of government. Excluding political issues from judicial scrutiny would denote the end of constitutional review. Hence, the question can only be whether operations that judges undertake in order to find the law and apply it to political issues are of a political or a legal character.

This question arises because every analysis of the process of law application to concrete issues illustrates that the text of the law is unable to determine judicial decisions entirely. One of the reasons is that the law in general and constitutional law in particular is neither void of gaps and contradictions nor always clear and unambiguous, and it can hardly be different, given the fact that a legal system is a product of different times, reacting to various challenges, inspired by different interests or concepts of justice and depending on the use of ordinary language. Filling the gaps, harmonizing contradicting provisions, rendering them precise enough for the decision of an issue is the task of the law applicants, in the last resort of the courts, which, in turn, profit from the efforts of legal science.

But even if provisions are formulated as clearly and as coherently as possible, they can raise questions when it comes to solving a concrete case. This incapacity to guarantee a full determination of legal decisions, even in

[3] 531. U.S. 98 (2000).

the case of seemingly clear provisions, is inherent in the law because a law is by definition a general rule applicable to an indefinite number of cases arising in the future. This is why it must be formulated in more or less abstract terms. Consequently, there will always remain a gap between the general and abstract norm on the one hand and the concrete and individual case on the other. The judge has to find out what the general norm means with regard to the case at hand. This is achieved by interpretation, which always precedes the application of the norm. The general norm must be concretized to a more specific rule before the individual case can be decided.

Like the task of filling gaps, harmonizing contradicting provisions, clarifying vague norms, concretization contains a creative element. Norm application therefore is always, to a certain extent, norm-construction. The fact as such is undisputable. The degree can vary. It depends on a number of variables. The most important one is the precision of a norm. A narrowly tailored norm leaves less room for the constructive element whereas a broad or even vague norm requires a lot of concretization before it can be applied to a case. Usually a constitution will contain more vague norms than, say, the code of civil procedure. This is certainly true for guiding principles and for fundamental rights, less so for organizational and procedural norms. Another variable is the age of a norm. The older a norm, the larger the number of problems that were not or could not have been foreseen by the legislature-thereby raising questions of meaning and applicability.

The mere fact that the law does not fully determine the judgment in individual cases is not sufficient to transform the application of law from a legal into a political operation. It remains a legal operation if what the judge adds to the text of the law in the process of interpretation has its basis in the text and can be derived from it in a reasonable, argumentative manner. If not, it becomes a political one. The task therefore is to distinguish between legal and non-legal arguments, be they political, economic, or religious. This decision can only be taken within the legal system. No other system is competent to determine what counts as a legal argument. Within the legal system the distinction between a legal and a non-legal argument rests with methodology. In so doing, methodology attempts to eliminate subjective influences from the interpretation of the law as far as possible. This is why the distinction between legal and non-legal operations in the course of law application becomes largely a question of legal method.

Yet, different from the text of the law that is the product of a political decision and thus not at the disposition of judges, legal methodology is itself a product of legal considerations. It emerges in the process of interpreting and applying the law or is developed in scholarly discourse, but nowhere is it decreed authoritatively. This means at the same time that various methodologies can coexist and so can different variations of a certain methodological creed. Method is a matter of choice within the legal system. All historical attempts by legislators to prohibit interpretation or to prescribe a certain method have proved fruitless. They were themselves subject to interpretation. But the lack of one authoritative method does not mean that methodology can justify any solution and thus loses its disciplining effect on judges. Just as certain legal systems have their time in history, methodologies have their time, too. There is usually a core of accepted arguments or operations and a number of arguments or operations that are regarded as unacceptable. The extent to which a method can succeed in eliminating all subjective elements from interpretation is controversial. There were and are methods that claim this capacity.

2. A historically influential method that promised to eliminate subjective influences was legal positivism, not in its capacity as a theory of the validity of law opposed to all natural law theories, but in its capacity as a theory of legal interpretation. For a positivist in this sense, the legal norm consists of its text and nothing else, and the only instruments for discovering the meaning of the text are philology and logic, i.e. not the legislative history, not the motives or the intent of the legislature, not the values behind the norm, not the social reality that brought forth the problems the norm was meant to solve and in which it is to take effect, not the consequences the interpretation may entail. There can be but one correct understanding of a norm and this remains correct as long as the norm is in force, no matter how the context changes.

The problem with positivism was that, on the one hand, it could not fulfil its promise to eliminate all subjective influences on interpretation. Rather, these influences were infused into the interpretation in a clandestine way, mostly in connection with the definition of the notions used by the legislature. On the other hand, positivism prohibited an adaptation of the law to social change by way of interpretation. Since the social reality in which the norm was to take effect was regarded as irrelevant to interpretation, a positivist could not even perceive social change. Of course, a positivist would not have denied that, because of social change, a legal norm might not fulfil its purpose and produce dysfunctional results. But this was regarded as a matter for the lawmaker, not for the law-applicant. It was this deficit that largely contributed to the decline of positivism after the far-reaching social change in the wake of the Industrial Revolution and World War I.

There is yet another influential theory of interpretation that claims to preclude all subjective influences, namely originalism. Different from positivists, originalists believe that only a historical method is the right way to ascertain the meaning of a legal norm. The law-applicant must give a norm, in particular a norm of the constitution, no meaning other than that which the framers had in mind. Sometimes originalism appears in a crude way that excludes the application of a norm to any phenomenon of which the framers could not have been aware. If the First Amendment to the US Constitution protects the freedom of the press, this would not allow the law-applicant to extend its protection to radio and TV by way of interpretation. Sometimes originalism appears in a more enlightened form. The law-applicant is then permitted to ask whether the framers clearly would have included a new phenomenon had they known it at the time when the law was enacted. In this case it would be methodologically permissible to include radio and TV into the protection of the First Amendment by way of interpretation. But like a positivist, an originalist is not prepared to acknowledge that there can be more than one sound interpretation of a norm and that the interpretation can legitimately change when the circumstances in which it is applied change.

The problem with originalism is first a practical one. In most cases it is difficult or even impossible to know what the original understanding or the original intent was. It is even more difficult if many persons are involved in the process of constitution-making, many of whom may not have expressed their understanding or intent. For this reason ascertaining the original intent or understanding is often a highly selective process, in which some utterances of some actors are singled out and ascribed to the whole. The second problem is the same as that encountered by positivism. There is extremely limited or even no room at all for the adaptation of legal norms to social change. If social change affects the constitution adversely, the only remedy would be to amend the text, which can be extremely complicated in a country like the United States. The constitution tends to petrify, in opposition to the theory of a living constitution.

Although one would have difficulties in finding positivists or originalists in Germany, these methodologies are by no means of historical interest only. Positivism, or more precisely a crude literal understanding, plays a considerable role in a number of post-communist countries and in parts of Latin America. Originalism has a stronghold in the United States in reaction to the activist Warren Court of the 1950s and '60s. In Germany, the idea that a legal method exists that can exclude any subjective element from the interpretation of legal norms is no longer upheld. The same is true for the majority of American legal scholars. But the consequences drawn from this premise differ considerably in the two countries. A very powerful school in the United States, Critical Legal Studies, is of the opinion that not only law-making is a political operation, but also the interpretation and application of law, the only difference being that the legislature operates in a political setting while judges operate in a judicial setting. As a further consequence, the focus of academic interest in the law differs. The question many American jurists tend to ask is: How will the courts decide? The dominant question in Germany would be: What is the correct decision?

In the last resort, a different attitude toward the autonomy of the law appears behind the two concepts. While the adherence to Critical Legal Studies does not leave much room for scholars to recognize the autonomy of the legal system, in Germany at least a relative autonomy of the law is widely accepted. This concept acknowledges on the one hand that law is a political product. It emerges from the legislative process, where political arguments dominate. On the other hand, once enacted, the law is disconnected from politics. It is up to the legislature to decide whether a legal norm remains in force or not. But as long as it is in force, its application does not follow political criteria. It is not only a difference in the institutional setting of political and judicial decisions. There is also a specific rationality of the legal system, which differs from the rationality of the political system.

The difference is not without consequences for the recruitment and the behaviour of judges. If interpretation and application of the law is regarded as a political operation, then the political preferences and affiliations of the judges are important, whereas they do not matter as much when the neutralizing effect of the legal rationality is recognized. The degree of politicization of the judiciary is linked to this. It explains at the same time the constant concern of the American constitutionalists as well as the American public with the so-called counter-majoritarian difficulty or the undemocratic character of judicial review, which is more or less absent in Germany and other countries where the establishment of judicial review was a reaction to the experience with non-democratic regimes.

An inside perspective of a constitutional court can confirm to what extent doctrine and methodology are able to bridge ideological differences. During my term on the bench I could observe that decisions were not necessarily result-driven. Legal arguments mattered and it happened quite often that members of the court changed their minds because of the arguments exchanged in the deliberation. Of course, this observation in one court cannot be generalized. Yet, what it certainly shows is how important it is that judges state the reasons for a decision. It is true that there may be good reasons for different results, but it is also true that not every result can be supported by legal reasons.

3. Which method guides the German Constitutional Court when it decides in matters involving constitutional conflicts? Authentic guidelines by the Court itself are rare, and where they appear in an opinion, they do not assume the form of a systematic and coherent explanation. Courts hardly discuss methodological questions, let alone describe in their opinions which method they followed. The method is practiced, not theoretically developed. This means that it must be inferred from the way a court usually arrives at its decisions. Easier than a positive statement on which method the Court adopts is the negative statement on what it avoids: There are neither positivists nor originalists on the bench in Germany, which neither means that the text of the constitution is neglected nor that historical arguments are absent.[4]

[4] *See* Life Imprisonment Case, (1977) 45 BVerfGE 187: "Neither original history nor the ideas and intentions of the framers are of decisive importance in interpreting particular provisions of the Basic Law. Since the adoption of the Basic Law, our understanding of the content, function, and effect of basic rights has deepened," *in* D. P. Kommers, The Constitutional Jurisprudence of the Federal Republic of Germany 307 (1997). (Editor's Note)

In very general terms the method can be described as purposive or functional. Constitutional norms are regarded as expressions of values or principles that society wanted to establish at the highest legal level. These values, in turn, inform the concretization of those constitutional provisions that apply to a concrete case. The goal of interpretation is to give utmost effect to these values or principles behind the text. Whenever the meaning of a constitutional provision vis-à-vis a concrete issue is to be determined, the Court asks for the objective to be pursued by a constitutional provision or for the function that it is to fulfil in society. Why do the media enjoy freedom of expression? Why does the family enjoy the special protection of the state? Why are the powers of parliament limited when delegating legislative power to the executive? Why are political parties obliged to organize themselves democratically and disclose their sources of finance and expenditure?

The result of the value search matters. It makes a difference whether the idea behind freedom of the media is to give the owners and journalists the possibility to disseminate their individual opinions to a larger public; or whether it aims to allow the owners to make as much profit as possible; or whether it is meant to enable the individual recipient to form his or her opinion and to guarantee that society gets the information it needs in the interest of self-government. In the first two cases, media regulation would present a constitutional problem, in the third case it may be a constitutional obligation. If a conflict between constitutionally protected values arises, the Court does not establish a hierarchy among them but tries to harmonize them in such a way that both retain as much as possible of their content. Thus, balancing becomes an important tool for the Court when it adjudicates fundamental rights issues.

The methodological maxim according to which the purpose of the constitutional provision at stake shall be given the utmost effect generates a further consequence that characterizes the methodological attitude of the German Court: What the utmost effect is cannot be ascertained without knowledge of the segment of social reality in which the constitutional provision is to take effect. Legal norms are formulated in view of a certain state of social reality. Next to text and purpose, this context is constitutive for the meaning of the legal norm. But different from the text and the purpose, which are determined by the legislature and remain the same as long as the norm is in force, the context is subject to social change. As a consequence, an interpretation that served the purpose best under certain conditions may cease to do so under changed conditions.

If this is so, adhering to the original interpretation could lead to suboptimal results. It could even overlook the function of the norm completely and produce dysfunctional results. It characterizes the jurisprudence of the Court that it takes social reality into account in order to ensure that the law can stand up to new challenges and that it retains its normative force also vis-à-vis new problems. The Court goes even one step further and asks for the probable consequences of alternative interpretations in the real world and chooses the interpretation whose consequences are closer to the normative purpose. In this way, it reacts in particular to new threats to constitutionally protected liberties, arising from scientific and technological developments and their commercial use, and thus broadens the protective scope of fundamental rights.

In sum, this method endows the constitution with high practical relevance. A number of important doctrinal innovations owe their existence to this approach, such as the principle of proportionality, the horizontal effect of human rights, the constitutional obligation of the legislature to protect fundamental rights against menaces from private actors or societal forces. They were meanwhile adopted in many new constitutions or in the jurisprudence of many constitutional courts. Yet, it is just this dynamic interpretation of the Court that brings back the question of the law-politics-divide. At what point does a new interpretation amount to an amendment of the constitution? Of course, in a formal sense an amendment requires a textual change of the constitution. This cannot be undertaken by a court. In a more substantive sense, however, changes in the meaning of a given text may have a bigger impact than textual changes.

The Basic Law has been formally amended 52 times in almost sixty years. Yet, the changes by way of interpretation, particularly in the field of fundamental rights, are certainly of a similar if not greater impact. Is there a point at which interpretation turns from a legal into a political operation? The answer cannot be different from that which was given earlier. As long as the interpretation is derived from the text in a legally acceptable way it remains within the realm of the law. The political consequences may nevertheless be severe. Every new content that a court derives from constitutional norms changes the balance between the political branches of government and the judiciary, mostly in favour of the latter. Sometimes this is called judicial imperialism. But it seems necessary to distinguish between intent and effect. The intent of courts usually is to give effect to constitutional requirements. The effect is often an increase in judicial power that corresponds with a loss of power on the side of the legislature. Still it seems very difficult to convince courts not to enforce what for them follows from the constitution.

In this situation many authors resort to judicial self-restraint as a remedy. Yet self-restraint, as recommendable as it may be, is but an appeal to professional ethics, not a legal rule. Descriptively, one can distinguish between active and deferential courts. Prescriptively, no operational criteria are visible. Too many factors are at stake, and often closer analysis reveals that an interpretation which looks extremely bold is well-founded under the circumstances in which it was taken. In addition, it is by no means clear whether there is a connection between judicial self-restraint and the degree of politicization of courts. The

German Constitutional Court, for example, is more active than the US Supreme Court, but it is less politicized.

The amending power is a more promising tool for limiting the expansion of judicial power. Courts are bound by the text of the law. Changing the text belongs to the politics. The political powers can re-program the judiciary whenever they disapprove of their jurisprudence. There is, however, one important difference between ordinary courts and constitutional courts. If the legislature is of the opinion that the interpretation of a law runs contrary to its legislative intention, it can change the law through a simple majority. For good reasons, constitutional courts apply the constitution whose amendment is usually more difficult. Yet, only by amending the constitutions can the political branches of government correct or re-program constitutional courts. Therefore, amendments should not be made too difficult. Where they are very difficult, like in the United States, the burden of the adaptation of the constitution to new challenges lies on the judges' shoulders and makes them more political. If judges shy away from carrying this burden, say for methodological reasons like originalism, and the amendment procedure is extremely difficult, it is to the detriment of the normative force of the constitution.

Amendments are an external corrective to the power of courts. However, there is also an internal corrective: Even if it is true that what is legally acceptable and what is not can only be defined in the legal system, it is never defined once and for all and judges are not the only actors to take part in the ongoing discussion. It is therefore extremely important that constitutional courts are embedded in a lively discourse in which the division of functions between the political and the juridical branches of government, the acceptability of legal methods, and the soundness of interpretations are constantly evaluated and readjusted. Judicial independence is not in danger when judges pay attention to society's reaction to their decisions.

Armand de Mestral & Jan A. Winter

The Law/Politics Distinction in the Experience of the European Court of Justice and the Supreme Court of Canada: A Comparative Study

1. The Experience of the Supreme Court of Canada

1.1. Introduction

The Supreme Court of Canada has in recent years assumed a key role in resolving issues that are of great political significance. This has in large part stemmed from the expansion of judicial review power which came about with the enactment of the *Charter*.[1] As a result, the Court has increasingly been called upon to adjudicate an increasing number of politically-sensitive Charter cases.

Aside from Charter litigation, the Supreme Court of Canada has, for a very long time, also been called upon to assume a role in dealing with often highly politicized federal-provincial conflicts of diverse nature.

Finally, the increasing numbers of references that have been submitted to the Supreme Court for adjudication have also had the effect of placing the Court at the center of politically charged matters. Although the Supreme Court of Canada has strived to maintain its function as an independent body, the court has in general not shied away from tackling the wide array of issues that have been brought to its attention.

[1] Canadian Charter of Rights and Freedoms, Part I of the Constitution Act, 1982, Schedule B to the Canada Act 1982 (UK), c.11.

Bogdan Iancu (Ed.), The Law/Politics Distinction in Contemporary Public Law Adjudication, 35-65.

1.2. The Impact of the Charter – A More Politicized Role for the Supreme Court of Canada?

The *Canadian Charter of Rights and Freedoms* not only protects fundamental rights and freedoms constitutionally, but it predicates a constitutional duty on courts to invalidate laws enacted by Parliament or by a provincial legislature, that do not accord with the values enshrined in the Charter. As Justice Bertha Wilson once observed:

> What right have [judges] to frustrate the will of the people's duly elected representatives? None, I would say, except for the fact that in enacting the Charter these same duly elected representatives conferred not just the right but that duty upon them.[2]

This idea was reiterated by Justice Iacobucci, who asserted that the enactment of the Charter was a deliberate choice of the legislatures, which conferred upon Courts the roles of being both the trustees of the Charter and the mediators of disputes arising from the interpretation of these rights.[3] It follows therefore that Courts "in their trustee or arbiter role must perforce scrutinize the role of the legislature and executive not in the name of the courts, but in the interests of the new social contract that was democratically chosen."[4]

The enactment of the *Charter* did indeed significantly expand the scope of judicial review of the Supreme Court of Canada over the substance of government actions, taking it beyond the scope of review of legislative jurisdiction under federalism, into the realm of substance and values under the *Charter*. The Supreme Court of Canada has in this regard been called upon to decide and influence important issues of public policy. The "judicial activism" critics argue that the Supreme Court's interventionist approach in Charter interpretation has exceeded the bounds of judicial authority and in so doing has usurped the roles of democratically elected governments.[5] Others contend that the Supreme Court's enhanced role simply reflects a necessary response to changing values whose protection depends on a heightened involvement of the judiciary. As will be seen in greater detail below, this issue remains a source for a heated debate among various commentators, whose views commonly lie at opposite ends of the spectrum.

At the one end, Hogg and Bushell have proposed the "dialogue" approach to *Charter* decisions in response to those who maintain that the enactment of

---

[2] B. Wilson, *We Didn't Volunteer*, *in* Howe & Russel (Eds.), Judicial Power and the Canadian Democracy 73, at 75 (2001).

[3] Vriend v. Alberta, [1985] 2 S.C.R. 486, at 497. *See also* D. McAllister, *Mackin: Of Sterile Rules and Real People*, 21 Sup. Ct. L. Rev. 340, at 362 (2003).

[4] *Vriend*, *id.*, at 564.

[5] *See, e.g.*, M. Mandell, The Charter of Rights and the Legalization of Politics in Canada, 2nd ed. (1994); R. Martin, The Most Dangerous Branch: How the Supreme Court of Canada Has Undermined Our Law and Our Democracy (2003).

the *Charter* represents the handing over of political decisions to unelected courts from elected representatives.[6] The dialogue approach argues that when courts invalidate a law, the legislature can still opt to reverse the decision, or even ignore the decision.[7] Thus according to Hogg and Bushell, a dialogue takes place in that the courts directly engage the legislatures to consider and argue for or against a decision rendered by the Courts. Other commentators, however, disagree with that assertion on the basis that a decision rendered by the Supreme Court of Canada creates a new policy *status quo*, in which the legislature has no say at all.[8] In this regard Manfredi and Kelly, leading political scientists, have suggested that the legislature is relegated to the simple role of being the passive observer of what the authors describe as the monologue of the Court.[9]

It is certainly incontestable that the constitutional issues that have been brought to the attention of the Supreme Court are essentially political in nature.[10] The fact is that "the very process of defining the contents of the rights protected by the *Charter* seems inherently political."[11] Peter Hogg, leading legal commentator, goes even further and affirms that:

> There can be no doubt that judicial review permits, indeed requires non elected judges to make decision of great political significance. Yet Canada's adoption of the *Charter of Rights and Freedoms* in 1982 was a conscious decision to increase the scope of judicial review.[12]

What this effectively means is that the constitutional issues that reach the Supreme Court are fundamentally and inescapably political. This is so because "[c]onstitutional arguments ask the Court to help define who we are as individuals and as a people. Such questions cannot be answered through the application of some specialized or technical brand of expertise. What

[6] P. W. Hogg & A. A. Bushell, *The Charter Dialogue Between Courts and Legislatures (Or Perhaps the Charter of Rights Isn't Such a Bad Thing After All)*, 35 Osgoode Hall L. J. 75 (1997).

[7] Sec. 33 of the Charter allows the federal Parliament or the provincial legislatures to pass legislation which is exempt (for a limited, renewable period of five years) from certain fundamental rights Charter provisions.

[8] T. Morton & R. Knopff, The Charter Revolution and the Court Party (2000).

[9] C. P. Manfredi & J. B. Kelly, *Dialogue, Deference and Restraint: Judicial Independence and Trial Procedures*, 64 Sask. L. Rev. 323 (2001).

[10] Peter Hogg notes "The addition of the Charter's grounds of judicial review has proved to be a substantial expansion of judicial review. Not only are the Charter cases more numerous than federalism cases, they are also more policy-laden. This is because many of the Charter rights are expressed in exceedingly vague terms, and all of the rights come into conflict with other values respected in Canadian society. The result is that judicial review under the charter involves a much higher content of policy than any other line of judicial work." P. Hogg, Constitutional Law of Canada (5th Edition Supplemented) at 36-6 (2007).

[11] P. Monahan, Politics and the Constitution: The Charter, Federalism and the Supreme Court of Canada 53 (1987) [emphasis in original].

[12] Hogg, *supra* note 10, at 5-29.

is demanded are political choices and acts of political will."[13] Chief Justice McLachlin also explicitly recognized that the adjudication of Charter cases necessarily requires that the Court make decisions that are political in nature. She thus makes the point that:

> This requires the Court to weigh the significance of the infringement of the individual right against the collective interests of the State in continuing the infringement. This is a judgment of political rather than judicial nature. The answer cannot be determined by logic or *stare decisis*.[14]

The Supreme Court of Canada has treaded carefully in the exercise of its function and has avoided interfering in political debates unless these debates raise significant legal issues or controversies that the Court believes it can address without overstepping the bounds of its competence. The attitude of the Supreme Court is in keeping with the principle of parliamentary sovereignty, which continues to delineate the division of authority between the courts and the legislatures. As one commentator notes "the *Charter* may be seen as another step in that process of defining roles. It has expanded the mandate of the judiciary as interpreter and guardian of constitutionally-protected human rights."[15]

The Supreme Court of Canada, while often referring to the American "political questions doctrine," has however not articulated a similar approach to clearly communicate what criteria it uses to determine if a given question is too political to be justiciable.[16] The case of *Operation Dismantle* stands as the leading authority for the proposition that the Supreme Court of Canada has not officially recognized and articulated the existence of a "political

[13] Monahan, *supra* note 11, at iii.

[14] B. McLachlin, *The Charter of Rights and the Freedoms: A Judicial Perspective*, U. B. C. L. Rev. 579, at 583-584 (1988-9).

[15] McAllister, *supra* note 3, at 361.

[16] It is a well established principle of American constitutional law that there are certain kinds of "political questions" that a court ought to refuse to decide. In *Baker v. Carr*, 369 U.S. 186 (1962), at 210-211, Brennan J. discussed the nature of the doctrine in the following terms:

> 'In determining whether a question falls within [the political question] category, the appropriateness under our system of government of attributing finality to the action of the political departments and also the lack of satisfactory criteria for a judicial determination are dominant considerations.' Coleman v. Miller, 307 U.S. 433, 454-455. The nonjusticiability of a political question is primarily a function of the separation of powers. Much confusion results from the capacity of the 'political question' label to obscure the need for case-by-case inquiry. Deciding whether a matter has in any measure been committed by the Constitution to another branch of government, or whether the action of that branch exceeds whatever authority has been committed, is itself a delicate exercise in constitutional interpretation, and is a responsibility of this Court as ultimate interpreter of the Constitution.

question" doctrine.[17] It was also established in this case that the Court may declare a question to be non-justiciable if it pertains to "moral and political considerations which it is not within the province of the courts to assess."[18] Justice Wilson stated that Section 1 of the *Canadian Charter of Rights and Freedom* frames the parameters under which courts can decide on the "judiciability" of a matter:

> Section 1, in my opinion, is the uniquely Canadian mechanism through which the courts are to determine the justiciability of particular issues that come before it. It embodies through its reference to a free and democratic society the essential features of our constitution including the separation of powers, responsible government and the rule of law.[19]

Wilson J. was of the view that "it [Section 1 of the *Charter*] obviates the need for a 'political questions' doctrine and permits the Court to deal with what might be termed 'prudential' considerations in a principled way without renouncing its constitutional and mandated responsibility of judicial review."[20]

In *Operation Dismantle v. The Queen*, the Supreme Court of Canada decided that the issue brought to its attention could not be construed as a political question and that it hence fell within the acceptable boundaries of review of the Court. Wilson J. stated to this effect that:

> [I]t seems to me that the legislature has assigned to the courts as a constitutional responsibility the task of determining whether or not a decision to permit the testing of cruise missiles violates the appellants' rights under the *Charter*. The preceding illustrations indicate why the legislature has done so. It is therefore, in my view, not only appropriate that we decide the matter; it is our constitutional obligation to do so.[21]

As one author aptly noted:

> *Operation Dismantle* both represents the leading authority for the proposition that Canadian courts do not recognize "a political question doctrine" as well as a leading authority for the proposition that certain types of political questions are not appropriate for judicial determination and a court should decline jurisdiction over them under Canadian law.[22]

The attitude adopted by the Court in *Operation Dismantle* is at first sight indicative of the fact that the Court shows a leveled openness to dealing with the variety of cases that are presented to it. As will be demonstrated in the subsequent sections, the Court has in general maintained this stance

---

[17] Operation Dismantle v. The Queen, [1985] 1 S.C.R. 441, at 472.
[18] *Id.*
[19] *Id.*
[20] *Id.*, at para. 104.
[21] Operation Dismantle, *supra* note 17, at 492.
[22] L. Sossin, Boundaries of Judicial Review: The Law of Justiciability in Canada 149 (2001).

except in cases pertaining to socio-economic rights and intergovernmental relations where the Court often avoids substituting its judgment to that of the legislatures.

1.3. Cases Dealing with Judicial Review of Federal/Provincial Arrangements

The Supreme Court of Canada has been called upon to engage in judicial review to settle fed+eralism disputes of various sorts since its creation in 1875. The questions that come before the Court often involve delineating the proper boundaries of action of each government. These questions are inescapably highly politicized and thus demand of the Court to approach them with restraint and caution.

On several occasions, the Court has stood by the statement that its "primary concern is to retain its proper role within the Constitutional framework of our democratic form of government."[23] The Supreme Court of Canada strongly reiterated this stance in *Amax Potash Ltd. v. Government of Saskatchewan* where it stated that:

> A state, it is said, is sovereign and it is not for the Courts to pass upon the policy or wisdom of legislative will. As a broad statement of principle that is undoubtedly correct, but the general principle must yield to the requisites of the constitution in a federal state. By it the bounds of sovereignty are defined and supremacy circumscribed. The Courts will not question the wisdom of enactments which, by the terms of the Canadian Constitution are within the competence of the Legislatures, *but it is the high duty of this Court to ensure that the legislatures do not transgress the limits of their constitutional mandate and engage in the illegal exercise of power.* [24]

In *Air Canada v. British Columbia*, a majority of the Court affirmed the constitutionality of the 1981 amendments to the *Gasoline Tax Act*, which retroactively taxed certain companies in the airline industry.[25] The amendments were strictly meant to defeat three companies' claims, brought in 1980, for reimbursement of gasoline taxes paid between 1974 and 1976, the collection of which had previously been found to be *ultra vires* the legislature of British Columbia. The legislative amendments, in addition to being retroactive, were for the benefit of the Crown, aimed at a particular industry with readily identifiable members and totally destructive of that industry's

[23] Reference Re Canada Assistance Plan (B.C.), [1991] 2 S.C.R. 525. *See also* Canada (Auditor General) v. Canada (Minister of Energy, Mines and Resources), [1989] 2 S.C.R. 49, at 90-91, and Borowski v. Canada (Attorney General), [1989] 1 S.C.R. 342, at 362.

[24] Authors' emphasis. Amax Potash Ltd. v. Government of Saskatchewan, [1977] 2 S.C.R. 576, at 590.

[25] Air Canada v. British Columbia, [1989] 1 S.C.R. 1161; Gasoline Tax Act, 1948, R.S.B.C. 1960, c. 162.

ability to successfully pursue their claims filed a year earlier. Nonetheless, the constitutionality of those amendments was affirmed by a majority of the Court.[26]

In *Finlay v. Canada (Minister of Finance)*,[27] the Supreme Court of Canada further articulated the criteria upon which the Court could decline to decide a matter on "political questions" grounds. The applicant, Finlay, was a welfare recipient under Manitoba's social assistance scheme. As a result of an early overpayment, the Province deducted a portion of his allowance over a period of time. One notable fact in this case was that the province of Manitoba operated its welfare program with significant financial contributions from the federal government. The financial contribution of the federal government consisted of an initiative aimed at encouraging provinces to develop welfare and social assistance programs according to certain standards and conditions. These conditions were imposed by statute. Finlay contended that the federal payments were illegal given that the province of Manitoba had breached certain sections of the agreement between the province and the federal government. Commenting on whether the issue was political rather than legal, Le Dain J. held that the Court should not "decline to determine it [the case] on the ground that because of its political context or implications it is better left for review and determination by the legislative or executive branches of government." As a leading constitutional law scholar commented on this case:

> Prudential reasoning does not have a significant part in the application of the "political questions" doctrine. In other words, it would appear not to be open to a court to decline to hear a matter because the political dimensions it raises could be more effectively considered by another branch of government. While courts can avoid political controversies on this basis the view, I think, is that pragmatic if not prudential, reasoning still has a role to play in the determination of justiciability, but that role should be confined to the determination of whether or not a matter is appropriate for the Court to decide.[28]

In *Canada (Auditor General) v. Canada (Minister of Energy, Mines and Resources)*, pursuant to an investigation in regards to certain acquisitions by Petro-Canada, the office of the Auditor General asked a cabinet minister to disclose some documents. The minister refused. The Auditor General brought a challenge to the Supreme Court to compel disclosure of the document. The Court in response stated that "an inquiry into justiciability is, first and foremost, a normative inquiry into the appropriateness as a matter of constitutional judicial policy of the courts deciding a given issue or, instead, deferring to other decision-making institutions of the polity."[29] Dickson C.J.

[26] *Air Canada*, *id.*

[27] Finlay v. Canada (Minister of Finance), [1986] 2 S.C.R. 607.

[28] Sossin, *supra* note 22, at 153.

[29] Canada (Auditor General) v. Canada (Minister of Energy, Mines and Resources), [1989] 2 S.C.R. 49.

writing for the majority argued that the Auditor General could not compel the minister to disclose the document for judicial review given that the *Auditor General Act* explicitly provided for a political rather than legal remedy for non disclosure.[30]

1.4. Reference Litigation

The *Supreme Court Act* imposes on the Supreme Court the duty of providing advisory opinions on questions referred to the court by the federal government.[31] Section 53 of the *Supreme Court Act* provides that "The Governor in Council may refer to the Court for hearing and consideration of important questions of law or fact" and that "it is the duty of the Court to hear and consider [the reference] and answer each question so referred."[32]

In the *Reference re Secession of Quebec* the Supreme Court of Canada provided an analysis on the circumstances under which the Province of Quebec would be justified in international and constitutional law in seeking secession from Canada and establishing itself as a sovereign state. The Court once again acknowledged the importance of respecting its proper function in the democratic framework of government but stated that it could address the questions brought to its attention for they not only were susceptible of legal analysis but they also lay under the legal framework of the democratic decision over secession.[33]

The court justified its approach in the following terms:

> As to the 'proper role' of the Court, it is important to underline, contrary to the submission of the *amicus curiae*, that the questions posed in this Reference do not ask the Court to usurp any democratic decision that the people of Quebec may be called upon to make. The questions posed by the Governor in Council, as we interpret them, are strictly limited to aspects of the legal framework in which that democratic decision is to be taken. The attempted analogy to the U.S. 'political questions' doctrine therefore has no application. The legal framework having been clarified, it will be for the population of Quebec, acting through the political process, to decide whether or not to pursue secession. As will be seen, the legal framework involves the rights and obligations of Canadians who live outside the province of Quebec, as well as those who live within Quebec. As to the 'legal' nature of the questions posed, if the Court is of the opinion that it is being asked a question with a significant extralegal component, it may interpret the question so as to answer only its legal aspects; if this is not possible, the Court may decline to answer the question. In the present Reference the questions

---

30 *Id.*, at 91-92.
31 Hogg, *supra* note 10, at 8-15.
32 Supreme Court Act R.S., 1985, c. S-26, s.53.
33 Reference re Secession of Quebec, [1998] 2 S.C.R. 217.

> may clearly be interpreted as directed to legal issues, and, so interpreted, the Court is in a position to answer them.[34]

As one commentator observed:

> [T]rue, the court in the secession reference may have been acting as politicians rather than as judges in formulating a duty to negotiate secession that applies following a clear majority on a clear question. But the pragmatic would respond that the court had no role but to respond to the high political sensitivity of the question before it.[35]

The decision clearly demonstrates that the Court's consideration of political questions is "neither inappropriate nor easily avoided" when important decisions of political significance are brought before it.[36] In *Reference re Canada Assistance Plan (British Columbia)*[37] the Court put this test into practice and accepted to look at the terms of federal-provincial agreements on the grounds that a form of contract had an adequate legal component to justify the Court's intervention. The question at issue pertained to a dispute between the provinces (represented by British Columbia) and the federal government over the federal government's limiting of transfer payments under the former *Canada Assistance Plan (CAP).* Under the *CAP*, each Province entered into a separate agreement with the federal government pursuant to which the federal government agreed to share the cost of social assistance on a 50/50 basis. As a result of the fiscal crisis of the late 1980s, the federal government unilaterally altered the agreement between it and three Provinces, placing a limit on its contribution to social welfare spending in those provinces. In the Supreme Court of Canada, the Attorney General for Canada argued that the dispute was a political matter and should not be heard by the Court. The Court argued in this regards that:

> [I]n considering its appropriate role the Court must determine whether the question is purely political in nature and should, therefore, be determined in another forum or whether it has a sufficient legal component to warrant the intervention of the judicial branch.[38]

The Court thus held that the subject at bar was a legal question and that it could hence effectively be answered by the Court. As the one commentator noted on the case, the question at hand could have been deemed to be non-justiciable if the "court had been asked whether the federal parliament should as a matter of policy reduce its contributions to provincial social programmes."[39]

[34] *Id.*, at paras. 27-28.
[35] P. Monahan, *The Public Policy Role of the Supreme Court of Canada in the Secession Reference*, 11 NJCL 65, at 92 (1999).
[36] Sossin, *supra* note 22, at 157.
[37] *Reference Re Canada Assistance Plan (B.C.)*, [1991] 2 S.C.R. 525.
[38] *Id.*
[39] Hogg, *supra* note 10, at 36-21.

In the *Manitoba Reference*, Freedman C.J.M, responding to a submission asking the Court to refrain from responding to a question on the grounds that it was a purely "political question," stated that:

> In my view, this submission goes too far. Its characterization of Question 2 as 'purely political' overstates the case. That there is a political element embodied in the question, arising from the contents of the joint address, may well be the case. But that does not end the matter. If Question 2, even if in part political, possesses a constitutional feature, it would legitimately call for our reply. In my view, the request for a decision by this Court on whether there is a constitutional convention, in the circumstances described, that the Dominion will not act without the agreement of the Provinces poses a question that is [*sic*], at least in part, constitutional in character. It therefore calls for an answer, and I propose to answer it.[40]

The reference cases suggest that the Supreme Court of Canada far from refuses to answer questions on the sole basis that they raise political matters. The cases reviewed suggest instead that the open-mindedness of the Supreme Court is tempered by a cautious attitude not to exercise its judicial authority outside the acceptable parameters of judicial review. As will be shown in the following section, the Supreme Court of Canada has accorded substantial deference in its handling of the various socio-economic cases that have been brought to its attention.

1.5. The Supreme of Court of Canada Handling Disputes Involving Socio-Economic Rights

The Supreme Court of Canada has accorded greater judicial deference to legislative choices in "socio-economic" cases where a government is asked to strike the balance between the legitimate claims of competing groups in society for limited resources. The Court has taken the view that most issues pertaining to property, contract and social welfare are outside the acceptable limits of judicial review. The Court has refused to interpret the open-ended wording of Section 7 of the *Charter* as including the right to property, or as a tool to review laws regulating certain socio-economic rights, such as the right to welfare. The Supreme Court has in so doing consciously and deliberately avoided dealing with a set of significant public policy matters.[41]

The Supreme Court's decision in *Gosselin* v. *Quebec (Attorney General)* aptly attests to this as the Court explicitly rejected a challenge to the Quebec

[40] Reference Re Amendment of the Constitution of Canada (1981), 117 D.L.R. (3d) 1 (Man. C.A.).

[41] Sec. 7 of the *Charter* provides that: "[e]veryone has the right to life, liberty and security of the person and the right not to be deprived thereof except in accordance with the principles of fundamental justice." D. Wiseman, *Competence Concerns in Charter Adjudication: Countering the Anti-Poverty Incompetence Argument*, 51 McGill L.J. 503 (2006).

government's use of reduced rates of social assistance as an incentive for welfare recipients to participate in employability programs.[42] The *Gosselin* case raised the critical issue of whether the right to "security of the person" in Section 7 of the *Charter* and the right to equality under Section 15 impose positive legal obligations upon governments to ensure an adequate level of income for Canadians who depend on government assistance.[43] Chief Justice McLachlin, writing for the majority, noted that "one day s. 7 [the right to life, liberty and security of the person] may be interpreted to include positive obligations." However, she found that there was "insufficient evidence" in that case to support adopting such a "novel" interpretation. Justice Arbour wrote a strong dissent calling for a *Charter* right to adequate social assistance. She nonetheless recognized that the Court did not have the competence to define the appropriateness of the social assistance program.[44] Her rationale was that, given that the issue at stake involved a question of resource allocation, the decision should be left to the legislative branch because it alone has the mandate from taxpayers to deal with these types of questions. This rationale is based on the premise that questions of resource allocation require the kind of value and policy judgments on the extent of social obligation, which can only be efficiently addressed by the legislatures and not the courts. Some critics endorse such a stand on the basis that protections of socio-economic rights "are too vague to guarantee anything of substance, do not touch the complicated causes of poverty and disadvantage and their symbolic message is at best ambiguous."[45] For some commentators, this reluctance was seemingly in part due to competence concerns. Nonetheless, as Wiseman notes:

> The Supreme Court itself has rightly questioned some of its own earlier conceptions of the attributes that signal incompetence, particularly the social policy/criminal justice distinction. Second, in other types of *Charter* cases, where competence challenges similar to those that can arise in anti-poverty cases have arisen, the courts have been willing to respond to those challenges in ways that provide more fulsome *Charter* protection.[46]

[42] Gosselin v. Quebec (Attorney General), 2002 SCC 84, [2002] 4 S.C.RJ 42985.

[43] Sec. 15 of the *Charter* provides that: "(1) Every individual is equal before and under the law and has the right to the equal protection and equal benefit of the law without discrimination and, in particular, without discrimination based on race, national or ethnic origin, colour, religion, sex, age or mental or physical disability.
(2) Subsection (1) does not preclude any law, program or activity that has as its object the amelioration of conditions of disadvantaged individuals or groups including those that are disadvantaged because of race, national or ethnic origin, colour, religion, sex, age or mental or physical disability."

[44] *Gosselin, supra* note 42, at para. 357.

[45] J. Bakan, What's Wrong with Social Rights 86 (1992). *See also* M. Mandel, The Charter of Rights and the Legalization of Politics in Canada (1994).

[46] D. Wiseman, *Competence Concerns in Charter Adjudication: Countering the Anti-Poverty Incompetence Argument*, 51 McGill L. J. 503 (2006).

Wiseman thus argues that the competence problem may be overstated as an argument militating for a non-interventionist court approach in dealing with issues related to socio-economic rights. Nonetheless, the Supreme Court decision in *Mahe v. Alberta (Attorney General)* speaks to an explicit recognition of the challenges that courts face in reviewing the balances struck by governments in designing and implementing social programs. Specifically, in opting for a declaratory remedy, the Court in *Mahe* expressly chose to leave it to the government, at least in the first instance, to identify and balance the relevant interests and considerations.[47]

The Court has continually been reluctant to engage in issues pertaining to socio-economic rights on the basis that these questions are too political and therefore are better addressed by the legislative branch.

1.6. Conclusion

The Court has successfully dealt with politically sensitive questions by creating an intricate distinction between questions that are purely political and those that are political but with sufficient legal components to warrant the judicial intervention. The Supreme Court of Canada seems to have articulated its own test in determining under what conditions the Court should accept or refrain from answering a political question. The test consists of identifying if the question under consideration contains a *sufficient legal element* to warrant its consideration. Lorne Sossin defines the essence of the various additional strands of analysis that the court utilizes to deal with political questions as comprising:

(1) matters which fail to raise legal issues, including (i) purely political disputes; (ii) disputes relating to the legislative process; and (iii) disputes involving the wisdom or desirability of legislation or government policy; (2) disputes involving constitutional conventions; (3) disputes regarding Parliamentary privileges and Crown prerogatives; (4) disputes involving intergovernmental relations; (5) disputes involving social and economic rights and; (6) disputes involving the enforcement of international agreements, the application of international law or the actions of foreign states.[48] The Supreme Court of Canada has thus effectively charted its own course in dealing with issues of "political nature" that it has been called upon to adjudicate. Rather than adopting a stance that outrightly refrains from answering questions that bear political connotations, the Supreme Court of Canada has devised a kind of "purely political question" test that has enabled it to address important issues without deviating from its essentially judicial function within the constitutional framework of Canada's federal system of government. The advent of the

[47] *Mahe v. Alberta* (A.G), [1990] 1 S.C.R. 34.
[48] Sossin, *supra* note 22, at 145.

Charter has also significantly expanded the Court's judicial review power and has forced the Court to confront an increasing number of politically charged questions. The attitude of the Supreme Court is emblematic of the fact that the Court is mindful of the political importance of its decisions and in very rare situations sets limits to what it is called to rule on. The circumstances where the Court has refrained from intervening most notably include disputes arising from federal-provincial arrangements and disputes pertaining to social and economic rights. A review of the case law emanating from the Supreme Court of Canada nonetheless suggests that the Court does not shrink from ruling simply because of the political significance of its role.

In recent years, the Supreme Court of Canada has used procedural means to temper the impact of politically sensitive decisions. Thus it has made increasing use of its inherent power to suspend the operation of its decisions temporarily, in order to give governments the time necessary to proceed with the delicate and complex work of implementation. The most notable case in point is the *Bilodeau Case*[49] but, as this technique has not been limited to sensitive language cases, it seems that the Court considers that it has wide latitude to rule on the mode of implementation as well as the substance of a case.

2. The European Court of Justice and the Distinction Between Law and Politics

2.1. Introduction

The European Court of Justice (ECJ) is charged with the task of ensuring that in the interpretation and application of the European treaties the law is observed.[50] The Court does not only have extensive powers of administrative and constitutional review over Community acts, it also has jurisdiction over matters relating to compliance by states with their Community obligations and, through the system of preliminary references, it provides national courts with interpretative rulings enabling them to apply Community law correctly in cases before them.

Obviously, the ECJ is only called upon to perform a judicial function. It therefore must refrain from invading the domain that the European treaties reserve to the political institutions of the European Union. Indeed, according to Article 7 of the EC Treaty: "Each institution shall act within the limits of the

[49] Bilodeau v. A.G. (Man.), [1986] 1 S.C.R. 449.

[50] EC, Consolidated Versions of the Treaty on European Union and the Treaty Establishing the European Community, Official Journal C 321E of 29 December 2006, art. 220, *available at* EURlex, http://eur-lex.europa.eu/en/treaties/index.htm. [EC Treaty].

powers conferred upon it by this Treaty."[51] However, even though the Court will not take political decisions, its judgments will often have a considerable political impact. This is especially so when the court assigns a wide scope to the prohibitions or obligations imposed on the Member States and defines the scope and the nature of EC's competences in a manner contributing to strengthening the Community's capacity for action. There are also instances where the ECJ has shown restraint.[52]

Western constitutional systems normally consider foreign policy issues to be "political questions," which are not within the courts' jurisdiction. In the EU, the Court was initially confronted with questions concerning the general scope of EC competences in the field of foreign relations. There seems to be a certain measure of judicial retrenchment since the 1970s – period which saw the emergence of the doctrine of "*in foro interno, in foro externo*." Matters relating to judicial deference for assessments made by political authorities in the Member States and the Community and – indirectly – in the United Nations Security Council have arisen in connection with decisions implementing UN sanctions against Yugoslavia and decisions pursuant to UN Security Council resolutions concerning the fight against terrorism. Likewise, the refusal by the Community judiciary to review the legality of Community actions in terms of their compatibility with WTO law may be explained by the courts' wish not to restrict the freedom of action of the EC's political authorities.[53]

The generalization of judicial review of legislative and administrative actions and the increased importance of general principles of law and human rights as grounds for review of such actions have enabled the Community judiciary to develop a critical attitude and to probe deeply into matters which were previously considered to fall squarely into the area of political or administrative discretion.[54]

2.2. Judicial Contributions to Strengthening the Foundations of the Community Legal Order

2.2.1. Basic Features of the Community Legal Order

The Court has made a major effort to turn the Communities into an effective supranational and quasi-federal polity. This inevitably means that Member States must accept a concomitant loss of autonomy. In certain areas their powers are extinguished (*e.g.*, trade policy measures, agriculture), in other areas they have retained their powers but their exercise is only allowed subject to severe

[51] *Id.*, art. 7.
[52] *See* part 2.2., below.
[53] *See* part 2.3., below.
[54] *See* part 2.4., below.

restrictions (*e.g.*, taxation, state aids). Generally speaking, the Court has not hesitated to affirm in appropriate cases that the Community is an autonomous legal order and that membership of the Community entails consequences that Member States might not have anticipated. Although this could have elicited some resentment from Member States, it did not change the fact that these states were bound by Community rules – explicit or implicit ones – as interpreted by the Court. The ECJ, from the early days of the Communities' existence, has construed the Treaties in such a way as to promote as much as possible the chances that the treaties would achieve their purposes. Pursuant to the principle of effectiveness and the principle of Community loyalty, the obligations of Member States must be interpreted broadly and the areas of reserved powers narrowly.[55] Although the Community is based on the principle of attributed competences, the Court has shown a great determination to ensure that the achievement of the Community's goals would not be jeopardized by a narrow interpretation of the Community's competences.[56] The Court has thus filled gaps, interpreted widely and in a teleological fashion, and has "unearthed" implied powers for the Community. In this connection one can mention its case law concerning the general structural underpinnings of the Community legal order, such as direct effect, supremacy, the creation of new legal remedies (*e.g.*, in connection with the liability of a Member State for failure of its institutions to comply with Treaty obligations). Through its case law, the Community judiciary has greatly enhanced the legal position of private individuals under the Treaties. Individuals can invoke many provisions of Community law in the face of domestic law rules that are incompatible with the Community provisions, a situation that ensures that Member States authorities would abide by their obligations under Community law. The vigilance of individuals to protect their own rights is a most useful addition to the power of the Commission to ensure respect for Treaty obligations.[57] By the same token, the position of the judiciary in the Member States is reinforced. Domestic courts are entitled – and required – to enforce provisions which the political departments of the states have not implemented correctly or within the appropriate time limits and which are sufficiently specific to lend themselves for such direct application by the courts. This "judicialization" of the execution of Community obligations has therefore resulted in a rearrangement of constitutional functions in the Member States. Domestic courts have been required to step in where national legislators or governments have failed to adopt the necessary measures for implementing Treaty obligations.

---

[55] *See* EC Treaty, art. 10.

[56] *Id.*, art. 5.1

[57] Van Gend en Loos v. Nederlandse Administratie der Belastingen (Case 26/62); [1963] ECR 1; [1970] C.M.L.R. 1.

2.2.2. Negative Integration

The scope of the prohibitions the Treaty imposed on the Member States in relation to the Common Market has often proven to be more extensive than States thought they had bargained for. For instance, negative integration in relation to the rules hindering cross-border trade, establishment, services and capital movements does not only pertain to discriminatory measures. The Treaty rules in this area also prohibit measures that are not only applicable to foreign goods, persons or capital but also and "indistinctly" to domestic goods, persons and capital.[58] It is true that such measures can be saved if they pursue legitimate aims defined in the Treaty or recognized in the Court's case law. The important point, however, is the fact that such measures are reached by the Treaty prohibitions and that Member States must be able to produce grounds for justification and also to show that the measures in question satisfy a test of proportionality.

There is no doubt that in many cases these requirements are seen by political authorities in the Member States as irritating constraints on their freedom to pursue domestic policy objectives that are not directly related to intra-Community movements of products or people. The same observation applies if the European Commission advises Member States that public funding of social housing activities or of public health care is to be subjected to scrutiny under the provisions relating to State aid. The provision of services by public organs in markets where private operators also offer services is not exempt from the rules of competition. Neither are services of general economic interest immune from scrutiny under the Treaty rules. Member States are not always ready to embrace such conclusions and would prefer to limit the scope of their obligations. The Court, which is generally in favor of giving a wide scope to the Treaty prohibitions, is sometimes seen as overly responsive to free market interests.

2.2.3. A Cautious and Traditional Approach to Questions of Community Competence

It would be incorrect to mention the tendencies toward judicial activism referred to in the preceding paragraphs without indicating that there are also a number of cases where the ECJ has shown great reticence and where it has declined to interpret the Community legislative powers broadly at the expense of Member States competences. An illustration of this attitude may be found in the *Grant Case*.[59] The complainant in this case had submitted that, like certain provisions of national law or of international conventions, the Community provisions on equal treatment of men and women should be interpreted as

[58] *See* EC Treaty, arts. 28, 43, 49, 56.

[59] Case C-249/96 Grant v. South West Trains, [1998] ECR I-621.

covering discrimination based on sexual orientation. The Court disagreed: "[A]lthough respect for the fundamental rights which form an integral part of those general principles of law is a condition of the legality of Community acts, those rights cannot in themselves have the effect of extending the scope of the Treaty provisions beyond the competences of the Community."[60]

Similarly, in the celebrated *Tobacco Cases*, the Court limited the scope of what can be done by the Community legislator on the basis of article 95 (the "general" equal basis for measures of harmonization of laws).[61]

Reference should also be made to the very cautious and wise judgment of the court in Case 13/83, *EP v. Council*.[62] The case concerned the failure of the Council to adopt measures in the transport field within a certain time limit. The Court was careful to avoid substituting its own views for those of the Council, but was able to give a clear indication of the contents of the measures the Treaty required the Council to adopt.[63]

On the other hand, the Court has, in a recent case, greatly upset certain Member States and criminal lawyers.[64] In this case, the Commission successfully challenged the Council's choice of Article 34 of the Treaty on EU as the legal basis for a number of legal provisions prescribing that Member States establish as criminal offences certain offences in the field of the environment. The Court agreed with the Commission that the measures in question came within the scope of the Community's powers on the environment and that the Council had erred in not opting for a genuine Community act but rather for a framework decision under the less supranational Third Pillar of the EU Treaty.

2.3. Judicial Review of Decisions in the Field of International Relations

2.3.1. Scope of Community Competences

The express powers conferred on the Community to act in the international sphere were very limited under the original EEC Treaty. The Community was only recognized an express external power as regards commercial policy (Article 133) and with respect to association agreements designed to establish a close relationship with third countries (Article 310). In spite of the principle that the Community only possesses the powers specifically granted to it, so that all other powers must be deemed to have remained vested in the Member

[60] *Id.*, at para. 45.

[61] *See* Case C-376/98 Germany v. Parliament and Council [2000] ECR I-8419; *also see,* Germany v. EP and Council, [2000] ECRI-8419.

[62] Case 13/83, EP v. Council, [1975] ECR 1514.

[63] EC Treaty, art. 71.

[64] Case C-176/03, Commission v. Council, [2005] ECR I-7879.

States (Article 5), the Court has gradually developed a comprehensive theory of implied external powers. This was a sensitive political enterprise, because Member States in general were very reluctant to relinquish the power to conduct policies in the international sphere. Through a number of high profile pronouncements, the Court has extended the Community's competence in the external field so substantially that the external powers of the Community were virtually coextensive with its internal competences.[65] Those early judgments were widely seen as unwarranted judicial interference with the political powers of the Treaty's founding nations. Especially in France, the Court's judgments were regarded as "le gouvernement des juges."

During the 1990s, the Court may have shown greater reticence with regard to questions concerning the scope of the external competences of the European Community. Thus, in Opinion 1/94, the Court refrained from extending the scope of the common external policy to include trade in services and commercial aspects of intellectual property rights in Article 133.[66] This Opinion may be regarded as evidence of judicial retrenchment and deference by the Court to the need for political consensus on an issue involving a significant transfer of powers from the Member States to the Community. The fact that the Commission, a few years earlier, had failed to persuade the Member States to broaden the commercial policy powers of the Community through an amendment of Article 133, may perhaps have convinced the Court that an important expansion of Community competences ought to be brought about by political decision-making and not by judicial verdict.

Be that as it may, the Court's judgments in the air transport cases,[67] demonstrated again the Court's willingness to ensure that Member States adhered to the basic tenets of the internal market and that they did not frustrate the need for unified external action as regards air traffic rights by an unlawful exercise of powers they no longer possessed in this area.

2.3.2. Unilateral or UN-inspired Sanctions

The Court has recognized that Member States possess a certain room for maneuver in matters involving issues of defense and national security. When, in the early 1990s, the break-up of Yugoslavia led to the formation of new states, including the Former Yugoslav Republic of Macedonia (FYROM), Greece objected against the use of the name Macedonia, which, in its view, promoted the idea of a unified Macedonia and constituted a threat to its territorial integrity. In February 1994, in breach of EC external trade instruments, Greece unilaterally prohibited trade with FYROM. Greece invoked Article 297, which

---

[65] *See* Case 22/70, Commission v. Council (ERTA), [1971] ECR 263; Cases 3, 4 and 6/76, Kramer, [1976] ECR 1279; Opinion 1/76 (Laying-up fund), [1977] ECR 741.

[66] [1994] ECR I-5267.

[67] Case C-466-476/98, Commission v. UK *et al.*, [2002] ECR I-9427.

allows Member States to take safeguard measures in the event of serious internal disturbances affecting the maintenance of law and order, in the event of war, serious international tension constituting a threat of war, or in order to carry out obligations undertaken for the purpose of maintaining peace and security. The Commission brought an action under Article 298 but the case was withdrawn after Advocate-General Jacobs delivered his opinion.[68] In this case, the Advocate-General argued that the scope and intensity of the Court's power to review Greece's conduct was subject to important limitations on account of the nature of the questions raised. The questions as to whether serious international tension existed and whether such tension constituted a threat of war involved a political assessment of an eminently political question. Hence there were no proper juridical tools and criteria that could be used for dealing with such a problem. This Opinion is the EC judicial text, which comes closest to establishing some kind of "political question" doctrine under EC law. The way in which the Advocate-General approached the problem was strongly deferential to the right of the Greek authorities to make their own appraisal. It has been observed, however, that in spite of this deferential attitude, a closer analysis revealed that there was substantial review of the factors that were alleged as justification for Greece's conduct.[69]

However, the Court is not invariably generous when it comes to deciding whether a Member State has retained authority to adopt autonomous measures on public security grounds. The political nature of a problem to be addressed does not give a Member State freedom to disregard binding Community law. In Case C-124/95, *Centro-Com*,[70] the UK tried to strengthen the effectiveness of trade sanctions against Serbia and Montenegro as laid down in a Council Regulation.[71] This regulation implemented a UN Security Council Resolution. Exports of medical products and foodstuffs were exempted from the trade embargo. Centro-Com, an Italian company, had exported exempted products to Montenegro. It requested payment from an account with a bank in London. As a result of a new Treasury policy, developed in response to reports about abuses of exceptions to the embargo, funds from a UK bank could only be transferred if the exports had been made from the UK. The UK argued before the Court that the national measures were taken by virtue of its national competence in the field of foreign and security policy and that performance of its obligations under the UN Charter and under the United Nations resolutions fell within that competence. The Court recognized in this case that the Member States had indeed retained power to conduct their own policies in the field of foreign and security policy but such powers must be exercised in a manner

[68] Case C-120/94, [1996] ECR I-1513.

[69] *See* P. Eeckhout, Does Europe's Constitution Stop at the Water's Edge? Law and Policy in the EU's External Relations (2005).

[70] [1997] ECR I-81.

[71] Council Regulation 1432/95 (OJ 1992, L 151/4).

consistent with Community law. Article 11 of the Community's general export regulation allowed Member States to restrict exports on grounds of public security. A national measure intended to apply sanctions prescribed by a UN Security resolution could therefore fall within the exception laid down in Article 11. However, a Member State could no longer rely on Article 11 once the public security concerns mentioned in that provision had been comprehensively addressed by a Community instrument such as the Council's sanctions regulation.

Considering the political nature of sanctions decisions, it appears very improbable that private parties can successfully bring legal challenges against such decisions before the Community Courts. In this connection it is important to refer briefly to another case, *Bosphorus*,[72] in which the Court was asked to review the validity of Community measures adopted for the implementation of UN Security Council sanction resolutions.

Whereas the FYROM and Centro-Com cases were both concerned with unilateral acts of a Member State, in the *Bosphorus* case the Court was faced with a challenge to EC legislation, namely Regulation 990/93 concerning trade between the EEC and the Federal Republic of Yugoslavia (Serbia and Montenegro) (FRY).[73] Yugoslav Airlines (JAT) had leased two aircraft to *Bosphorus*, a Turkish air charter company. The leases were not in breach of the sanctions rules but when in April 1993 one of the aircraft was flown to Dublin Airport for the purpose of maintenance, the Irish authorities impounded the aircraft, in implementation of article 8 of the EC Sanctions Regulation. This provision, in virtually the same terms as those used in the UN Resolution, stipulated that all vessels, vehicles, rolling stock, and aircraft in which the controlling interest was held by a person or undertaking in or operating from the FRY had to be impounded by the competent authorities of the Member States. The case hinged on the question whether for the application of article 8 it was enough that ownership of the aircraft was vested in JAT or whether the term "interest" meant that actual control was required. The Court interpreted the regulation in line with the UN resolution and found that actual control was not necessary for justifying the impounding of the aircraft owned by JAT.

However, *Bosphorus*' claims also raised the important issue of whether sanction decisions could be reviewed by reference to general principles of law and fundamental human rights, such as legal certainty, the proportionality principle, and the right to property. The Court confirmed that such decisions could be subjected to this type of review. It found that according to settled case law, the fundamental rights invoked were not absolute, since their exercise was capable of being subjected to restrictions justified by objectives of general interest. Balancing the claimant's private interest against that of the international community and of the European Union, the impounding of the aircraft could

[72] Case C-84/95, Bosphorus, [1996] ECR I-3953.
[73] OJ 1993, L 102/14.

not be considered either an inappropriate or a disproportionate measure. In the *Bosphorus* case, the Court showed deference to the predominance of the policy-makers but it did not abdicate its judicial functions. Sanctions decisions are not immune from judicial scrutiny for conformity with general principles of law and human rights.

In the recent terrorism cases,[74] the Court of First Instance dismissed an action brought by alleged terrorists, whose assets had been frozen against a Council Regulation[75] imposing specific restrictive measures directed against certain persons and entities associated with Osama bin Laden, the Al-Qaeda network, and the Taliban (OJ 2002 L 139/9). The Court clearly wanted to avoid any interference with the execution by the Member States of their obligations under the UN resolutions. In contrast to the *Bosphorus* decision, the Court refused to subject the Community regulations implementing UN sanctions resolutions to review on grounds of general principles of Community law and human rights:

> Any review of the internal lawfulness of the contested regulation, especially having regard to the provisions or general principles of Community law relating to the protection of fundamental rights, would [...] imply that the Court is to consider, indirectly, the lawfulness of those resolutions. In that hypothetical situation, in fact, the origin of the illegality alleged by the applicant would have to be sought, not in the adoption of the contested regulation but in the resolutions of the Security Council which imposed the sanctions [...]. In particular, if the Court were to annul the contested regulation, as the applicants claim it should, although that regulation seems to be imposed by international law, on the ground that that act infringes their fundamental rights which are protected by the Community legal order, such annulment would indirectly mean that the resolutions of the Security Council concerned themselves infringe those fundamental rights. In other words, the applicants ask the Court to declare by implication that the provision of international law at issue infringes the fundamental rights of individuals, as protected by the Community legal order.[76]

The only remedy it could offer the claimants was a review of the lawfulness of the UN and the Community measures in question by reference to *ius cogens*:

> None the less, the Court is empowered to check, indirectly, the lawfulness of the resolutions of the Security Council in question with regard to *jus cogens*, understood as a body of higher rules of public international law binding on all subjects of international law, including the bodies of the United Nations, and from which no derogation is possible.[77]

[74] T-306/01, Yusuf, and T-315/01, Kadi, [2005] ECR II-3532 and 3649.
[75] Council Regulation (EC) No 881/2002 of 27 May 2002.
[76] Yusuf and Kadi, *supra* note 74, at paras. 266, 267.
[77] *Id.*, at para. 277.

2.3.3. Compliance with WTO Law; Deference to Political Authorities

Judicial deference to political authorities is clearly discernible in the Court's approach to the possibility of judicial review of Community acts on grounds of incompatibility of such acts with WTO law. In Case C-149/96, *Portugal v. Council*,[78] the Court confirmed its long standing case law according to which multilateral trade agreements do not have direct effect in the Community legal order. It will only review the legality of a Community measure in light of the WTO rules in situations where the Community intended, by means of that measure, to implement a particular obligation assumed in the context of the WTO, or where the measure refers expressly to the precise provisions of the WTO agreements. There is no doubt that the refusal to attribute direct effect to WTO law can be explained in large measure by the fact that major trading partners such as the US and Canada do not accept that WTO law can have direct effect. It is also clear that, in this area, the wishes of the Community's political authorities carry great weight. In the preamble to the Council Decision[79] concerning the conclusion of the agreements reached during the Uruguay Round negotiations, the Council had stated that the WTO Agreement was not susceptible of being directly invoked in Community or Member State courts. If the Court were to accept the direct effect of this type of international agreements, there would obviously be a lack of reciprocity. European judges clearly indicate that they do not wish to tie the Council and the Commission's hands:

> To accept that the role of ensuring that Community law complies with those rules devolves directly on the Community judicature would deprive the legislative or executive organs of the Community of the scope for manoeuvre enjoyed by their counterparts in the Community's trading partners.[80]

The Court of Justice has not changed its views in a number of cases where private parties have complained about non-compliance of the EC with WTO dispute rulings. In 1997 the Dispute Settlement Body (DSB) ruled against the EC bananas regime. A ruling of the WTO must be complied with within a reasonable time. In 1999, the EC measures taken to comply with the Ruling were found wanting. In the *Van Parys* case,[81] and in the *Chiquita* case,[82] the claimants sought damages from the Community for the period after the reasonable time for compliance had expired. The courts dismissed the claims. They pointed out that the Dispute Settlement Understanding provided that the issue of compliance remained on the agenda of the DSB as long as the parties

[78] [1999] ECR I-9519.
[79] 94/800, [1994] OJ L 336/1.
[80] *Portugal*, *supra* note 78, at para. 46.
[81] Case C-377/02, Van Parys, [2005] ECR I-1465.
[82] Case T-19/01, Chiquita, [2005] ECR II-315.

did not reach an agreement on compliance. Therefore, the courts cannot interfere with the leeway required by EC political institutions for negotiating a settlement, even after the expiry of the reasonable period.

2.4. Judicial Review of the Exercise of Discretionary Powers

2.4.1. General Considerations

It is generally recognized by courts that they should respect the freedom of the legislator and the administration to fulfill the tasks assigned to them, i.e., to adopt legislation and to execute rules. The very nature of theses activities severely limits the possibility of judicial scrutiny. This is not because the problems to be solved are too political for courts to handle but because courts have not been called into existence in order to deal with these problems.

However that may be, judicial review is not just a matter of testing the compatibility of legislative acts with the constitution or the conformity of subordinate administrative acts with enabling laws. Law is not just the consequence of what legislative bodies lay down in their enactments. Certain legal principles, in particular those embodying human rights and the fundamental guarantees of the rule of law, are considered as "supralegal." Political institutions may be tempted occasionally to disregard these fundamental requirements. Only the judiciary will then be able to recall the limits that supralegal rules impose on politics. This is all within their traditional role of being "guardians of the rule of law."[83] In spite of the fact that European courts will sometimes curb actions of political institutions that affect human rights or run counter to general principles of law, these courts are very much aware of the fact that the legislative and executive bodies are entitled to a margin of appreciation free from judicial interference and that they should therefore refrain from evaluating a situation, simply because there are no legal standards that can be applied to that situation.

2.4.2. The Search for the Limits of the Area of Discretion

The theory of discretion provides the theoretical framework for determining whether there is room for courts to substitute their own assessment of a situation for that reached by the legislator or the administration. If an authority goes beyond the limits of its discretion, its decision is reviewable by the courts. It is now settled case law of the Court of Justice that in reviewing an act, which has necessitated a complex economic or social appraisal, the Court must confine itself to verifying whether the relevant rules governing procedure and

[83] *See*, T. Koopmans, Courts and Political Institutions 107 (2003).

the statement of reasons were complied with, whether the facts on which the contested finding was based have been accurately stated, and whether there has been any manifest error of assessment or a misuse of powers.[84]

If a court finds that an authority has adopted a measure in a field where it enjoys genuine discretion – i.e., where it has freedom to act (or not to act) and freedom to assess – judges still have some important tasks to fulfill. In the first place, they have to verify whether formal requirements have been properly respected (*e.g.* provisions on time-limits, publication requirements, mandatory consultation of certain advisory bodies etc.). Secondly, the requirement as to the statement of reasons permits courts to strike down administrative decisions or legislative norms if such acts do not sufficiently set out the principal issues of fact and of law upon which they are based; or if the rationality of the choices made is not supported by the reasons provided.[85] All this does not pertain to the area of discretion, which courts must respect. Third, courts need not refrain from ascertaining whether the decision-making body has based its decision on a correct determination of the relevant facts. Fourth, an authority does not act within its area of discretion if it has misused its discretionary powers. There is room for judicial control if powers are deflected from the purposes for which they have been granted. In other words, as was stated by the Court of Justice "an act of a Community institution is vitiated by a misuse of powers if it has been adopted with the exclusive or main purpose of achieving ends other than those stated or evading a procedure specifically prescribed by the Treaty for dealing with the circumstances of the case."[86]

2.4.3. Discretionary Powers and Indeterminate Concepts

The fact that an enabling constitutional provision or the applicable statute uses indeterminate legal concepts, which require further interpretation and concretization before they can be applied, does not necessarily mean that representative bodies or administrative authorities have unlimited freedom of appreciation and that courts must defer completely to the assessments made by these bodies and authorities. If powers of public bodies have been defined in imprecise terms this does not mean that courts must act upon the assumption that the legislator has used vague concepts deliberately so as to confer discretionary powers on the administration. Open concepts ("unbestimmte Rechtsbegriffe") such as "reasonable care," "acting fairly," "public order" or "public security" etc., are often used not because they intend to grant discretion to administrative bodies but because these notions are meant to cover a great variety of situations that cannot be foreseen or defined in advance.

[84] *See* Case C-56/93, Belgium v. Commission, [1996] ECR I-723.
[85] *See* EC Treaty, art. 253.
[86] Case C-84/94, UK v. Council, [1996] ECR I-5755.

Generally speaking, nowadays courts have abandoned the view that judicial deference is necessary in areas of discretionary exercise of powers because supervision of the way in which discretion is used is better left in the hands of representative bodies. In France, Germany, the United Kingdom, and in other Member States the vague or open character of notions used in the applicable legislation does not secure decisions against judicial review.[87] The same holds true for the Court of Justice. As indicated above, if legal enactments use broad and indeterminate terms, the Community Courts feel free to determine the meaning of broad and indefinite legal characterizations by deciding if the relevant facts could reasonably be covered by the notions used. If this is not the case, the act under review may be annulled because its validity is affected by a manifest error of judgment.

2.4.4. General Principles of Law and Human Rights as Standards for Judicial Review

Increasingly, standards for determining whether policy-makers or the administration have committed an error of appreciation have come to include general principles of law and human rights protection. There was hardly any reference to these principles and basic human rights in the original treaties. After initially resisting attempts by private individuals to persuade the Court of Justice to rule on the compatibility of Community measures with fundamental rights guaranteed by the German constitution, the Court recognized for the first time in 1969 that "fundamental human rights [are] enshrined in the general principles of Community law and protected by the Court."[88] In subsequent cases, the Court emphasized the autonomous nature of these Community general principles of law. In Case 4/73, *Nold*,[89] it specified that "[i]n safeguarding these rights, the Court is bound to draw inspiration from constitutional traditions common to the member States, and it cannot therefore uphold measures which are incompatible with fundamental rights recognized and protected by the constitutions of those States. Similarly, international treaties for the protection of human rights on which the member States have collaborated or of which they are signatories, can supply guidelines which should be followed within the framework of Community law." This formula is reflected in the text of Article 6(2) of the Treaty on European Union. This provision specifically mentions the European Convention of Human Rights, highlighting its singular importance as a key source of inspiration for determining the scope and intensity of human rights protection.

It is to be noted that the protection of general principles of law and fundamental human rights does not merely impose restraints upon the powers

---

87 *See* Koopmans, *supra* note 83, at 112.

88 Case 29/69, Stauder, [1969] ECR 419.

89 Case 4/73, Nold, [1974] ECR 491.

of the Community institutions. The Court has also ruled that any action by Member States taken within the scope of Community law must be susceptible of being reviewed for conformity with general principles and fundamental rights.[90] This situation occurs especially in cases[91] where Member States implement Community rules or when they rely upon derogations from the Treaty rules relating to free movement of goods, persons, services, and capital.[92]

It is difficult to overestimate the importance of the potential inroads into the national sovereignty and the prerogatives of policy-makers, which judicial review on grounds of human rights protection and fundamental principles of law can produce. The list of fundamental human rights invoked by litigants in relation to acts of the Community and of the Member States is a long one.[93] In addition, the courts frequently have to rule on complaints about alleged infringements of general principles such as legal certainty and protection of legitimate expectations, equal treatment, access to justice, fair trial and rights of the defence, transparency, the proportionality principle, and many other principles of administrative legality.

In this connection, the requirement of proportionality is particularly liable to impose significant limitations on the decision-makers' freedom of choice. For example, the Court has often had to apply a proportionality test in cases where challenges were brought against Community agricultural policy measures, which involved heavy financial burdens on producers, distributors, exporters, etc.[94] In this area, the Community institutions enjoy a wide discretion. As a result, the proportionality inquiry in such areas of economic regulation will be less rigorous than in cases where there is less discretion. However, in other cases, especially when Member States seek to restrict the exercise of free movement rights under the Treaty (Articles 28, 43, 49, 56), the Court tends to examine thoroughly whether the arguments adduced by Member States support the contention that the measures taken are justified on grounds of public health, public policy or any other imperative requirement in the general interest. The intrusive nature of the proportionality test applied to Member State actions is readily apparent from the four factors which judges will commonly have to evaluate. The measure under review must be suitable to attain the desired objective; the measure must be necessary to achieve the desired end; there must not be another measure capable of achieving the objective sought, which constitutes less of a hindrance to free movement; and

[90] Case 222/84, Johnston, [1986] ECR 1651.

[91] Case 5/88, Wachauf, [1989] ECR 2609.

[92] Case C-260/89, ERT, [1991] ECR I-2925.

[93] *See*, for a survey of rulings of the Court of Justice on a wide range of fundamental rights, K. Lenaerts & P. van Nuffel (Eds.), Constitutional law of the European Union 548-550 (1999).

[94] *See* Case C-331/88, Fedesa, [1990] ECR 4023.

the measure must not impose a burden, which is excessive in relation to the objective sought to be attained (proportionality in a narrow sense).[95]

2.5. Conclusion

The European Community, like many European countries, Canada, and the USA, has instituted a system ensuring that the final say on the compatibility of legislation with provisions of a constitutional nature or the conformity of executive action with an empowering act does not rest with the legislative power but with the judiciary. Inevitably, the power to review legislation and administrative action has reinforced the position of the judiciary. This type of jurisdiction provides courts with an important tool for exercising influence over matters, which used to be considered essentially political. The European Court of Justice, including the Court of First Instance, shows great awareness of the need to use this power sparingly and to respect the prerogatives of the political institutions of the EU. However, their judgments, even if they do not encroach on the policy-making powers of the European institutions and Member States, frequently have a considerable political impact.

The Court of Justice has consistently tended to enhance the effectiveness of the Treaties by placing a wide interpretation on the powers of the Community and by reducing the scope of the powers left to the Member States. The extension of the Community's external competences to match its powers of internal legislation has been especially controversial and was widely perceived as exceeding the limits of judicial discretion.

In the field of defence and public security matters, the European Courts are reluctant to substitute their own assessment for that made by the political institutions of the Community or the Member States.

The European judiciary, as a matter of principle, is disinclined to criticize choices of economic or social policy made by legislative or executive authorities. Courts will confine their review to checking whether a measure suffers from procedural defects and whether there has been misuse of power, an error in establishing the relevant facts, or a manifest error in applying the law to these facts.

The European courts show great deference to respecting the area of discretion enjoyed by the other branches of government. However, this does not amount to judicial abdication. If an enabling provision uses indeterminate concepts and broad legal characterizations, judges no longer assume automatically that there has been an intention to grant discretionary powers to the authority entrusted with powers of application. Open concepts, which require an "evaluative assessment," are not beyond judicial interpretation.

---

95 *See* for more on this point, J. Schwarze, European Administrative Law 685 (1992); P. P. Craig & G. de Burca, EU Law 370 (2002).

Human rights protection and review on grounds of general principles of law has tended to reinforce the position of the judiciary throughout the world. In the European Community, judicial review on these grounds is a standard feature of challenges brought before the courts in regard to legislative policy measures and individual administrative acts. Undeniably, the possibility that Community acts and national measures within the scope of Community law are annulled for failing to conform to human rights or other fundamental general principles of law imposes important restraints on the political freedom of decision-makers.

When courts apply a general principle such as the requirement of proportionality, this may lead to a different assessment of the adequacy of the means used to secure an end than that reached by the author of the disputed act. Yet, the interpretation and enforcement of these principles, be they written or unwritten, is part of the judicial function and excessive judicial deference is unnecessary and inappropriate.

3. Some Comparative Conclusions

Very few people today would argue that when judges are called upon to apply treaties, statutes and other legal norms in disputes before them, they are engaged in an operation of an essentially mechanical nature. The idea defended by the formalist school of thought since the time of Montesquieu that the judge merely is "la bouche qui prononce les paroles de la loi" and that courts act as a blank slate when discerning the meaning of words and ascertaining the intention of the legislator is no longer the prevailing view of the nature of judicial decision making. Since roughly the middle of the twentieth century most legal scholars and theorists belong to the school of legal realism. They acknowledge that constitutional provisions and pieces of legislation leave gaps that must be filled by courts and that the manner in which different judges will discharge this task may be influenced by the values and the philosophies that are dear to them. But the role of the judge is to give to the law its truest meaning. Therefore, even though the best possible interpretation of the law may vary somewhat from judge to judge, judges will generally be aware of the need to show considerable restraint and to steer clear of legal decisions based on political views rather than on legal arguments. Law and politics are distinct, but issues that are politically controversial frequently also become legal issues submitted to courts for resolution. The arguments made in the political arena by political actors often bear a striking resemblance to those presented in the judicial forum. Nevertheless, judges must be able to explain and justify their conclusions as the product of legal reasoning. They are bound by legal acts, prior judgments and fundamental legal principles to a degree that political actors are not. Every important court decision is likely to have political importance. It does not follow, however, that such a decision extinguishes the law/politics distinction.

In the preceding comments on the experience of the Supreme Court of Canada and of the European Court of Justice we have shown that both courts are engaged in judicial review to settle disputes in matters which are often highly politicized. The settings within which these courts operate are of course very different. Canada is a federal state while the European Union is a work in progress devoid of statehood. At most, the EU can be characterized as a halfway house between an international organisation and a federal state. Since none of the current Member States is prepared to give up its position as a sovereign State with legal personality under international law, the EU is best described as a very advanced form of international organisation, or as a quasi-federal polity in which sovereignty is shared between the Union and its constituent Member States. In spite of these differences between Canada and the European Union, the way in which their courts operate appears to be very similar. Both courts have wide powers of constitutional and administrative review. The Supreme Court of Canada, in contrast to the European Court of Justice, also has criminal and civil jurisdiction. Both courts have considerable powers in regard to commercial matters and both courts, in their handling of issues with political implications, are concerned to isolate the legal questions from those that do not have a sufficient legal component. In short, while it is true that one is federal and the other is supranational, these courts share many common traits flowing from the judicial function.

One essential element which the legal order of the EU clearly has in common with the constitutional order of Canada is that in both cases the judiciary has been given primary responsibility for settling disputes over the interpretation and application of the fundamental rules delineating the boundaries of action of the respective governments. Wisely, the founding fathers of the European Union have recognised the need to avoid a situation where the courts of the Member States would be responsible for construing the European Treaties autonomously. If these national courts had been given the right to determine themselves the extent to which the States could be deemed to have abandoned sovereignty for the benefit of the European Community, this would inevitably have resulted in divergent and potentially destructive interpretations of the Treaties. So, "auto-interpretation" was ruled out and compulsory jurisdiction was vested in the Court of Justice. Member States undertook not to submit a dispute concerning the interpretation or application of the Treaties to any method of settlement other than those provided therein (Article 292 EC). This means that, in the same way as the Supreme Court of Canada is the guardian of the borderline between federal and provincial powers, the European Court of Justice is the final arbiter on issues regarding the delimitation of the respective spheres of authority of the European Union and its Member States. Both courts have made important pronouncements on the nature of their respective legal orders and have contributed decisively to clarifying and strengthening the legal underpinnings of the federal system in Canada and the basic tenets of the Community construction in Europe. Although there has occasionally been public outcry in certain quarters over cases where the European Court of Justice has construed Community powers widely and residual powers of member States narrowly ("le gouvernement des juges !"), there never has been a serious attempt to curtail the Court's jurisdiction by way of an amendment to the Treaties. At the same time, it is not difficult to find cases in Canada and in Europe where the respective courts have handled issues presenting sensitive political aspects with great caution and substantial deference.

One such field in which both courts have shown particular restraint is that of foreign affairs. Neither the Supreme Court of Canada, nor the European Court of Justice has officially recognized and articulated a "political question" doctrine, but both courts show a clear disinclination to review measures when these are manifestly within the sphere of authority of the political departments and when satisfactory legal criteria for a judicial determination are lacking. The European Court of Justice tends not to accept the justiciability of GATT provisions and has consistently rejected challenges relating to the validity of Community legislative acts adopted in violation of WTO obligations. More recently and in connection with the legality of UN-inspired sanctions against Serbia and against the Al Qaeda network, the Community courts have emitted confusing and conflicting signals. On the one hand, the Court of Justice has confirmed that sanctions measures taken in pursuance of UN decisions can be reviewed by reference to general principles of law and fundamental rights, such as legal certainty, proportionality, and protection of property. On the other hand, the Court of First Instance, in the recent judgments *Yusuf* and *Kadi* has shown excessive deference for the authors of the UN sanctions resolutions. It has declined to review the Community regulations implementing the resolutions of the Security Council on grounds of general principles of Community law and fundamental rights protection. This judgment has been appealed to the Court of Justice.

Both in Canada and in the European Union the judiciary is committed to upholding the primacy of fundamental rights and freedoms. The enactment of the *Canadian Charter of Rights and Freedoms* has significantly expanded the scope of judicial review of the Supreme Court of Canada over the compatibility of federal or provincial legislative and executive action with the values enshrined in the Charter. The gradual strengthening of the powers and the role of the European Court of Justice with regard to human rights issues has probably not been as spectacular and as contentious as was the case in Canada. In the absence of a written catalogue of fundamental rights in the Treaties, the European Court of Justice has reviewed Community legislation by reference to the European Convention of Human Rights and Fundamental

Freedoms (1950) and by reference to the rights and freedoms resulting from Member States' constitutional traditions. Even if, as may be expected, the Treaties will soon incorporate a proper Charter of Fundamental Rights, in Europe pride of place for the protection of human rights and fundamental values will rest with the European Court of Human Rights and the domestic courts of the 46 Member States of the Council of Europe. The European Court of Justice will be able to exercise review over legislation and administrative action of Union institutions and it can influence the way in which Member States implement their obligations under the Treaties. In this respect, the powers of the Supreme Court of Canada clearly exceed those of the European Court of Justice. The Canadian court is competent also to scrutinize the laws and executive action of the provinces. In the European Union the judiciary must refrain from reviewing government action of the Member States that raises questions in relation to fundamental rights in policy areas not covered by the Treaties.

Finally, both courts perform important functions in controlling the way in which legislation or government policy in the socio-economic field is shaped. The courts in Canada and in the EU will never sit directly in judgment over the wisdom or the desirability of political choices or over the exercise of discretionary authority by the political and executive organs of the State. Nevertheless, judicial intervention may be warranted whenever the choices of economic or social policy made by the legislative or executive branches of government raise issues that are within the bounds of judicial review. Indeed, neither the Supreme Court of Canada nor the European Court of Justice exceeds the limits of the judicial function if it assesses the validity of a public measure by checking whether its author has respected procedural requirements, whether it has used its powers for the proper purposes and whether the grounds and the reasoning on which the measure under attack is based are not manifestly erroneous.

Christian Joerges

Judicialization and Transnational Governance: The Example of WTO Law and the GMO Dispute

The title of my chapter requires a number of interpretative efforts. Firstly, "governance" is not (yet?) a legal concept. The term has come in use for arrangements that do not respect the public/private distinction – a major reference point of the law/politics distinction. Secondly, "governance" – at least in the parlance of one of the most influential proponents of this term, the European Commission – designates an *ersatz* for a well-defined activity, namely regulation. The judiciary, however, is adjudicating, neither regulating nor governing. Thirdly, transnational governance is a term which has replaced the notion of "regime," first in international relations theory and then in specialized fields of international law. Last but not least, "judicialization" is a term which has started its very remarkable career in the conceptualisation of the formative era of the European integration project, with law as a decisive parameter. In all the reconstructions of this "integration through law" saga, the European Court of Justice is presented as the noble hero, who managed prudently and patiently to transform the European Treaty into a quasi-federal order.[1] Legal scholarship, empirical research, and political theory have followed suit.[2] Could what had proved to be so successful in the EU be repeated at an

[1] "Tucked away in the fairytale Duchy of Luxembourg and blessed, until recently, with benign neglect by the powers that be and the mass media, the Court of Justice of the European Communities has fashioned a constitutional framework for a federal type Europe," thus famously and beautifully E. Stein, *Lawyers, Judges and the Making of a Transnational Constitution*, 75 Am. J. Int'l L. 1, at 1 (1981).

[2] *See* A.-M. Slaughter, A. Stone Sweet & J. Weiler (Eds.), The European Court and the National Courts – Doctrine and Jurisprudence: Legal Change in its Social Context (1998). *Also see* A. Stone Sweet's recent retrospection, *The Juridical* Coup d'État *and the Problem of Authority:*

Bogdan Iancu (Ed.), The Law/Politics Distinction in Contemporary Public Law Adjudication, 67-84.

international level? The "legalization" of international relations has become an important field of research,[3] and judicialization an intensively examined candidate for potentially promising legalization strategies.[4]

These are all good reasons to accept my assignment. But from my brief remarks one can already infer that it would be a hopeless effort to try to provide an overview over the many facets of pertinent research activities and debates. One way to bring the debate to manageable proportions is to restrict it to a specific field. This I have done through my sub-theme. World Trade Organization (WTO) law and the genetically modified organisms (GMO) dispute provide an example from the world of trade and contested regulatory concerns. That narrows our enquiry drastically.

Concreteness comes at a price, however. I will have to expose my readers in some detail to a field of knowledge with complexities of its own. In the following, I will first complement my introductory remarks with an excursion into a widely forgotten discipline, *i.e.*, conflict of laws scholarship, and point to the work and theses of one important (yet, in Europe, hardly appreciated) American scholar, namely Brainerd Currie. On that basis I will, as a .+second step, present my theoretical concerns, dealing with the "mother and father" of judicialization, namely the notion of constitutionalization, at all levels of governance. The following third step of the argument will be strictly juridical. I will re-translate and rephrase in legal terms my theoretical premises and positions. Here, I will take up the conflict of laws tradition again but adapt it to the European multi-level system of governance. In a fourth stage of my argument, I will deal with a widely discussed sector of transnational governance, namely WTO law. My specific focus, at that juncture, will be the recent GMO dispute. Can what we observe in this dispute be called judicialization or are we rather observing a return to politics?

1. An Idiosyncratic Preliminary: The Brainerd Currie-Led American Conflict of Laws' Revolution of the 1960s

Conflict of laws, *Kollisionsrecht*, is not an idiosyncratic term; the field associated with it is much better known as Private International Law (PIL) in all

CILFIT *and* Foto-Frost, *in* M. Poiares Maduro & L. Azoulai (Eds.), *The Past and Future of EU Law: the Classics of EU Law Revisited on the 50th Anniversary of the Rome Treaty* (2009).

3 *See* Abbott *et al.*, *The Concept of Legalization*, 54 International Organization 401 (2000).

4 An authority on the topic has become by now Bernhard Zangl, *Courts Matter! A Comparison of Dispute Settlement under GATT and the WTO*, contribution to the workshop "Gutes Regieren durch Deliberation und Entscheidungsverfahren," 9-10 February 2007, Bamberg [paper on file with the author], Die Internationalisierung der Rechtsstaatlichkeit. Streitbeilegung in GATT und WTO [The Internationalization of the Rule of Law. Settlement of Disputes in GATT and WTO Law] (2006), and *Judicialization Matters! A Comparison of Dispute Settlement Under GATT and the WTO*, 52 International Studies Quarterly 825 (2008).

of Continental Europe. PIL determines the applicable law in cases with foreign elements, *i.e.*, with "links" to or relationships with different legal systems. If a Romanian drives his car to Italy and has an accident somewhere in Austria, in which a driver from France is involved: What law do we apply? PIL provides us with rules of rule-selection. Its rules are, in principle, indifferent as to the contents of the potentially applicable laws. PIL-justice is categorically different from substantive justice: what it seeks to determine is not which law is better or more just but, rather, which legal system should govern. It is exactly this indifference towards content that enables national courts to accept and apply foreign law. Indeed, it is thanks to this indifference that PIL rules can be accepted by all jurisdictions, thus furthering the uniformity of decisions over legal controversies all over the world, the famous "*Entscheidungseinklang.*"

In 1958 the American law professor Brainerd Currie published the first of a series of articles, in which he explained his "misgivings concerning our inherited method of handling problems in the conflict of laws."[5] Currie started what was to become heralded and criticised as the American conflicts revolution, a break with older (esp. Bealian) American traditions and their European (esp. Savignian) counterparts.

The strength of this influence and the success and defeat stories about the revolution need not concern us here in any detail.[6] However, two elements of his approach are of crucial importance to my argument. The first is quite simple: Modern law, even our private law, has become "politicised." It expresses and pursues "policies." This is why we can attribute an "interest" to a jurisdiction of a polity in the application of its policies. The second follows from this insight with great stringency. Courts are bound to follow the policies of their own jurisdiction. They have no mandate to evaluate the policies of a foreign jurisdiction. Let me cite from Currie's summary:

> 1. Normally, even in cases involving foreign elements, the court should be expected, as a matter of course, to apply the rule of decision found in the law of the forum.
>
> 4. ["False problems"] If the court finds that the forum state has no interest in the application of its policy, but that the foreign state has, it should apply the foreign law.

[5] For a brief summary, B. Currie, *Notes on Methods and Objectives in Conflicts of Laws*, *in* Selected Essays on the Conflict of Laws 177 (1963).

[6] To my knowledge, the most constructive recent contributions to this "revolutionary" tradition are by L. Kramer, *More Notes on Methods and Objectives in Conflict of Laws*, 24 Cornell Int'l L. J. 245 (1991), and, by the same author, *Rethinking Choice of Law*, 90 Colum. L. Rev. 277 (1990).

> 5. ["True conflicts"] If the court finds that the forum state has an interest in the application of its policy, it should apply the law of the forum, even though the foreign state also has an interest in the application of its contrary policy…[7]

All of these directives, amounting as they did to an assault on the most precious values and achievements of PIL, namely, its tolerance towards foreign law, provoked heated debates. They brought a political dimension into the citadel of private law without indicating how the law could cope with this unruliness. Currie moderated his positions somewhat in his later writings,[8] but his concern about the epistemic and constitutional limits of the judiciary remained in place:

> [C]hoice between the competing interests of co-ordinate states is a political function of a high order, which ought not, in a democracy, to be committed to the judiciary: … the court is not equipped to perform such a function; and the Constitution specifically confers that function upon Congress.[9]

Brainerd Currie was writing for a federal system. Even in such a system, he asserted, the "politicisation" of modern law (its social functions) has transformed the choice-of-law problem into a delicate task, which courts are ill-equipped for and not legitimated to perform where the "governmental interests" of the concerned states are in conflict. I will not defend this position. But I believe that we should take Currie's queries seriously: Is transnational governance a proper task for a judicial, let alone quasi-judicial, body? Is judicialization of trasnational governance at all conceivable?

2. Constitutionalization

Governance must not be equated with government. It is, nevertheless, a response to functional needs, which arises out of necessity, even where there is no government in place to take action. This is what James Rosenau, to whom we owe the idea of "governance without government" in the international system, has famously observed and explained.[10] If it is functionally similar to government – insofar as it is an exercise of public power –, we need bodies to supervise that exercise. These bodies need to be authorized to exercise such supervision. They need to operate in a "constitutional" framework.

[7] *See* Currie, *supra* note 5, at 183-184. *See also* his *Comment on Babcock v. Jackson*, 63 Colum. L. Rev. 1233, at 1242 *et seq.* (1963).

[8] B. Currie, *The Disinterested Third State*, 28 Law & Contemp. Probs. 754 (1963).

[9] B. Currie, *The Constitution and the Choice of Law: Governmental Interests and the Judicial Function* (1958), *in* Currie, *supra* note 5, at 272.

[10] J. N. Rosenau, *Governance, Order, and Change in World Politics*, *in* J. N. Rosenau & E.-O. Czempiel (Eds.), Governance Without Government in World Politics 1, at 3 (1992).

2.1. Democratic Constitutionalism and Globalising Markets

Constitutionalization has become the most prominent of all "buzzwords" in legal discourses. For a decade or so, we have read of the constitutionalization of what was formerly purely legal: all branches of national law, including private law. Libraries could be filled with the proposals that have been advanced for curing Europe's democracy deficit by constitutionalization. In the wake of that debate, international law is developing its own constitutionalization agenda, which is extending into its sub-disciplines, most notably WTO law. Let me also mention societal constitutionalism, a theoretical vision to which I will return.

Clearly, it is impossible to summarize all these debates in any meaningful way. Let me therefore start with my own very strong normative notion of constitutionalism and constitutionalization. I reserve this term for law that seeks justify law-making processes, a "law of law production" to use Frank Michelman's formula.[11] This is what we expect the constitutions of democratic states to accomplish. This is the normative premise to which I refer in my understanding of constitutionalization. This premise implies that the citizens of a democratic polity have a claim to determine the economic and social conditions in which they live. This is not a social right, which would prescribe and guarantee social justice. It is a right to participate in democratic processes, which form and shape these conditions. To put it slightly differently: constitutionalism must reach down into the economic system and the social fabric of society. If it fails to do so, it loses its democratic credentials.[12]

This is a strong statement, to be sure. It rests upon an understanding of the project of political modernity as collective self-determination, and is at odds with the economic definition of modernity as the "autonomous determination of the ways in which human needs are satisfied."[13] But this statement also

[11] F. I. Michelman, Brennan and Democracy 48 (1999). As a close equivalent, in German jurisprudence there is the term "*Rechtfertigungs-Recht*" or *Rechtsverfassungsrecht* coined by Rudolf Wiethölter. *See* his *Just-ifications of a law of Society*, *in* O. Perez & G. Teubner (Eds.), Paradoxes and Inconsistencies in the Law 65 (2005), *also available at* http://www.jura.uni-frankfurt.de/ifawz1/teubner/RW.html. *Also see* C. Joerges, *Constitutionalism in Postnational Constellations: Contrasting Social Regulation in the EU and in the WTO*, *in* C. Joerges & E.-U. Petersmann (Eds.), Constitutionalism, Multilevel Trade Governance and Social Regulation 491, at 493 (2006).

[12] P. Wagner, *Introduction. The Political Construction of Contemporary Capitalism*, *in* C. Joerges, B. Stråth, & P. Wagner (Eds.), The Economy as a Polity x (2005); A. Somek, *Dogmatischer Pragmatismus. Über die Normativitätskrise der Europäischen Union [Dogmatic Pragmatism. On the Normativity Crisis in the European Union]*, *in* Hammer *et al.* (Eds.), Demokratie und sozialer Rechtsstaat in Europa. Festschrift Theo Öhlinger [Democracy and Social Rule of Law State in Europe. Festschrift for Theo Öhlinger] 41 (2004); C. Joerges, *What is Left of the European Economic Constitution? A Melancholic Eulogy*, 30 Eur. L. Rev. 461 (2005).

[13] F. Block, *Towards a New Understanding of Economic Modernity*, *in* C. Joerges *et al.*, *supra* note 12, at 3.

helps us understand the difficulties of the protagonists of the project of political modernity with the post-national constellation, with Europeanization, and even more so with globalisation. To take just one example, at least in Germany, particularly prominent: Jürgen Habermas argues that Europe needs a constitution if it is to preserve the European "social model."[14] Yet this claim is by no means as naïve as it has been portrayed to be by certain critics, Habermas adding, at an early stage, the further condition that "any assessment of the chances for a European-wide democracy depends in the first place upon empirically grounded arguments."[15]

2.2. Democratic Constitutionalism and Transnational Governance

Applied at the global level, constitutionalism, in the sense I set out above, appears to be at best a utopian project. Those advocating such use of the term need to re-define it. One famous suggestion is to proclaim an "international community" as the basis and object of constitutionalization.[16] I will not engage in a discussion of such suggestions,[17] because my concern here is to understand the sociological basis of law, the linking of validity to facticity. More so as a private lawyer, I do not shy away from exploring a possibility, which Habermas himself categorically rejects: "markets, unlike polities, cannot be democratized."[18]

My starting point here is the phenomenon of an intensifying "embedding" of markets at the international level via governance arrangements established through and alongside WTO law. The background to the strong development of international trade law is well known: under the 1947 General Agreement on Tariffs and Trade (GATT) regime, objections to free trade were essentially economic and tariffs were a nation state's primary means of protecting its interests. However, by the early 1970s, tariffs had been substantially reduced and, subsequently, the imposition and removal of non-tariff barriers (NTBs)

[14] J. Habermas, *Warum braucht Europa eine Verfassung?*, *in* Zeit der Übergänge [Age of Transformations] 104 (2001), (*So, Why Does Europe Need a Constitution*, http://www.iue.it/RSCAS/e-texts/CR200102UK.pdf).

[15] J. Habermas, *The Inclusion of the Other: Studies in Political Theory*, *in* C. Cronin & P. de Greiff (Eds.), at 158 (1998); *see also*, the precise analysis by J. P. McCormick, *Habermas, Supranational Democracy and the European Constitution*, 2:3 European Constitutional Law Review 398 (2006).

[16] For a review of pertinent contributions, *see* B. Fassbender, *The United Nations Charter as Constitution of the International Community*, 36 Colum J. Transnat'l Law 529 (1998); on Christian Tomuschadt in particular *cf.* A. von Bogdandy, *Constitutionalism in International Law: Comment on a Proposal from Germany*, 47 Harv. Int'l L. J. 223 (2006).

[17] A. Fischer-Lescano, Globalverfassung. Die Geltungsbegründung der Menschenrechte [Global Constitutionalism – The Foundational Validity of Human Rights] 253 *et seq.* (2005).

[18] J. Habermas, *The European Nation-State and the Pressures of Globalization*, 235 New Left Review 46 (1999). *Also see* McCormick, *supra* note 15, at 402, n. 25.

that reflected a wide range of domestic concerns about the protection of health, safety, and the environment have come to dominate trade agreements and their implementation. The growing impact of NTBs on international trade is hence indicative of the latter's politicization. The law of the new WTO 1994 stands for a juridification/legalisation and judicialization of this new reality.

Do these developments, to take up another Habermasian formula,[19] "deserve recognition"? Or, more specifically, by which criteria should we assess their normative quality? This second dimension of the discussion is, in my understanding, the agenda driving recent controversies concerning the constitutionalization of international trade law.

To rephrase, the core issue of WTO law is its relation to national law. Can national regulatory policies survive WTO law? Does WTO law overrule and thereby erode the regulatory politics of WTO members? Or, to turn the question around, will WTO law survive the steady growth of regulatory law in national or regional legal systems? This is a question of clear constitutional dimensions. The constitutionalization debate is, so-to-speak, a logical consequence of the emergence of transnational governance structures, and an indispensable one – at least if one continues to believe that the type of power which is administered through these arrangements should be legitimated and that we should at least try to defend the idea of law-based legitimacy.

But what promise is there of fulfilling such ambitions? Not a great deal, in my view, if we continue to seek the type of legitimacy constitutional democracies can claim, while refusing to be content with the type of "constitutional talk,"[20] which decouples normativity from facticity. My thesis is that we can avoid both Scylla and Charybdis through the adoption of an alternative approach, which I call "conflict of laws as constitutional form."

3. Conflict of Laws as Constitutional Form: The Case of the EU

The second step of my argument will be more demanding. I will again operate with that not so well known legal discipline to which I have referred at the beginning. I will also seek to revise it, to get even beyond Currie, and to overcome his destructive normative nihilism. What I set out to do is a Hegelian move: on the one hand, a synthesis of the theses of traditional PIL and, on the other hand, the antitheses of the American conflict revolution. The synthesis is what both traditions could not imagine: conflict of laws of supranational validity. This revised understanding of conflict of laws supplies us with a new

[19] J. Habermas, *Remarks on Legitimation through Human Rights*, *in* The Postnational Constellation. Political Essays 113-129 (2001).

[20] N. Walker, *Globalization and Transnational Constitutionalism* (Manuscript Florence 2007, on file with the author).

perspective on transnational constitutionalism. Last but not least, I will argue that my legal conceptualisation is not only normatively attractive but also compatible with the structures and function of transnational governance at both European and international levels – and even has the potential to reflect their specifics.[21]

Let me start with Europe and my thesis that we can, and indeed should, understand European law as a new species of supranational conflict of laws. I open with this bold thesis because I want to underline that the conflict-of-laws approach to European constitutionalism is not a matter of simply selecting the law of one particular jurisdiction. Its objective is rather to turn the debate on the democracy deficit in European governance upside down. It does not start with the much-deplored democracy deficits of the Union but, contrariwise, focuses on those of constitutional nation states. The kernel of the argument may date back to Rousseau[22] and is not as idiosyncratic as my terminology:

> The legitimacy of governance within constitutional states is flawed in so far as it remains inevitably one-sided and parochial or selfish. The taming of the nation-state through democratic constitutions has its limits. [If and, indeed, because] democracies presuppose and represent collective identities, they have very few mechanisms to ensure that 'foreign' identities and their interests are taken into account within their decision-making processes.[23]

[21] I refrain from a discussion of similarities and differences with the work of G. Teubner & A. Fischer-Lescano, *cf.* most recently *Fragmentierung des Weltrechts: Vernetzung globaler Regimes statt etatistischer Rechtseinheit [The Fragmentation of World Law: The Interconnectedness of Global Legal Regimes instead of State-Centered Legal Unity], in* M. Albert & R. Stichweh (Eds.), Weltstaat und Weltstaatlichkeit: Beobachtungen globaler politischer Strukturbildung [World-State and World-Statehood: A Study of the Global Political Texture] 37 (2007). *See also,* Lescano & Teubner, *Regime-Collisions: The Vain Search for Legal Unity in the Fragmentation of Global Law*, 25 Mich. J. Int'l L. 999 (2004). As is plainly visible, my theoretical framework is indebted to the discourse theory of law of Jürgen Habermas. But just as I have to depart from the efforts he made to adapt this framework to Europeanization and globalization, Gunther Teubner and Andreas Fischer-Lescano have to make a very creative use of systems theory in general and Luhmann's theory of the world society in particular. Constitutions, Luhmann has explained, bridge the legal and the political system (N. Luhmann, Law as a Social System (2004)). That formula is simply inapplicable at international level. The *Ersatz* there is "the search for a structural coupling of global law and global governance," explains Lescano, *supra* note 17, at 210. This definition is not too remote from my conceptualisation of the constitutionalization of transnational governance through a second order conflict of laws (*see* C. Joerges & M. Everson, *Re-conceptualising Europeanisation as a Public Law of Collisions: Comitology, Agencies and an Interactive Public Adjudication, in* H. C. H. Hofmann & A. H. Türk (Eds.), EU Administrative Governance 512 (2006). *See also* C. Joerges, *Rethinking European Law's Supremacy: A Plea for a Supranational Conflict of Laws, in* B. Kohler-Koch & B. Rittberger (Eds.), Debating the Democratic Legitimacy of the European Union 311 (2008).

[22] *See* R. Grant & R. A. Keohane, *Accountability and Abuses of Power in World Politics*, 99 Am. Pol. Sci. L. Rev. 29 (2005).

[23] C. Joerges & J. Neyer, *From Intergovernmental Bargaining to Deliberative Political Processes: The Constitutionalisation of Comitology*, 3 Eur. L. J. 273, at 293 (1997).

If the legitimacy of supranational institutions can be so designed as to cure these deficiencies – as a correction of "nation-state failures," as it were – they may then derive their legitimacy from this compensatory function. As I have recently put it:

> We must conceptualise supranational constitutionalism as an alternative to the model of the constitutional nation-state, which respects that state's constitutional legitimacy but, at the same time, clarifies and sanctions the commitments arising from its interdependence with equally democratically legitimised states and with the supranational prerogatives that an institutionalisation of this interdependence requires.[24]

What should that postulated design have to do with conflict of laws? That discipline is concerned with differences between legal systems. Its vocation is – in my understanding – the disciplining through law of conflicts arising out of these differences. This law is to transform international anarchy into what Kant, however tentatively, envisaged as a cosmopolitan '*Rechtszustand*.' Conflict of laws "juridifies" the Union through rules and principles, which resolve the paradoxical task of creating "unity in diversity." This is its constitutional function. It does what traditional conflict of laws, and in particular international administrative (public) law in the continental tradition, refused to do. In that tradition the application of foreign public law seemed irreconcilable with the sovereignty of the forum state. "Kein Staat macht sich zum Büttel eines anderen Staates," ("No State will allow itself to become the bailiff of another.") we still read in Germany's leading treatise.[25] This is precisely what my supranational conflict of laws asks them to do. This authority has its positive basis in the "Bund" which the European Treaty has established.[26]

---

[24] *See* C. Joerges, *Deliberative Political Processes Revisited: What Have we Learnt About the Legitimacy of Supranational Decision-Making*, 44 JCMS 779, at 791-795 (2006).

[25] G. Kegel and K. Schurig, Internationales Privatrecht [Private International Law] 1094 (2000): "Jeder Staat … ist frei …, duldet keine Richter über sich" ["Any state is … autonomous … [and] allows no judge above itself"].

[26] On that notion, *see* C. Schönberger, *Die Europäische Union als Bund. Zugleich ein Beitrag zur Verabschiedung des Staatenbund-Bundesstaat-Schemas*, 129 Archiv des öffentlichen Rechts 81, at 88 *et seq.* (2004). The term has previously been used by C. Schmitt, Verfassungslehre [Theory of the Constitution] 363 (1993): "Der *Bund* ist eine auf freier Vereinbarung beruhende, dem gemeinsam Zweck der politischen Selbsterhaltung aller Bundesmitglieder dienende, dauernde Vereinigung, durch welche der politische Gesamtstatus jedes einzelnen Bundesmitgliedes im Blick auf den gemeinsamen Zweck verändert wird" ["The *Bund* is a stable association [of states], grounded on a freely entered into agreement, serving the common purpose of political self-preservation of all the *Bund* members, an association by virtue of which the general political status of each individual member will be changed in view of the common purpose"]. Schmitt's *Bund* presupposed a kind of homogeneity which the conflict-of-laws approach rejects, *id.*, at 375: "… jeder Bund [beruht] auf einer wesentlichen Voraussetzung, nämlich der *Homogenität aller Bundesmitglieder,* d.h. auf einer substantiellen Gleichartigkeit, welche eine konkrete, seinsmäßige Übereinstimmung der Gliedstaaten begründet und es bewirkt, dass der extreme Konfliktfall innerhalb des Bundes nicht eintritt" ["Any *Bund* rests on an essential assumption,

Why use the notion of conflicts in the first place rather than a more pleasant term like "horizontal constitutionalism"? What is specific about the EU is the need to deal continuously with a variety of conflict patterns, namely vertical conflicts (the realm of supremacy), horizontal conflicts (the realm of mutual recognition), and diagonal conflicts.[27] In all of these constellations, European conflict-of-laws can build upon legal commitments and principles furthering co-operative problem-solving, which are quite firmly enshrined in the Treaty and have been further developed in Europe's *praxis*.

I refrain from any further elaboration here, but I will underline two potentials of the EU, which are either not present or considerably weaker at an international level. First, Europe can turn to secondary legislation as a means of ensuring stable and long-term coordinated problem-solving.[28] Second, Europe has the means to organise a cognitive opening of the legal system for scientific and other expertise without subjecting itself to technocratic governance.

---

namely the *Homogeneity of all Bund-members, i.e.*, it presupposes a substantive uniformity which underlies the concrete, mutual understanding of the member states and thus guarantees that the extreme case of a conflict within the *Bund* does not occur"]. The "unity" which that approach seeks to ensure can content itself with a Habermasian constitutional patriotism; *see* most recently J. Habermas, Zwischen Naturalismus und Religion [Between Naturalism and Religion] 111 (2005): "Entgegen einem weit verbreiteten Missverständnis heißt, Verfassungspatriotismus, dass sich Bürger die Prinzipien der Verfassung nicht allein in ihrem abstraktem Gehalt, sondern konkret aus dem geschichtlichen Kontext ihrer jeweils eigenen nationalen Geschichte zu Eigen machen. Wenn die moralischen Gehalte von Grundrechten in Gesinnungen Fuß fassen sollen, genügt der kognitive Vorgang nicht. Moralische Einsichten und die weltweite Übereinstimmung in der moralischen Empörung über massive Menschenrechtsverletzungen allein würden nur für die hauchdünne Integration der Bürger einer politisch verfassten Weltgesellschaft genügen (wenn es sie denn eines Tages geben sollte). Unter Staatsbürgern entsteht eine wie immer auch abstrakte und rechtlich vermittelte Solidarität erst dann, wenn die Gerechtigkeitsprinzipien in das dichtere Geflecht kultureller Wertorientierungen Eingang finden" ["Contrary to a widespread misunderstanding, constitutional patriotism means that citizens embrace the principles of the Constitution not only in their abstract content but also concretely, out of their own national historical context. If the moral content of fundamental rights is to take practical root, the cognitive process does not suffice. Moral intuitions and the universal agreement which arises as indignation towards massive human rights violations, as such, would suffice only for the very superficial integration needs of the politically created world society citizenry. Between state citizens arises in truth a solidarity – as always, partially abstract and legally-mediated – only when the principles of justice find an entry point into the network of cultural value-orientation"] [author's translations].

[27] To explain the third category at least briefly: since the Member States have delegated legislative competences only in limited fields, responses to functionally interdependent problem constellations often require a co-ordination of different, semi-autonomous levels of governance.

[28] This possibility and functional necessity does not compromise the conflict-of-laws approach. Suffice it here to recall the insights of Ernst Steindorff's amazingly modern *Habilitation* thesis: Sachnormen im internationalen Privatrecht [Substantive Rules in Private International Law] (1958).

4. Juridification and Its Limits at an International Level

Beyond the EU issues are more complex. Yet the conflict-of-laws approach can be brought to WTO law and adapted to the specifics of WTO-governance. Let me explain this thesis with the help of two cases, the "Hormones Case" and the GMO dispute.

4.1. Hormones in Beef: A Case of Manageable Proportions and Prudently Managed

The core issue of the Hormones Case[29] was similar to that of the GMO dispute but of less troubling proportions. In *Hormones*, the subject matter was the administration of growth hormones to cattle – illegal in the EU, but a common practice in the US. Which law is applicable? This is the question traditional conflict of laws would pose. But this is not the question the Appellate Body had to answer. The Appellate Body had to look for guidance in the *The WTO Agreement on the Application of Sanitary and Phytosanitary Measures (SPS Agreement)*. Trade restricting measures cannot be "maintained without sufficient scientific evidence" (Article 2.2) and must be based on the risk assessment methods of the relevant international organizations (Article 5): These provisions can be interpreted as the search for a transnationally acceptable, meta-norm institutionalising "science" as peacemaker. All WTO lawyers know about the indeterminacy of scientific authority. Science typically provides no clear answers to questions posed by politicians and lawyers; it cannot resolve ethical and normative controversies about numerous technologies; and consumer *angst* might be so significant that neither policy-makers nor the economy can ignore it.

All these difficulties, however, do not stand in the way of applying a conflict-of-laws approach to transnational trade governance. The Appellate Body wisely refrained from referring to science as the ultimate authority, which would be legitimated to resolve the conflict. It nevertheless channelled the ongoing controversy thus promoting a civilized conduct of the conflict.[30]

[29] Appellate Body Report *EC – Measures Concerning Meat and Meat Products (Hormones)*, WT/DS26/AB/R and WT/DS48/AB/R, 16 January 1998.

[30] This type of restraint was wise for an additional reason. The standards to which the Technical Barriers to Trade and the SPS Agreements refer are produced "outside" any legal system. At national and European level, the generation of non-state "law" is operating in the shadow and under some supervision of politically accountable actors, courts and other authorized bodies. At the international level, conflict of laws can again deliver an *ersatz*. It can develop the conditions – especially procedural requirements – under which "private transnationalism" (as in standardisations) or more intergovernmental systems (like the Codex Alimentarius Commission) "deserve recognition." The parallel to the recognition of foreign law and foreign judgments seems obvious but is rarely drawn. *See* E. Schanze, *International Standards –*

4.2. The Example of the GMO Dispute: Are International Markets "Socially Embedded"?

Foodstuffs are in general highly politicised products. No legal system has ever ceased to subject them to a degree of regulatory supervision. GMOs are in that sense nothing new. But they are the most technologically advanced and most controversial of all foodstuffs, if not of all consumer products. GMO production is led by the US but has also been mastered by countries such as Brazil and India, occasioning very ambivalent socio-economic implications, as development imperatives clash with agrarian employment concerns not only in international trade but also within these countries.[31] The most famous debate, however, focuses on risks posed by GMOs. Both GMO sceptics and GMO adherents agree that there is little evidence that GMO food poses an appreciable risk to health.[32] Nonetheless, a major concern remains that non GMO-crops will be contaminated by GMOs released in the environment. Likewise, conflict rages on the meaning of consumer anxiety and choice: do we have a 'right to know' what we are eating;[33] might governments demand GMO labelling, since the majority of their citizens refuse to accept GMO products;[34] is the EU correct to have 'perfected' its authorization procedures by means of the establishment of an ethical advisory body?[35]

For all these reasons the GMO case is a touchstone for competing views on the constitutional status of WTO law and my analysis focuses on this aspect.[36] However, neither this intense debate nor the socio-economic dimensions of

Functions and Links to Law, *in* P. Nobel (Ed.), International Standards and the Law 84, esp. at 90-91 (2005) and J. Scott, *International Trade and Environmental Governance: Relating Rules (and Standards) in the EU and the WTO*, 15 EJIL 307 (2004).

[31] *See* S. Zarrilli, *International Trade in GMOs: Legal Frameworks and Developing Country Concerns*, *in* F. Francioni & T. Scovazzi (Eds.), Biotechnology and International Law 231 (2006).

[32] *See* W. van den Daele, *Legal Framework and Political Strategy in Dealing with the Risks of New Technology – The Two Faces of the Precautionary Principle*, *in* H. Somsen (Ed.), The Regulatory Challenge of Biotechnology 118 (2007).

[33] *See, generally*, on this controversy P. H. Sand, *Labelling Genetically Modified Food: The Right to Know*, 15 Review of European Community & International Environmental Law 185 (2006).

[34] *See* Europeans and Biotechnology in 2005: Patterns and Trends, 64.3 Eurobarometer (2006).

[35] *See* P. Dabrowska, *Hybrid Solution for Hybrid Products? EU Governance of GMOs* (EUI PhD Thesis on file with the author).

[36] To name just three analyses: O. Perez, *Anomalies at the Precautionary Kingdom: Reflections on the GMO Panel's Decision*, 6 World Trade Review 265 (2007); C. Conrad, *The EC-Biotech Dispute and Applicability of the SPS Agreement: are the Panel's Findings Built on Shaky Ground?*, 6 World Trade Review 233 (2007); D. Prévost, *Opening Pandora's Box: The Panel's Findings in the EC-Biotech Products Dispute*, 34 Legal Issues of Economic Integration 67 (2007).

the GMO controversy are explicitly addressed in the more than 1000 pages of the report finally delivered by the panel in September 2006.[37] To the contrary, the panel took great pains at underlining that it did not address a series of issues of obvious importance.[38] However, the intended (quasi-)judicial self-restraint was not achieved in practice. The panel adopted partisan positions, albeit partly indirectly and implicitly.

This is not what a conflict-of laws approach would have recommended.

4.2.1. The Authority and Austerity of Science

The US and the EU, main actors in the dispute, differ in their regulatory approaches to GMOs in two significant respects: whereas the US focuses on health risks posed by food, the EU follows a more comprehensive approach, placing an additional and greater emphasis upon environmental risks.[39] US authorities will approve products *unless* evidence exists confirming a risk. By contrast, the 1992 Treaty on European Union constitutionalized the "precautionary principle," so that all legislative, administrative, and judicial decision-making within Europe must respect the notion that *any* indistinct hazard must be guarded against (Article 174 (2) EC Treaty).

Can this type of conflict be resolved by "science"? Science has been portrayed and invoked as an objective and non-partisan authority by the ECJ in conflicts over the limits of national regulatory autonomy and the EU commitment to free intra-community trade.[40] The ECJ certainly knows that risk

---

[37] *European Communities – Measures Affecting the Approval and Marketing of Biotech Products,* (DS291, DS292 and DS293). Findings and conclusions: http://www.wto.org/english/tratop_e/dispu_e/291r_conc_e.pdf. Full panel report: http://www.wto.org/english/news_e/news06_e/291r_e.htm.

[38] "[T]he Panel did *not* examine: whether biotech products in general are safe or not; whether the biotech products at issue in this dispute are "like" their conventional counterparts. Although this claim was made by the Complaining Parties (*i.e.*, the United States, Canada and Argentina) in relation to some aspects of their complaints, the Panel did not find it necessary to address those aspects of the complaints; whether the European Communities has a right to require the pre-marketing approval of biotech products …; whether the European Communities' approval procedures as established by Directive 90/220, Directive 2001/18 and Regulation 258/97, which provide for a product-by-product assessment requiring scientific consideration of various potential risks, are consistent with the European Communities' obligations under the WTO agreements …; the conclusions of the relevant EC scientific committees regarding the safety evaluation of specific biotech products …" Panel-Report 8.3.

[39] G. C. Shaffer & M. A. Pollack, *Reconciling (or Failing to Reconcile) Regulatory Differences: The Ongoing Transatlantic Dispute over the Regulation of Biotechnology*, *in* Andrews *et al.*, The New Transatlantic Agenda and the Future of Transatlantic Economic Governance 167 (2005).

[40] *See* C. Joerges, *Scientific Expertise in Social Regulation and the European Court of Justice: Legal Frameworks for Denationalized Governance Structures*, *in* C. Joerges, K.-H. Ladeur, & E. Vos (Eds.), Integrating Scientific Expertise into Regulatory Decision-Making. National Traditions and European Innovations 295 (1997).

assessment and management also entail political and ethical issues.[41] Nobody questions these dimensions seriously. This does not affect the readiness to assign trans-legal and meta-political authority to scientific discourses. Science itself and science-led techniques of risk assessments derive this prominent position from the fact that, even where scientists fail to agree, disagreements are conducted within a shared and constantly re-assessed scientific logic.

Why should this not be possible at international level? Why should WTO members who refuse free access to their markets not be expected to justify such restrictions on the basis of scientific evidence? This is exactly what the SPS agreement, which the panel held applicable after very lengthy deliberations,[42] provides.[43] This, however, is not all we need to know. We also have to decide, what these provisions mean in cases when science "runs out." Scientists agree that general hazards cannot be transformed into specific risks, since they cannot hope to gather sufficient data with which to conduct a scientific risk assessment.

Within the EU the precautionary principle governs such dilemmas, without, however, providing much guidance.[44] In the Hormones Case, the WTO Appellate Body found that the "[precautionary] principle [had] not been written into the SPS Agreement as a ground for justifying SPS measures that [were] otherwise inconsistent with the obligations of Members set out in particular provisions of that Agreement."[45] The panel, in the GMO case, went an important step further. Recalling "that, according to the Appellate Body, the precautionary principle [had] not been written into the *SPS Agreement* as a legitimate ground for justifying SPS measures," the panel proceeded to explain that "even if a member follows a precautionary approach, its SPS measures need to be 'based on' a ('sufficiently warranted' or 'reasonably supported') risk assessment."[46] This is a constitutionalizing move. It seems readily apparent that the WTO panel is not prepared to recognise the constitutional

---

[41] *See* A. W. Gouldner, *Cosmopolitans and Locals: Towards an Analysis of Latent Social Roles*, Administrative Science Quarterly 281 (1957) and 444 (1958).

[42] *See* the critical comments of Conrad, *supra* note 36.

[43] "Members shall ensure that any sanitary or phytosanitary measure … is based on scientific principles and is not maintained without sufficient scientific evidence …" (Article 2 (2)) "In cases where relevant scientific evidence is insufficient, a Member may provisionally adopt sanitary or phytosanitary measures on the basis of available pertinent information, including that from the relevant international organizations as well as from sanitary or phytosanitary measures applied by other Members. In such circumstances, Members shall seek to obtain the additional information necessary for a more objective assessment of risk and review the sanitary or phytosanitary measure accordingly within a reasonable period of time." (Art. 5 (7))

[44] *Cf.*, most prominently, ECJ, Case C-236/01, *Monsanto v. Italy*, [2003] ECR I-8105.

[45] WTO Appellate Body Report, *European Communities – Measures Concerning Meat and Meat Products (Hormones) ("EC - Hormones")*, WT/DS26/AB/R and WT/DS48/AB/R, adopted 13 February 1998.

[46] Para. 7.0365, note 1905.

commitment to precaution of any of its members. "Supremacy" of WTO standards over European constitutional commitments – this is the implication and the message.

4.2.2. The Distortion of Political Authority

It is instructive to contrast the European and WTO constellations at this point. Both the European and the international system share free trade commitments. Within a system so clearly predicated on establishment of a *common* market, diversity seems hard to accept. Accordingly, the ECJ has imposed significant burdens on Member States while invoking their autonomy in risk assessments. It has underlined that safeguards based on the precautionary principle may justify a temporary derogation, but *only* where "it proves impossible to carry out as full a risk assessment as possible … because of the inadequate nature of the available scientific data."[47] There are limits to the political autonomy of Member States. However, with respect to such limits, the ECJ has prudently declined to draw any rigid lines.

Why do the two systems react differently, and what difference does it make? This seems to lead us to the core problem. Europe has been struggling over GMOs for many years. Even though the EU claims that intense political debate has led to a definitive settlement,[48] it is far from clear whether this new regime will be easy to administer or instead will serve as a framework, within which competing positions are continuously discussed and negotiated. In my view the most problematic aspect of the panel report is that it seeks to delegitimatize even that type of indeterminate response to scientific controversies and political contestation. Exercising prudence of a different kind, the panel decided that the SPS Agreement was applicable to the authorisation of GMOs and could then point to Article 8 of the SPS Agreement, whose provisions require that applications must be processed without "undue delay." This, again, is a constitutionalizing manoeuvre, albeit one less plainly visible. The private right of applicants seeking authorisation for their products trumps political sensitivities; it is irrelevant that time may be needed to debate domestic political and ethical issues. Constitutions, Niklas Luhmann has explained to us, confer on political systems the right to take binding decisions.[49] Is that a valid diagnosis for a Union of political systems? Should such a Union have the right *not* to decide? These are subtle questions, to be sure. The panel found that completion of the approval process had been "unduly delayed" in 24 cases. Accordingly, it requested that the EU bring its measures "into conformity with

[47] Case C-236/01, *Monsanto v. Italy*, [2003] ECR I-8105, at para. 109.

[48] *See* the detailed analysis by Dabrowska, *supra* note 35, at 71-278.

[49] *E.g.*, in *Verfassung als evolutionäre Errungenschaft [The Constitution as an Evolutionary Achievement]*, 9 Rechtshistorisches Journal 176 (1990). *Cf.* Fischer-Lescano, *supra* note 17, at 208 *et seq.*

its obligations under the SPS Agreement," in effect asking the EU to complete approval procedures for outstanding applications.

The panel's critique of EU member state autonomy in relation to safeguard measures was equally indirect but effective. French, German, Austrian, Italian, Luxembourgish, and Greek bans on the marketing and import of EU-approved biotech products were held incompatible with WTO law. Again the panel arrived at this result in an indirect way. It did not question the validity of the European regulatory framework and its institutional balancing. It nonetheless opined that, since the EU's scientific committee had judged relevant biotech products to be safe, the named states had failed to undertake risk assessments that would "reasonably support [their] prohibitions" under the SPS Agreement. SPS standards overruled Europe's precarious institutional settlement.

4.2.3. Where the Law Ends

What would a conflicts-of-law approach have to offer as an alternative? This alternative has become visible in the settlement of the "Hormones" dispute. There, the Appellate Body ruled against the EU, without however depriving it of the right to develop new arguments and to refine its positions. In an analysis written prior to publication of the panel report, Nico Krisch argued that the GMO controversy showed that global governance must live with "a constant potential for mutual challenge of decisions with limited authority that may be contested through diverse channels until some (perhaps provisional) closure might be achieved."[50] Is this a conflict-of-laws solution? It is a response that reflects and respects the limits of transnational governance. No authority (certainly not a WTO panel) is entitled to rewrite European law of constitutional dimensions in the name of sound science.

Is it adequate to suggest that there is a legal duty not to decide? A positive answer is not incorrect but incomplete. The answer is "hard" law in that it acknowledges that, especially at an international level, one has to acknowledge that there are both factual and normative limitations to "legalization" and "judicialization." It is incomplete in that it fails to characterize that non-legalized sphere in any constructive way. The proper characterization of that sphere may be diplomacy[51] or, closer to the traditions of conflict of laws, *comitas*. As Jona Israël recently put it,[52] the *comitas* of the European Member States has mutated into a legal duty of co-operative problem-solving. At the WTO level, the wide-ranging general conversion of *comitas* into mandatory commitments is not conceivable.[53]

[50] *See* his *The Pluralism of Global Administrative Law*, 17 EJIL 247, at 266 (2006).

[51] J. H. H. Weiler, *The Rule of Lawyers and the Ethos of Diplomats: Reflections on the Internal and External Legitimacy of WTO Dispute Settlement*, 35 Journal of World Trade 191 (2001).

[52] J. Israël, European Cross-Border Insolvency Regulation 123, 150-152, 325-334 (2005).

[53] There are striking parallels between my suggestions and the version of global administrative law recently presented by Krisch, *supra* note 50, according to whom the difficulties of regulation

5. Concluding Remark

Markets, Karl Polanyi has famously assured us,[54] will always be "socially embedded." Do WTO law, in general, and the GMO controversy, in particular, confirm that assertion? The panel report, it may be noted, favours law over politics, opting for juridification in a very specific sense: restrictions on free trade, on the freedom of producers, exporters and traders can be imposed only where they are supported by "sound science." Sound science, rather than politically accountable regulation, has become the guardian of the common good and of the consumer. In a series of lectures on the "*naissance de la biopolitique*" delivered to the *Collège de France* in 1979, Michel Foucault warned that neo-liberalism would replace the supervision of markets by the state with the supervision of states by the market – and by sound science, we may now add.[55] Would this gloomy conclusion take the panel report too seriously? The differences between panel reports and the Reports of the Appellate Body are often significant, and were probably of importance in this case. The EU, however, has decided not to appeal the panel report[56] and a recent, highly detailed comment underlines: the report is "not too difficult for the EC to accept, since the Commission has been trying, and failing, to get the Member States to remove their safeguard measures for some time now."[57]

and its juridification in international arenas result "from fundamental and durable contestation over the tight constituency of global governance … [A]ttempts at 'constutionalizing' the political order by forcing it into a coherent, unified framework are problematic as they tend to downplay the extent of legitimate diversity in the global polity …" (at 248). Nowhere does Krisch mention "conflict of laws." However, his insight that global governance is confronted with "competing constituencies" insisting on their competence to define legitimacy autonomously (at 253) rephrases the core problem of conflict of laws. Neither does Krisch refer to the *comitas* tradition in international law. And yet, his insight that global governance has to live with "a constant potential for mutual challenge: of decisions with limited authority that may be contested through diverse channels until some (perhaps provisional) closure) might be achieved" portrays precisely the space between law and the state of nature which the notion of *comitas* designates.

[54] K. Polanyi, The Great Transformation: The Political and Economic Origins of Our Time, esp. at 45-58, 71-80 (1992).

[55] "… [A]u lieu d'accepter une liberté du marché, définie par l'État et maintenue en quelque sorte sur surveillance étatique … eh bien, disent les ordolibéraux, il faut entièrement retourner la formule et se donner la liberté du marché comme principe organisateur et régulateur de l'État … Autrement dit, un État sous surveillance du marché plutôt qu'un marché sous surveillance de l'État " [Instead of accepting market freedoms as defined by the state and maintained through state regulation, the ordo-liberals propose that one turn the formula upside down and take the free market as a founding principle which controls the state. Otherwise put, they promote the regaulation of states by markets rather than markets regulated by states.] (thus, Michel Foucault, *Naissance de la biopolitique.* Cours au Collège de France, Seuil/Gallimard 2004, Leçon 5, 120) [author's translation].

[56] *See*, http://www.euractiv.com/en/trade/eu-accepts-trade-ruling-gmos/article-159918.

[57] Prévost, *supra* note 36, at 84.

Does this indicate that the EU, or at least its officials, are ready to comply, and will use the report to discipline recalcitrant member states? Perhaps both Polanyi and Foucault captured an element of truth: The GMO market is at any rate "politically embedded." Can one call this constitutionalization? The law of constitutional democracies provides a structuring framework for political processes and decision-making, which ensures their legitimacy. WTO law, in our example, cannot make such claims.

András Sajó

The Judicialized Handling of Global Risk

In his discussion of the WTO GMO Dispute Professor Christian Joerges addresses the interaction of two fundamental concepts of contemporary regulatory law, namely judicialization and transnational governance. A word count in the contemporary scholarly literature would probably indicate that 'judicialization' and 'transnational governance' keep appearing with a very high frequency in the area. There are, however, two more words that I think have the same likelihood of appearance. These are 'network' and 'globalization'.

As a consequence two questions arise: Why do we encounter this governance problem? Why are we facing a crisis of sovereignty? The evasive answer is globalization and we must ask ourselves what is the specific globalization problem in this context.

People and countries simply cannot live anymore in a splendid isolation. Isolation was perhaps the case in the relationship between China and France or Persia and France in the days of Montesquieu. At the time of the emergence of the concept and reality of "world literature," the 'world' meant primarily an intellectual community of men of letters but not much more than that. Today countries are interrelated and people are interconnected. This is called globalization. Whatever globalization means, there is an increasing community of fate and faith. The community of fate relates for instance to global warming. We also have a problem of global market failures, a case of disturbed coordination that creates a need for political coordination. Yet the real issue is the extent to which political coordination results in legal coordination. This is the problem that lies at the heart of Professor Joerges' concerns.

One of the regulatory answers is given in the form of 'federation' formation at regional and even global levels. There are important objections to this regulatory model: there is not enough community of fate at the international level.

Bogdan Iancu (Ed.), The Law/Politics Distinction in Contemporary Public Law Adjudication, 85-87.

International law is certainly not solving the coordination problem. Additionally, given all the assurances – or false assurances – coming from the judicial involvement in handling global risk-related conflicts there is a chance that coordination through law will mean increasingly coordination by courts – or quasi-courts – and tribunals, which operate with independence and according to certain concepts of the rule of law. Given the nature of the judicial process and the nature of judicial cognition, judicialized coordination may not be possible at a transnational level. That is basically the challenge addressed in Professor Joerges' paper. There are obvious reasons to be very cautious and Professor Joerges, as always, was very cautious in his dialectical approach. After all, the WTO Panel is not a court and its independence is pretty questionable. Its reasoning is dubious too, at least from a strictly juridical perspective. It may well be that what seems today a step towards judicialization will not end up as part of juridification.

The specific coordination problem of the GMO release is related, among others, to risk management. Europeans opted for precaution. Cass Sunstein would claim that Europeans will lose because of that.[1] Europeans claim that Americans do not understand the need for regulatory precaution and, hence, approach the issue erroneously. Of course, Europe does not speak with one voice, and this is an additional complication. One reading of the WTO dispute is that the Commission is discretely siding with the 'global' risk-taking perspective and relies on the WTO mechanism to strengthen its own position vis-à-vis other European players. Behind the GMO dispute there is a value choice and now the questions arising are: Who should make that value choice? Whose evaluations matter in a global network? The standard (gut) reaction is that science is the appropriate forum to answer the GMO questions. I happen to be on a GMO release panel. I have to admit that I do not understand the science at stake there but one thing is sure: if you let three experts to be present at these national panels, you will get three different opinions and two of the scholars will take an oath that the third one is an idiot, who is paid by one of the special interest groups. Thus we may expect certainty while there is only a false certainty in science.

Second, risk management is a matter of value choices. What do we mean by values here? People have different cultures, both professionally and geographically, and different cultures have different ways to handle fear. Handling of fear is often through the democratic political process. As an alternative to science, democratic solutions imply that we let people voice their fear through democratic processes. Yet this approach may not make the GMO industry very happy. So what comes out of the democratic process? The message is: legal procedural rules, 'rule of law' requirements. Under judicialized governance, every procedure has to satisfy rule of law requirements. This may,

[1] C. Sunstein, Laws of Fear: Beyond the Precautionary Principle (2005).

or may not, correspond to businessmen's logic, despite the fact that, of course, businessmen's logic and rule of law are historically somewhat interrelated. In any case, there is a message of due process.

Furthermore, if we look at the European context, the juridification of global governance implies among others a 'right to know' concern. This results in additional, fundamentally procedural, requirements related to practical risk analysis. We do not know what the risks are but people should have the right to know at least that we *do not know*. Again, this is both a moral and procedural right that results in access to information. This right is what is generated by many of the decisions in the area of high risk, high uncertainty activities. The end result is a kind of right to globalized certainty handled to a certain extent by court-like organizations, which are unable to solve the issue for a number of reasons: partly because of uncertainty, partly because of the extremely dynamic nature of the whole process. As a result, interestingly, the message is that we should carry out what is procedurally more correct, more fair. I recall a decision of Judge Scalia, as he was at that time at the DC Court of Appeals. He had to decide a genetic modification release case in the mid-1980s and he decided the case along the same lines, namely, that the only question the law would consider was whether the administrative procedure was according to the requirements of the US Administrative Procedure Act and whether the procedural requirements of the law (hearing, etc.) were satisfied. As soon as the hearing requirement was satisfied, you had to allow that the administrative decision regarding the release was correct from a judicial perspective. So, it is once again a purely procedural control that we have.

What is the conclusion? In my opinion it is either too late or too early to get to conclusions from the perspective of globalization and juridification. It seems to me that given the enormous level of uncertainty and vast complexity resulting from the players, the only thing that emerges so far is a transnational rule of law without the need or the possibility for substance or for democratic decision-making. Nevertheless, these decisions, which are of doubtful substantive credibility, do have a great impact on the players at the regional or national level, as the WTO/GMO example indicates. In this sense, as the example shows, the European Commission jumped – not in a very discrete way – on the bandwagon. It seemed to use the Panel decision as a source of legitimation for a process which went against some of the Member States. This approach brings up the issue of Member State sovereignty, and so on and so forth. The game within the Community or in a region is changed by this new legitimacy. Is this judicial legitimacy? I am not so sure. Is this legal legitimacy? It sounds like judicial since it has an element of ultimate power – or we can at least construe it that way. Subsequently it has a strategic impact.

That is where we are, in light of Professor Joerges' inquiries.

Roderick A. Macdonald & Thomas McMorrow*

Myths of Miscegenation

Should the Concept of "Reasonable Accommodation" for Subordinated Groups and Minorities Be Constitutionalized?

1. Introduction

For the past two centuries most North-Atlantic democracies have, notwithstanding their implicit founding aspiration to be ethno-culturally homogeneous "nation"-States, been required to confront the linguistic, ethnic, religious, and cultural heterogeneity of their populations. Yet it is only in the past quarter-century that issues of social cohesion involving the integration of large numbers of immigrants of diverse, non-Christian, religious beliefs and manifold, non-European, cultural backgrounds have reached the centre of the political agenda. Broadly speaking, these States have pursued two general approaches to social inclusion. One, favored by countries including France and the United States of America, assumes that nationalism can be grounded in a relatively thin, but uniform and universally-shared, "legal republican" conception of citizenship. It appropriates the label "civic nationalism" as a way of transcending historical ethno-cultural homogeneity and recreating a new nationalism, often under the guise of a rhetorical "melting pot." The other, perhaps best exemplified in Canada, assumes a thicker, but "legal pluralistic," conception of citizenship. This approach adopts the label "multicultural citizenship" or "multiculturalism" to fashion a differentiated nationalism, typically under the rhetorical guise of a "cultural mosaic."[1] This essay considers

* We are grateful to Fabien Gélinas, Hoi Kong and Robert Leckey for challenging conversations and helpful suggestions.

[1] The literature on these two conceptions of citizenship is voluminous. *See, generally*,

Bogdan Iancu (Ed.), The Law/Politics Distinction in Contemporary Public Law Adjudication, 89-113.

a number of aspects of what might be called the "multicultural approach" by focusing on a particular policy dimension of its current application in Canada: the legal concept of "reasonable accommodation."[2]

The term "multicultural" entered the Canadian policy lexicon in the late 1960s as a consequence of a dissenting opinion by a member of Ukrainian origin on the Royal Commission on Bilingualism and Biculturalism.[3] It rightly meant to challenge the, then predominant, view that Canada had only two cultures, reflecting its "two founding peoples." In the *bi*-national model of the Royal Commission itself, English and French were linguistically-based, spatially-dominant mono-cultures, and "multi" cultures and "ethnic"

C. Taylor, Multiculturalism and "The Politics of Recognition" (1992); W. Kymlicka, Multicultural Citizenship: A Liberal Theory of Minority Rights (1995); J. Tully, Strange Multiplicity: Constitutionalism in an Age of Diversity (1995); D. M. Weinstock, Le Défi du Pluralisme [The Challenge of Pluralism] (1993-1994); M. Minow, *Rights and Cultural Difference*, *in* A. Sarat & T. R. Kearns (Eds.), Identities, Politics and Rights 347 (1995); S. M. Okin, *Is Multiculturalism Bad for Women?*, *in* J. Cohen, M. Howard & M. Nussbaum (Eds.), Is Multiculturalism Bad for Women? 7 (1999); A. Shachar, Multicultural Jurisdictions: Cultural Differences and Women's Rights (2001); M. McAndrew, *Québec Immigration, Integration and Intercultural Policy: a Critical Assessment*, New Delhi: Paper Presented at The International Conference on *Multiculturalism, Public Policy and Problem Areas in Canada and India*, December 2005, on file with the authors; K. Banting & W. Kymlicka (Eds.), Multiculturalism and the Welfare State: Recognition and Redistribution in Contemporary Democracies (2006); E. Winter, *How Does the Nation State Become Pluralist?*, 7 Ethnicities 483 (2007); P. Shah (Ed.) Law and Ethnic plurality: Socio-legal perspectives (2007). On the terms "legal republicanism" and "legal pluralism" *see* R. A. Macdonald, *Legal Republicanism and Legal Pluralism: Two Takes on Identity and Diversity*, *in* M. Bussani & M. Graziadei (Eds.), Human Diversity and the Law 43 (2005). Of course, in adverting to notions of "civic nationalism," "melting pot," "multiculturalism," and "cultural mosaic" we do not mean to claim that these labels accurately capture either what official public policy seeks to accomplish, or how various policy instruments actually play out in particular states. Rather, the point is that the political and popular discourse of immigration and ethno-cultural, religious, and linguistic diversity in these states evokes these competing perspectives.

[2] The concept of reasonable accommodation as a means for negotiating the integration of subordinated groups and minorities into the cultural mainstream was developed in a series of Supreme Court of Canada decisions of the 1990s. *See*, notably, Multani v. Commission scolaire Marguerite-Bourgeoys, 2006 S.C.C., [2006] 1 S.C.R. 256, 264 D.L.R. (4th) 577 [hereinafter, *Multani*]; Syndicat Northcrest v. Anselem, 2004 S.C.C. 47, [2004] 2 S.C.R. 551, 241 D.L.R. (4th) [hereinafter, *Anselem*]; Eldridge v. British Columbia (Attorney General), [1997] 3 S.C.R. 624 [hereinafter, *Eldridge*]. For a discussion of the antecedents of "reasonable accommodation" in the law relating to disabilities in the workplace see D. Lepofsky, *A Report Card on the Charter's Guarantee of Equality to Persons with Disabilities After 10 Years – What Progress? What Prospects?,* 7 National Journal of Constitutional Law 5 and *infra*, text at notes 29-32 (1997).

[3] *See* the separate statement of J. B. Rudnyckyj on "regional languages" in Canada, Report of the Royal Commission on Bilingualism and Biculturalism, Vol. 1, at 155 (1967). Until then, the dominant metaphor for Canadian social structure was "mosaic." *See* J. Porter, The Vertical Mosaic: An Analysis of Social Class and Power in Canada (1965).

languages were deviants that must adapt to one or the other.[4] Since then, however, a different political understanding has emerged (at least outside Quebec). English remains the dominant language, but there is no dominant monoculture associated with it. In such a context, "multi" describes a complex cultural reality with multiple strands and multiple valences.[5]

Over the past two decades in Canada, multiculturalism has acquired a legal meaning as well. Here the term serves as shorthand for laws and policies that acknowledge the specificity of ethno-cultural minorities, often visible minorities, and particularly visible, religious minorities. As a legal concept, it has often been asserted in opposition to a dominant rights-based discourse conventionally described as "*Charter* patriotism." The 1982 *Canadian Charter of Rights and Freedoms*[6] proclaims that all Canadians have the same rights and are constitutionally equal. Since multicultural groups are, by definition, an aggregation less than the whole (and in practice, invariably a minority aggregation), for *Charter* patriots their constitutional recognition amounts to an inappropriate deviation from liberal universalism.[7]

On both the positive and negative readings of the constitutional concept of multiculturalism,[8] the current Canadian preoccupation with the idea of "reasonable accommodation" of ethno-cultural and religious minorities is

---

[4] The same conception of non-dominant cultures holds (even more strongly) in Quebec, where an alternative policy label – interculturalism – has been adopted. *See* Ministère des Relations avec les citoyens et de l'Immigration, *Shared Values, Common Interests – To Ensure the Full Participation of Quebeckers from Cultural Communities in the Development of Québec. Shine Among the Best*, Quebec: Gouvernement du Québec, 2004.

[5] In Quebec, by contrast, many claim that language and culture are so linked that there can only be a single Quebec culture. The argument tracks that made by members of First Nations communities and some groups of immigrants: the community is so small that it does not have the population to support significant variations in cultural forms, and consequently language maps culture in a close one-to-one relationship. For present purposes it is not necessary to explore the claim in relation to aboriginal peoples and small, discrete minority communities. The implications of this view for Quebec francophones are discussed *infra*, text at notes 39-48.

[6] Part I of the *Constitution Act, 1982*, being Schedule B to the *Canada Act, 1982* (UK).

[7] Paradoxically, another strand of *Charter* patriotism in Canada views the constitutional guarantee of equal protection in purely instrumental terms. The equality guarantee of Sec. 15 is meant to protect designated minorities and subordinated groups from oppression by majorities. On this reading, if an ethno-cultural-religious minority is able to frame its claims within one of the designated categories of Sec. 15, then the *Charter* can be wielded to support, rather than contest, the multicultural claim. Such a view also finds support in Sec. 27 of the *Charter*. Sec. 27 specifically constitutionalizes multiculturalism, providing: "This Charter shall be interpreted in a manner consistent with the preservation and enhancement of the multicultural heritage of Canadians."

[8] By "constitutional concept of multiculturalism" we mean to signal the view of multiculturalism in Sec. 27 of the *Charter* that "*Charter* patriots" contest, by contrast with three other uses of the term in Canada: (1) the original political meaning (i.e. one that challenges the "bicultural model" of Canadian identity); (2) the subsequent political meaning given to the concept (i.e. the

unfortunate. These readings imagine that the public policy issue is simply to delineate the circumstances under which exceptions from presumed *Charter* principles must be allowed on the basis of a religious or cultural claim: when is it "reasonable" to "accommodate" claims for exceptional treatment? Yet such an approach asks only some people to defend their cultural preferences. It seems to assume not only that all citizens have rights, not only that they all have the same rights, but also that these identical rights must be translated into identical practices. So, on this view of things, instead of simply changing a legal rule or modifying an administrative practice that is in some way failing some group, in order that the overall public policy objective in view can be more fully realized across the country's entire population, the dominant mono-culture must make an otherwise unwanted exception – must accommodate the specificity of immigrants, minorities, and religious dissentients.[9] The appeal to accommodation stigmatizes, for certain contexts, everyday features of legal life; it also reflects a curiously authoritarian view of law in the making. All legal rules change, all the time – whether through legislative amendment, judicial interpretation or simply changing practices. In other words, framing the beliefs and actions of citizens who may not share the assumptions of the majority as curiosities that must be accommodated is a bizarre response to the fact that all legal rules change, all policies evolve, and all absolutes become relativized through the experience of particularity.

To articulating an alternative conception of how the fundamental heterogeneity of human beings in contemporary democratic States may be acknowledged, this essay now turns. It begins by distinguishing between anti-discrimination law and anti-miscegenation law as responses to diversity (section 2). It then draws on a particular example of contemporary anti-miscegenation rhetoric in Canada to explore the tyranny of all mono-cultures (section 3). The essay next considers arguments for and against imposing a mono-culture of civic nationalism as a means of assimilating religious and cultural minorities (section 4). It argues for a recasting of the debate about reasonable accommodation in the mould of deep legal pluralism (section 5), and concludes with the claim that explicitly constitutionalizing the concept of reasonable accommodation as an approach to legitimating the heterogeneity of populations in contemporary liberal democracies would be a mistake.

complex cultural reality in Canada today); (3) its justiciable legal meaning (i.e. as short-hand for specific multiculturalism laws/policies).

[9] We acknowledge, of course, that some public policy objectives can be achieved by incorporating non-majority practices, while incorporation of such practices may be incompatible with other public policy objectives like, for example, public safety. In both cases, however, the issue is not one of "making an exception." Either the practice is consistent with the policy goal (which may be imperfectly instantiated in an existing regime that will, therefore, have to be modified in consequence) or the practice is inconsistent with a legitimate policy goal that does not directly or indirectly promote majority cultural practices and, as a result, the practice will have to be modified. This point is elaborated more fully *infra*, text at notes 49-51.

2. Myths of Miscegenation

The word miscegenation[10] was born of an especially deceitful act of political propaganda. During the US Presidential campaign of 1864 two anti-abolitionist newspapermen of the New York *World*, David Goodman Croly and George Wakeman, anonymously published a pamphlet entitled *Miscegenation: The Theory of the Blending of the Races, Applied to the American White Man and Negro*. The idea was simple: by circulating a tract as the work of pro-Republican abolitionists, in which racial intermarriage is not only praised but hailed as the glorious destiny of the United States (and thus logical conclusion of President Lincoln's anti-slavery policies), the authors could capitalize on the racist fears of white America to oppose Lincoln's campaign for re-election. Although the desired end was not met (the Republicans would win), the means were by no means inconsequential.[11]

The pseudo-scientific nomenclature was a perfect cover for the unstated but deeper fallacy at the heart of the concept of miscegenation: the racial superiority of whites and the racial inferiority of blacks.[12] This conception of a hierarchy of races is a persistent theme in human history although it reached a disastrous apogee in mid-19th century US.[13] Even among Northern abolitionists who supported the crusade against slavery, the belief of the

---

[10] The Oxford English Dictionary on-line defines miscegenation as: "The mixing or interbreeding of (people of) different races or ethnic groups, *esp.* the interbreeding or sexual union of whites and non-whites; a theory which advocates this as being advantageous to society; marriage or cohabitation by members of different ethnic groups."

[11] *See* S. Kaplan, *The Miscegenation Issue in the Election of 1864*, 34(3) Journal of Negro History 274 (1949). Prior to 1864, the deepest fear of defenders of slavery was expressed as the "amalgamation of the races." The conniving deceptiveness of the propagandists prefigures the increasing role that the deliberate manufacture of myth came to play in 20th century politics. *See also* E. Cassirer, *The Technique of the Modern Political Myths*, *in* The Myth of the State 277 (1946).

[12] A. F. Kinney, *Faulkner and Racial Mythology*, 5(2-3) Connotations 259 (1995-96). For contours of this debate during the US civil war, *see* P. Cleburne, "Memorial to the Commanding General, the Corps, Division, Brigade, and Regimental Commanders of the Army of Tennessee, January 2, 1864" (proposing the conscription and arming of slaves to fight for the southern Confederacy and their consequent emancipation, but denying the moral and political equality of the negro) and the response of Howell Cobb to a similar proposal by the Confederate government in a letter to Confederate Secretary of War, James Sedden, 8 January 1865: "If slaves will make good soldiers our whole theory of slavery is wrong." Both are reproduced in R. F. Durden, The Gray and the Black: The Confederate Debate on Emancipation, at 54-63 and 183-185 respectively (2000).

[13] For excellent studies *see* D. W. Howe, What Hath God Wrought: The Transformation of America, 1815-1848 (2007), and J. M. McPherson, Battle Cry of Freedom (1987) – two volumes of the Oxford History of the United States covering the periods 1815-1848 and 1848-1865 respectively.

inferiority of "negroes" was widespread, and "free blacks" in the northern states faced systematic social and legal exclusion.

Today, the word miscegenation is used figuratively as much as in its original acceptation, although invariably as a pejorative. The undesirable *métissage* of difference inflects discussions of religion, ethnicity, language, and social class. Occasionally the rhetoric is explicitly invidious and focuses on racial, religious or linguistic "purity"; most often, however, the poison is buried under a different contemporary preoccupation, both broader in scope and more diffuse in application. The late 18th-century conception of human equality, first reflected constitutionally in the French *Déclaration des droits de l'homme et du citoyen* and in the American *Declaration of Independence*, organized the mediation of human difference around a notion of individual equality and "equal protection of the laws." The legal tool was non-discrimination doctrine. Surprisingly, however, the constitutional approach to non-discrimination today is itself discriminatory – in two ways. First, unequal treatment is only invidious if its cause is identified as a prohibited ground of discrimination: typically, race, ancestry, place of origin, colour, ethnic origin, citizenship, creed, sex, sexual orientation, age, marital status, family status or disability.[14] Second, some countries (like the United States) draw distinctions even among grounds of discrimination, subject some claims of discrimination to closer scrutiny than others. Because the forces of American history have rendered discrimination on the base of race particularly harmful, courts consider that category more suspect than, for example, economic discrimination.[15]

This contemporary move to the language of non-discrimination, invariably praised as a triumph for democracy and the Rule of Law, obscures the central issue which the 1864 pamphlet sought to highlight. Treating others as legal equals will ultimately lead to treating them as social equals; and treating them as social equals will ultimately lead to cross-breeding, with its attendant debasement of the "gene pool."[16] Equal protection of the laws and non-

[14] *See*, for example, *Ontario Human Rights Code*, 1990 R.S.O. c. H-19, s. 1. The *Canadian Charter of Rights and Freedoms* identifies prohibited grounds as race, national or ethnic origin, colour, religion, sex, age or mental or physical disability, a list extended by the Supreme Court of Canada, using a concept of "analogous grounds", to among other bases of non-discrimination, sexual orientation, citizenship, and possibly, place of residence. Socio-economic status is not one of the enumerated grounds, nor has it been found to be an analogous ground by the Supreme Court. Consequently, most discussion of the justiciability of socio-economic rights focuses on Sec. 7 of the Canadian *Charter*, "the right to life, liberty and security of the person ..." *See* J. Glenn, *Enforceability of Economic and Social Rights in the Wake of* Gosselin*: Room for Cautious Optimism*, 83 Can. Bar Rev. 929 (2004).

[15] For a contemporary discussion of US anti-discrimination law, *see* R. D. Rotunda & J. E. Nowak, Treatise on Constitutional Law: Substance and Procedure, Ch. 18 "Equal Protection" (2007). Of course, the "tiers of scrutiny" approach arises because the XIVth Amendment to the US Constitution does not enumerate, as does the Canadian *Charter* and provincial *Human Rights Codes*, various prohibited grounds of discrimination.

[16] The social Darwinist conception also plays out in Holmes' dictum: "Three generations of

discrimination are handy covers, framed in the negative language of duty, for avoiding the positive aspiration, so nicely framed in the parable of the "Good Samaritan," of seeking to enlarge the moral community.

But the terrain of miscegenation has been significantly enlarged over the past 150 years. If the central issue in the United States in 1864 was one of latent biology, and rested on a distinction between what might be called "given" rather than "chosen" identities,[17] today, that distinction appears less clear cut, with the result that identity markers such as gender, sexual orientation, ethnicity, race, culture and religion are all seen to display elements of the "*donné*" and the "*construit.*"[18] Moreover, in 1864, notwithstanding how individual citizens may have felt, identities were lexically ordered by a community consensus. Very few Americans thought otherwise than that the most important differentiator of human beings was race, the excluded or subordinated being African slaves, Mexican *mestisos* and aboriginal peoples. Thereafter, religion (and, in particular, anti-Catholicism) served to separate communities. Distinctions between "nativists" and "immigrants" offered a further differentiator. And, particularly for the white male population, only thereafter did gender account for identity.[19]

A key feature of this conception of identity was the totalizing character of the primary claim. An African male slave could not easily claim identity affiliation with a free white woman on the grounds that both were Baptists. A Roman Catholic Irish immigrant could not easily claim identity affiliation with a native-born free-black Methodist on the grounds that both were women. Even Lincoln initially did not see the eradication of slavery as necessarily affirming the equality of Negroes. Nor, unsurprisingly, did he believe that legal equality would lead to social equality and, ultimately, to miscegenation.[20]

The moral and political universe of the 19th and 20th century nation State presumed racial, religious, cultural, and linguistic homogeneity. Indeed, the founding fiction of the nation State, maintained right through the Versailles

---

idiots are enough." *See* Buck v. Bell 274 US 200, at 207 (1927).

[17] On this distinction, its uncertain basis, and its contemporary use in constitutional adjudication, *see* R. Leckey, *Chosen Discrimination*, 18 Supreme Court Law Review (2d) 445 (2002). Of course, the idea that an identity could be chosen is not free from ambiguity. The choice is not just that of an individual whether to identify with a particular race, ethnicity or even religion. Indeed, whatever that personal decision, others often will impose on an individual various categories of their choice.

[18] An interesting parallel development can be seen in contemporary theories of molecular genetics. Few leading scholars today deny that environmental factors can actually modify genotypes – a heresy just a few decades ago. *See* the various papers *in* L. Maheu (Ed.), Beyond the Nature-Nurture Divide (2008).

[19] Howe, *supra* note 13. For an illuminating review of popular and elite opinion about the centrality of race and the moral and religious justifications for enslaving the "degraded negro," *see* B. Levine, Confederate Emancipation (2006).

[20] *See* D. K. Goodwin, Team of Rivals: the Political Genius of Abraham Lincoln (2006).

mantra of "national self-determination,"[21] through the egregious examples of ethnic cleansing during and after World War II, and right up to contemporary atrocities in the former Yugoslavia, Rwanda, and Darfur, was an assumption that an exact fit between ethno-cultural, religious, and racial character and political organization could be achieved. In the United States of the 19th century, the fiction was maintained by conceiving the more homogeneous federating States as the locus of sovereignty, and by denying the political rights of African slaves. In the 20th century the fiction was maintained by imagining federal citizenship in which the homogeneity of the population was reconceived as the constitutional and political equality of citizens. But even under the minimalist political equality conception of citizenship, the foundational myths of the miscegenationist fear can often be present. Patriotism – call it civic nationalism if you will – merely substitutes flags, national anthems, lapel pins, oaths of allegiance, military and sports circuses, and (typically) unread textual icons like "the constitution" for (to take the paraphernalia of Clan Ranald in the Scottish Highlands) kilts, bagpipes, toasts, Culloden, the caber toss, and so on.

The fear of miscegenation rests on a descriptive and a normative claim. Descriptively, the belief is that categories such as race and ethnicity are natural not constructed, necessary not chosen; in the same manner categories like religion (especially meta-religions like Christianity and Islam, rather than sects like Roman Catholic, Episcopalian, Baptist, Lutheran, Shiia, Sunni, Ismaili) are given by God, not chosen by humans. In brief, peoples are "naturally" different, from one another just as much as from other primates. Normatively, the claim is that heterogeneity of populations is dangerous since it inevitably leads to cross-breeding; and cross-breeding, or hybridization, equals impurity, an outrage against God and nature, and degradation.[22] Since population homogeneity is not only possible, but also desirable, opportunities for racial, ethnic and religious mixing must be eliminated, avoided, and denied.

There are, however, differences in the manner in which States may address the miscegenationist apprehension. These rest on whether they distinguish between (1) the *legal* concept of anti-discrimination as it may affect, on the one hand, legislation and the exercise of public power and, on the other hand,

---

[21] A fascinating account of the on-the-ground politics of national self-determination is given in M. MacMillan, Paris 1919: Six Months That Changed the World (2002).

[22] An underexplored aspect of the way the fear of miscegenation is expressed concerns its impact on those (especially children) who are of mixed blood. They are characterized either as belonging to the subordinated race, ethnicity, or language group (to be a mongrel is no better than to be a pure-blood inferior), or as constituting their own degraded, impure caste (in which case the child develops a divided, destructive self-image). Literary renderings are several, however. Consider the tragic end of Faulkner's "octaroon" anti-hero, Joe Christmas: W. Faulkner, Light in August: The Corrected Text 448-449 (1985). For a discussion of the complex relationship between Faulkner's own perspective and racist modes of thinking, *see* Kinney, *supra* note 12.

the non-governmental provision of goods, services, accommodation, and employment opportunities; and (2) the *socio-political* concept of miscegenation as a way of framing human relationships. Failure to attend to the distinction and to acknowledge that the former does not necessarily presume the latter is at the root of several problems collectively conceived as issues of "ethnic relations" or "cultural accommodation" or "religious toleration." The legal concept is autonomist – assuming that the role of the State is simply to avoid in its own actions, and constrain in the actions of others, excesses of intolerant behaviour. The socio-political concept (without the perverse undertones that accompanied its original usage) is relational – assuming a frank recognition and celebration of the necessary *métissage* of human populations.[23]

While anti-discrimination law rests on an affirmation of legal equality, it does not put into question the belief that there is a standard-instance (a typical citizen) that is naturally given and by reference to which discrimination is to be gauged. The challenge for contemporary liberal democratic States, therefore, is to formulate appropriate legal responses that will facilitate the celebration of appropriate social understandings of the complex, fluid, increasingly disaggregated, identities of human beings. Must all legal responses, in the manner of anti-discrimination law and the accompanying concept of reasonable accommodation, tend to a presupposition of essentialized, frozen, official identities and to require people to select for all purposes, and unless one is willing to become an apostate, for all time, only one of their multiple identities?

3. Heroes of Hérouxville

The myths of miscegenation, in both its racialized form and in its broader extension to ethnicity, religion, language and culture, have had a particularly evocative elaboration in contemporary Quebec. For some period Quebeckers have witnessed the growth of numerous communities of immigrants that are visibly different from the descendants of the Norman-Breton-Poitou settlers of 1608.[24] Most of these more recent immigrants settle in the greater Montreal

[23] It is important to emphasize that such recognition and celebration of *métissage* does not hinge on a dystopic vision of achieving a fully homogenized, golden race. The gene pool is far too diverse, and the combination of genes in any particular human being, for a standardized hybrid to emerge. More importantly, as moral agents, human beings are not simply the "sum of their genes." Environment and personality will inevitably contribute to the continuing diversity of human populations. For contemporary discussion of the effect if the nature-nurture interplay on the diversity of human beings *see* R. Plomin, Genetics and Experience: The Interplay between Nature and Nurture (1994), and M. Rutter, Genes and Behavior: Nature-Nurture Interplay Explained (2006).

[24] This statement compels two further observations. First, the issue is one of perception. Religious communities other than Roman Catholic have been present in Quebec since the later

area, although some have located in other larger cities. Unlike past waves of immigrants, many are not Christian, not of European provenance, and do not speak French (or English) as a first language (or even at all).[25] In colour of skin, manner of dress, dietary practices and public displays of gender roles, these immigrants appear different.

Occasionally, differences in perception and in the interpretation of action have led to requests by authorities for such immigrants to cease or modify their traditional religious and cultural practices, that are seen to be contrary to Quebec laws and values; also occasionally, differences in perception and the interpretation of action have led to requests by such immigrants for public authorities to change existing laws and practices that are perceived to be unnecessarily constraining of how they express their identity.[26] On rare occasions, these requests have culminated in litigation: almost never a criminal or regulatory prosecution; more often a civil action meant to overturn an enacted norm or to reverse a decision by a public administrator, school principal or municipal official. Nonetheless, the vast bulk of requests – be they from public officials or from citizens – are negotiated and settled through discussion, adjustment and mutual accommodation.

But whether these differences are litigated or resolved through discussion and adjustment, they can provoke resentment. Even when, for example, a regulatory prosecution succeeds or a civil action fails, many citizens feel offended that the prosecution was necessary or that the civil action was even launched.[27] In part, offence is taken because mainstream media have taken to framing issues involving religious and cultural difference as one of "survival," a

17th century. Even before the cession of New France to England in 1763, inhabitants of Quebec spoke European languages other than French: notably English, Spanish, Dutch, and German. Apparently a black, freeman translator accompanied Champlain in 1608, and there is evidence that a Portugese-born African slave was tortured and hanged for arson in 1734. *See* A. Cooper, The Hanging of Angelique: The Untold Story of Canadian Slavery and the Burning of Old Montréal (2006). For more than two centuries a black population has been present in Quebec and North African and East Asian immigrants began to settle in the early 19th century. Second, the "old stock" Quebeckers of Norman-Breton-Poitou origin cannot lay claim to "ethnic purity." Numerous studies indicate the extent of sexual relationships between Aboriginal peoples and earlier settlers, such that only a fraction of those who can trace their arrival to the time of New France do not also have aboriginal ancestors.

[25] We are drawing a distinction here between "waves" of immigration – Scots in the late 18th century, Irish in the mid 19th century, Germans, Italians and Greeks in the early 20th century, for example – and the constant trickle of worldwide emigration to Quebec noted in the previous note.

[26] In the next few paragraphs reference will be made to immigrants (implicitly recent immigrants) as the primary source of ethno-cultural and religious diversity. Interestingly, however, most "incidents" involve second and third generation Quebec citizens who are Muslims, Sikhs, Hassidic Jews, and Hindus, not recent immigrants.

[27] Consider, by contrast, general public reaction to criminal prosecution or civil actions. Citizens may lament that "biker gangs" exist and must be prosecuted criminally; however, they typically do not see ordinary criminal action as a moral outrage when the accused is convicted. Similarly,

longstanding preoccupation of francophones in Quebec.[28] When foregrounded against various inescapable uncertainties of life, the specific challenge posed by the unfamiliar other takes on major significance. Questions like the environment, drugs, crime, employment security, pension adequacy, health, and the cost of health care, relationships with parents, spouse and children vex contemporary society. But human beings have a limited capacity to deal with uncertainty, and rely on large symbol systems to park the uncertainties they would rather not confront.

Historically, in Quebec, religion and in particular the Roman Catholic faith provided the primary reassurance. In the City of God the tribulations of the City of Man will be absent. For the inescapable heartache of the City of Man, the confessional and the sacraments served to reassure. But with the Quiet Revolution of the 1960s, citizens abandoned the Church in droves and displaced the parking spot for their uncertainties to the State. While late in arriving in comparison with other North American political units, the social-welfare State quickly occupied a predominant role in Quebeckers' self-definition: public action, expressed in the slogan "maîtres chez nous," became Quebec's secular religion, and the Provincial government was its church. For many "sovereignty" (or political independence from Canada) was the approaching nirvana that would make today's *travails* tolerable. After two unsuccessful independence referendums (in 1980 and 1995) and a growing sense among Quebec's political leadership that the economy was either more important than (or at least that a healthy economy was a precondition to) independence, the reassurance provided by the State no longer resonated reassurance. Yet another displacement of uncertainty beckoned. If aspirational projects in the next life or in this life are unattainable, solutions to one's apprehension can often be found in scapegoating and blame. The cause of distress is the "other," the "immigrant," the "person that does not share my values."

---

citizens rarely fulminate about the collapse of civilization when labour unions launch public relations campaigns to seek a change to labour standards or minimum wage legislation.

[28] On media representation of the issues, *see* M. Potvin, *Les médias écrits et les accommodements raisonnables: L'invention d'un débat [Written Media and Reasonable Accommodation: The Invention of Debate]*, Montréal: Report No. 8 presented to the Bouchard-Taylor Commission on Reasonable Accommodation, 2008, online: Commission de consultation sur les pratiques d'accommodement reliées aux différences culturelles http://www.accommodements.qc.ca/documentation/rapports/rapport-8-potvin-maryse.pdf. On perceptions of identity and modes of nationalism chez les Québécois, *see* R. Cook (Ed.), French-Canadian Nationalism: an Anthology (1969); R. A. Stebbins, French Enigma: Survival and Development in Canada's Francophone Societies (2000); D. Salée, *Identity Politics and Multiculturalism in Quebec*, 18(2) Cultural Survival Quarterly 1994. Initially the survival was directed to the idea of preserving a French-speaking, Roman Catholic, and rural arcadia. Since the mid-1960s the objective has been predominantly linguistic, although some also claim that there is a cultural specificity to Quebec. *See*, classically, L. Groulx, Histoire du Canada-français [A History of French Canada] (1960); *see also* C. Dufour, Le défi québécois [The Quebec Challenge] (1989).

These various concerns found vivid expression in the adoption (and widespread dissemination) in the spring of 2007 of a "Code of Conduct" by the Municipality of Hérouxville, a town of 1300 people in the rural heartland of Quebec. This Code of Conduct purported to set out the basic values of Hérouxville and the norms that should be followed by its residents.[29] Not surprisingly, the litany of norms included in the Code of Conduct tracks the list of incidents reported in the popular press where courts, administrative agencies, municipalities, school commissions and private institutions like the YMCA or soccer leagues adjusted their practices at the request of a religious or cultural group. In each case, the Hérouxville prescriptions directly seek to contest the decision taken, to proscribe any such adjustments, and to reaffirm the *status quo ante* as a non-negotiable value. Occasionally, the norms of the Code of Conduct respond to practices that may be associated in the public mind with particular cultures and religions elsewhere in the world, but are unknown, rarely encountered, or illegal under the *Criminal Code* in Canada: female circumcision, polygamy, the sale of child brides, stoning, the chopping off of the hands of thieves, lashing, and so on.

Whatever the causes that led to the promulgation of the Code of Conduct, its central objective was not instrumental: there were, for example, no Sikhs, Muslims, Hindus, Hassidic Jews or Roma people inhabiting Hérouxville. Rather the goal was symbolic and polemical: the political objective was to stake out a position against the *manner* in which courts had come to justify decisions relating to the wearing of the hijab and the bearing of the kirpan in schools, the erection of a sukkah, and the proposal to permit religious courts to pronounce, via consensual arbitration, in matters of filiation, marriage, divorce, and successoral entitlement.[30] In a number of cases, the Supreme Court had, borrowing from arbitral jurisprudence in labour relations, characterized its approach to determining the constitutionality of various laws, regulations, by-laws and practices as requiring it to ask whether the requested attenuation of the norm constituted a "reasonable accommodation" of cultural

[29] *See* Municipalité de Hérouxville *Normes de vie*, online: http://municipalite.herouxville.qc.ca/normes.pdf. The Code of Conduct, were it not serious, could be seen simply as a modern day version of Merle Haggard's famous song "Okie from Muskogee," which notoriously opens: "We don't smoke marijuana in Muskogee, We don't take our trips on LSD, We don't burn our drafts cards down on main street, 'Cause we like livin' right an' bein' free." (composed by Merle Haggard and Roy Edward Burris, 1969). Whether the last line is intended as ironic remains an open question; in Hérouxville, the affirmation of "freedom" under the "Normes de vie" would be taken as self-evident.

[30] For further elaboration of these incidents *see* R. A. Macdonald & A. Popovici, *Le catéchisme de l'islamophobie [The Catechism of Islamophobia]*, *in* M. Jezequel (Ed.), La justice à l'épreuve de la diversité culturelle [The Justice System and the Challenge of Cultural Diversity] 19 (2007); R. A. Macdonald, *The Legal Mediation of Social Diversity*, *in* A. Gagnon, F. Rocher, & M. Monserrat Guibernau I Berdun (Eds.), The Conditions of Diversity in Multinational Democracies 85 (2004).

or religious practice.[31] For the municipal councillors of Hérouxville, however, these Supreme Court decisions were, rather, examples of "unreasonable accommodations"[32] that had to be resisted.[33]

In reaction to the promulgation of the Hérouxville Code of Conduct, and to the electoral politics of the time, the Government of Québec appointed a

[31] Ontario Human Rights Commission and Theresa O'Malley v. Simpsons-Sears, [1985] 2 S.C.R. 536 (where a work requirement imposed on all employees for business reasons discriminated against the appellant, a Seventh Day Adventist, because compliance required her to act contrary to her religious beliefs, *i.e.,* work on the Sabbath; the Supreme Court held that the employer did not take reasonable steps to accommodate the employee); Commission scolaire régionale de Chambly v. Bergevin, [1994] 2 S.C.R. 525 (where an absence of accommodation on behalf of their employer obliged Jewish teachers to take their religious holidays without pay, the Supreme Court restored the arbitration board's award requiring the employer to compensate the teachers when they were absent due to their observance of religious holidays); *Eldridge, supra* note 2 (where the Supreme Court held that the failure to provide sign language interpreters as an insured benefit under the Medical Services Plan violated the equality provision in Sec. 15(1) of the *Canadian Charter of Rights and Freedoms*). In *Anselem, supra* note 2, it was held that stipulations in the declaration of co-ownership of a luxury condominium complex that would prevent the Orthodox Jewish appellants from constructing Succah's (temporary shelters) on their balconies during the nine-day festival of Souccoth, infringed upon the appellants' freedom of religion under Sec. 3 of the Quebec *Charter.* In *Multani, supra* note 2, the decision by the governing board of the appellant's school to prohibit him from wearing a kirpan – that is, a Sikh religious object resembling a dagger that must be made of metal and worn at all times – for the stated purpose of ensuring school safety was held by the Supreme Court to be an unjustified infringement in a free and democratic society of the appellant's right to religious freedom. In both these recent cases coming from Quebec, *Anselem* and *Multani,* the majority opinion of the court employed the concept of reasonable accommodation to assess the limits that could reasonably be imposed on the exercise of minority religious beliefs. For discussion of the approach of the Supreme Court of Canada to equality rights and anti-discrimination norms *see* P. W. Hogg, Constitutional Law of Canada Ch. 52 (2005).

[32] Lurking in the reaction of the Hérouxville council also seemed to be the question of cost. In the disability setting where the concept first arose, the adjective "reasonable" was meant to provide a balance where the expenditure – for ramps, elevators, sign language, Braille translations, etc. – was beyond the capacity of the undertaking to absorb. Most accommodations on ethno-cultural and religious grounds do not require expenditure (although some do), so the concept of "reasonable" acquires a different valence: what deviations from the heretofore-assumed normative baselines are reasonable from a normative perspective? This necessarily turns the question into one of ethics (political theory) rather than economics.

[33] While the Code of Conduct was reactive to what was perceived as elite imposition of urban liberal values, the central point is that these public judgements and decisions provided a stimulus to Hérouxville municipal councilors to render explicit the underlying normativity of rural Quebec that until then had neither been revealed nor debated in an open, public, discursive form. Occasionally, Quebec artists, poets, musicians and authors attempted to expose (and critique) this implicit normativity, but the strong nationalist leanings of most in the artistic community significantly muted critique. The monologues of comedian Yvon Deschamps and the plays of Michel Tremblay are excellent examples of the genre and its limitations. *See* A. Gervais (Ed.), Emblématiques de l'époque de joual: Jacques Renaud, Gérald Godin, Michel Tremblay, Yvon Deschamps (2000); C. Paquette, Yvon Deschamps: un aventurier fragile (1997).

"*Commission de consultation sur les pratiques d'accommodement reliées aux différences culturelles*" (the Bouchard-Taylor Commission) to

> (a) take stock of accommodation practices in Quebec; (b) analyse the attendant issues bearing in mind the experience of other societies; (c) conduct an extensive consultation on this topic; and (d) formulate recommendation to the government to ensure that accommodation practices conform to the values of Quebec society as a pluralistic, democratic, egalitarian society.[34]

In late May 2008 the Commission released its report *Building the future: a time for reconciliation.*[35] Most of its 37 recommendations can be grouped in three themes. First, and most importantly, only three recommendations speak to legislative action: the Commission recommends one amendment to the *Quebec Charter of Human Rights and Freedoms* to provide for the equality of men and women (recommendation B6), another to prohibit public incitement to discrimination (recommendation E1), and a third to reinforce the protections given to social and economic rights in article 39-48, by extending the supremacy clause to them (recommendation E3). Second, the Commission recommends a focus on dejudicialisation (recommendation B2), local solutions (recommendations A2, B5), an office to collect and promote best practices (recommendation B4), and leadership by State organizations (recommendations B9, E2). Third, the Commission proposed that, to encourage better intercultural understanding, the government should encourage immigration outside large cities (recommendation C5), increase opportunities for such exchange (recommendation D3), and promote secularism (recommendation G1).

In brief the Commission sought (1) to expose the myths of miscegenation; (2) to counter myths about the idea of reasonable accommodation; (3) to reconstruct in a more positive way than the Hérouxville Code of Conduct the explicitation of the implicit values of Quebec society; and (4) to focus on strategies for mediating ethnic, religious, cultural, and linguistic diversity that do not require textual amendment to constitutional or quasi-constitutional documents. To a brief consideration of why such an approach is justified, this essay now turns.[36]

[34] The mandate of the Commission was established by Order-in-Council 95-2007 issued on 8 February 2007 and reproduced as Appendix A of the Commission's Report (*infra* note 35).

[35] Quebec: Éditeur official, 2008. A caveat is in order here. One of us, Roderick Macdonald, was a member of the 15-person Advisory Council to the Commission; accordingly, the interpretation conveyed here is obviously coloured by that experience. Nonetheless, the essay reflects the views of the authors, which should not, of course, be ascribed to the Commission.

[36] One of has previously treated many of these themes in several texts, including those cited *supra* note 30. *See* R.A. Macdonald, *Kaleidoscopic Federalism*, *in* J-F Gaudreault-DesBiens & F. Gélinas (Eds.), The States and Moods of Federalism: Governance, Identity and Methodology 261 (2005); *Triangulating Social Law Reform*, *in* Y. Gendreau (Ed.), Dessiner la société par le droit [Designing Society Through Law] 119 (2004); *European Private Law and the Challenge of Plural Legal Subjectivities*, 9:1 The European Legacy 55 (2004); *L'hypothèse du pluralisme dans les sociétés démocratiques avancées [The Hypothesis of Pluralism in Advanced Modern*

4. Ethics of Ethnicity

Before considering directly the manner in which the Bouchard-Taylor Commission addressed the question of reasonable accommodation, it is useful to consider the ethical positions (as a matter of social and political theory) that underlay comments made during the Commission's public hearings, and reactions to the Report when it was released. One may begin by recalling that mongrelization or *métissage* has traditionally had an unfavourable status in western culture. The Greeks, for example, considered crossbreeding of plants and animals as an outrage against nature.[37] In modern times, the fear is different. One does not worry about offending nature as such, but one does recoil from offending one's own nature: in the case of classical racial miscegenation, it is the blood of one's forefathers; in the case of cultural miscegenation, it is the 20th century cover for naturalism – personal identity.[38] In other words, the fear at the heart of the invention of the word miscegenation is the same fear of loss of identity at the heart of opposition to what has been characterized as the "reasonable accommodation" of ethno-cultural and religious difference.

During the public hearings conducted by the Commission, the recurrent question of identity, and loss of identity loomed large. Many "old stock Quebeckers" (a group that the Commission called "Quebeckers of French-Canadian ancestry") felt that the Commission too quickly dismissed their concerns about the rapidly changing face of Quebec and the weakening of Quebec's traditional culture. The theme was reiterated by public intellectuals. For example, Jacques Beauchemin, a sociology professor at the *Université du Québec à Montréal* and also a member of the Commission's Advisory Council, felt that the Commission left no room for "real" Quebeckers to defend their identity.[39] Similarly, Guy Rocher, a prominent sovereignist sociologist wrote that the Commission Report denigrated Quebeckers by constantly referring to them as minorities fearful about the loss of their cultural heritage.[40] True, the Commission did take the view that Quebec culture was in transition, as it had been since 1608. But the Commission also observed that since those who

Societies], 33 Revue de droit de l'Université de Sherbrooke 133 (2002); *The Design of Constitutions to Accommodate Linguistic, Cultural and Ethnic Diversity*, *in* K. Kulcsar & D. Szabo (Eds.), Dual Images: Multiculturalism on Two Sides of the Atlantic 52 (1996).

[37] *Cf.* C. Zirkle, The Beginnings of Plant Hybridization 41 (1935).

[38] *See* Taylor, *supra* note 1.

[39] *See* J. Heinrich, *Dissident Decries 'Whitewash': UQÀM Prof Targets Bouchard*, The Gazette, 17 May 2008, at A-6. Many also objected to the Commission's use of the term "Quebeckers of French-Canadian ancestry" since, for them, any reference to Canada was a reminder of the "conquest" of 1759 and two centuries of oppression by the English. In these circles "québécois de souche" or "québécois pure laine" are less offensive terms to identify "true Quebeckers."

[40] G. Rocher, *Rapport Bouchard-Taylor. Une Majorité Trop Minoritaire? [The Bouchard-Taylor Report: Too Minoritarian Majority?]*, Le Devoir, 12 June 2008, at A-7.

held to this culture were by far the dominant social, political, and (since the mid-1960s) economic force in Quebec, it was time to get over the inferiority complex.[41]

What, then, is the particular identity of "Quebeckers of French-Canadian ancestry" that is so fragile? Beauchemin states, as justification of the need to defend traditional old-stock culture:

> If that … [the non-necessity of defending this culture] … is true, why do we impose French in schools? English is infinitely more practical than French. We're in North America but we cling to another language. Why not just abandon it? For good reason: society isn't just some fashion: it's something that gives itself projects to do and sets out norms to live by. And here in Quebec we have something to preserve.[42]

In this comment, Beauchemin unwittingly expresses the same miscegenationist apprehension that prompted the Hérouxville Code of Conduct. It is normal to be afraid of losing that which one is socialized into believing is historically permanent, natural and beneficial. And it is normal to defend a purely conjunctural practice or perception by claiming that it is historically permanent, natural and beneficial.[43] If someone speaks condescendingly of that which one holds as natural and beneficial, the attack is on one's sense of self. One might ask, for example, if the historical permanence of Scottishness is something other than simply kilts and bag-pipes. The illusion is to consider that culture is something that is only reflected by some other something – a race, an ethnicity, a religion – that is its origin and sole generator. In this conceit, if one were to

[41] One of the particular difficulties faced by the Commission concerned the basic question of "cultural identity" and the way in which a "culture" could (or should) be described. No matter how Quebec culture is described, there is a risk of moral exclusion. The exclusion is obvious if Quebec culture means "old-stock culture." If the description embraces "francophone culture," then culture is tied to language, not geography. If the description is geographic, the diaspora of "Quebeckers of French-Canadian ancestry" presently living outside Quebec is excluded. In the end, the Commission sought (unsuccessfully) to deflect the critique by adopting an approach that did not require it to specify exactly what the "essential" components of Quebec culture were. *See Building the Future*, Part IV, *supra* note 35.

[42] Jacques Beauchemin as cited in J. Heinrich, *supra* note 39.

[43] Without in any way suggesting that Beauchemin or the municipal councillors of Hérouxville entertain a conception of race, religion, and culture remotely like that held by Southern élites in the era leading up to the Civil War, it is nonetheless useful to notice how the miscegenationist fear is rhetorically framed in the two cases. Between 1815 and 1830 the justification for African slavery in the United States underwent a significant transformation. From a Jeffersonian-type defence of the institution based on its toleration as a necessary evil that would eventually be overcome when no longer economically rational, John C. Calhoun came to articulate the "natural inferiority of the Negro race" and the "positive good" of slavery as a means for improving the condition of this "degraded race." *See* J. C. Calhoun, *Speech on the Reception of Abolition Petitions*, *in* Works (II) 625 (1851-1856).

lose racial, ethnic, and religious differentiation, one would lose one's culture – either permanently, or by it simply becoming a caricature of itself.[44]

But this perspective suffers from four analytical mistakes. First, it assumes an ahistorical and acontextual culture. Those who take this position would unhesitatingly acknowledge that "*Un canadien errant*" (a popular mid-19th century folk ballad about a "Patriote" exiled for his participation in the Rebellion in Lower Canada, written in 1842), Gilles Vigneault's nationalist anthem "*Mon pays, c'est l'hiver*" (1968) and Les Colocs' lament for the transformation of small-town Quebec, "*La rue principale*" (1991) are equally canons of Quebec musical culture. And yet, were the Quebec State to have protected a static culture, the latter two songs would never have been created. Both Beauchemin and the municipal councilors of Hérouxville have a presentist view of culture, in that they can only see what they now have; not only is the past collapsed into a singular present, the singular present is imagined as unchangeable. Because it is impossible to know the future, its influences, and its developments, it is impossible to know what the future of Quebec culture will comprise. There is another point about ahistoricism and acontextualism. Until now the dominant myth has been that Quebec culture is a one-directional, hermetically-insulated, self-generated project of those who arrived in 1608. This, of course, ignores the impact of aboriginal rhythms and chants on early Quebec folk music, of Appalachian music on Gilles Vigneault, and of contemporary US pop music on Les Colocs. But acknowledging these impacts invites the question why would it not be a black musician like Gregory Charles, or an as yet unnamed Muslim rocker, or perhaps a boulevardier of Vietnamese origin that provides the leavening of Quebec music of the future?

Second, this perspective assumes that cultures thrive primarily when they are protected from outside, corrupting influences. The assumption is that a culture is like a "perpetual motion machine" that keeps regenerating itself through its own endogenous mechanisms. Such a conception leads to defensiveness about what currently "is", and a continual quest for criteria to determine what about that "is" is "pure" and what is "impure." The point can be made by contrasting caricatured views of French and Quebec nationalism: the typical French parliamentarian cannot understand why the whole world does not want to be French; the typical Quebec sovereignist wishes everybody else would just go away. This defensiveness about culture also breeds an emotional conservatism. Sociologist Beauchemin claims that Quebeckers have something to preserve, as if preservation of that which now exists is the first goal of a polity. Thomas Aquinas rightly reminds us that if the goal of

[44] More importantly, it is less the object of loss than the manner of loss that is most troubling. It is the loss of agency, not identity as such that is the real problem: the idea that one never planned or consented for one's culture to go away. The implications of a loss of agency for members of an existing cultural mainstream are discussed in Section IV.

a ship's captain were simply to preserve a boat, it would never leave port.[45] Analogously, one would say, the point of a polity is not simply to survive; it is to provide the artefacts, activities and mechanisms through which members of a society may seek fulfillment, develop, flourish and move forward.

Third, this perspective assumes that there is "something" (an agent) called society. In Beauchemin's words, "Society isn't just some fashion. It's something that gives itself projects." Beauchemin is no doubt correct in asserting that societies are not just some fashion. But they do not give themselves projects. People act in concert to imagine and pursue collective projects – multiple projects that are as varied as the people comprising the collectivity themselves. Moreover, people do not act monolithically: they act in concert in multiple settings and multiple associations, conceiving and pursuing multiple collective projects. What might be called the "societal project" is a description of the ensemble of these individual and small group projects. It has no independent rationale or existence; and to the degree it is prescriptive, it can only be procedurally or formally prescriptive. The "societal project" may be captured in a political slogan concocted and imposed by political élites, but its content is necessarily open-ended and generated by citizens. The Code of Conduct in Hérouxville is, in this respect, epi-phenomenal.

Fourth, this perspective assumes that there is a moral claim that flows uniquely from history. To claim that "we" have something to preserve, "we" have projects to pursue, and "we" have norms to live by, begs the questions "who is we?" and "how did any particular we get to appropriate that status to itself?" At bottom, the claim is that "we were here first, so we get to control." And yet, such a claim betrays a selective view of history. Was the territory claimed by France in 1608 uninhabited? Ought not the Innu, Naskapi, Cree, Algonquin, Huron and Mohawks, among others, to have a better right to impose their language, their projects and their norms? Even assuming, for the sake of argument, that New France was *terra nullius* in 1608, whatever Quebeckers are in 2008 cannot simply be reduced to direct descendants of those settlers. If the moral claim is uniquely a claim of history, then the British of the 1760s and 1770s, the Irish of the 1830s and 1840s and the Italians of the 1920s and 1930s should have a greater right to impose their language, projects and norms than the Algerians, Lebanese and Moroccans of the 1970s and 1980s. Whatever claims may flow uniquely from history, they are not exclusionary moral claims.

This analysis of the manner in which some public intellectuals reacted to the Report of the Bouchard-Taylor Commission now permits the central question posed in the sub-title to this essay to be addressed: should the concept of 'reasonable accommodation' for subordinated groups and minorities be constitutionalized? In framing an answer it is helpful to begin by noting what a query formulated in this way presupposes.

[45] *Summa Theologica, prima secundae*, question 2, art. 5.

Obviously, the question presupposes that the concept of reasonable accommodation is not already constitutionalized. This assumption is doubtful. Exactly this type of relationship – the recognition and adjustment to another person's particularities – characterizes and constitutes human interaction, across and within groups, all the time.[46] Through these everyday interactions members of a society constitute a dynamic normative framework that is part of the implicit constitution of a State.[47] That is, the question to be addressed ought rather to be "should the concept of reasonable accommodation be elevated to the status of an explicit constitutional text"? And just as the heroes of Hérouxville seem to think that the Code of Conduct actually has significant instrumental (rather than symbolic) weight so too the proponents of explicit constitutionalization seem to think that adding the expression "reasonable accommodation" to a constitutional text will make a difference.[48] In this connection, it is worth recalling that the U.S. Bill of Rights was of little use in reigning in the excesses of McCarthyism in the 1950s while, at the same time, Canadian courts had no compunction about invoking an unwritten, implicit Bill of Rights to strike down anti-communist legislation in Quebec.[49]

In addition, the question presupposes that the concept of reasonable accommodation is a mechanism through which otherwise unacceptable deviations from a more general constitutional (or *Charter*) norm can be justified. But what is the norm from which exceptions must be allowed on the basis of a religious or cultural claim? It is nothing other than the claim to equality and equal protection of the laws. As understood in Hérouxville, the concept and import of reasonable accommodation is exactly backwards. Far from being an exception to the norm of constitutional equality (as the Code of Conduct would have it), reasonable accommodation is the practice through which that norm of equality is instantiated. The point is that an equality

[46] Most of the examples of "reasonable accommodation" cited in the Bouchard-Taylor Report involved situations where a request was made – for example, by a group of Muslims to have a "no-pork" menu for their visit to a sugar-shack – well in advance of the relevant interaction and an adjustment was made that did not require any other visitors to go without pork in their plates of baked beans. *See Building the Future*, *supra* note 35, Part Two: A Crisis of Perception, Chapter Two: A Chronology of Events. Does this request represent anything different from the continuing negotiation between customer and restaurant owner of decaffeinated coffee, artificial sweetener, vegetarian meals, and fair-trade fruits and vegetables?

[47] On the nature of a State's implicit constitution and the role of citizens in shaping that constitution through their day-to-day interactions, *see* Macdonald (1996), *supra* note 36.

[48] What does it say about a society that some of its constitutional scholars believe that an explicit constitutional text will be necessary in order to negotiate agreement on the principle that getting along together requires give and take? If, by contrast, the added text is meant solely as aspirational one wonders what a canonical formulation in a constitution adds to the discursive, contextualized statements that have already appeared in constitutional decisions of a State's Supreme Court. *See, for example*, the cases cited, *supra* note 31.

[49] *See, for example*, Saumur v. City of Quebec [1953] 2 S.C.R. 299; Birks v. Montreal [1955] S.C.R. 799; Switzman v. Elbling [1957] 2 S.C.R. 85.

norm should, as a theoretical proposition, require all citizens to defend their religious and cultural preferences, including those citizens who have taken their preferences for granted in the past because no-one has ever observed that they reflect the specificity of the dominant religion and culture.[50] However much "Quebeckers of French-Canadian ancestry" might assume that names like Rue Ste-Catherine, or Carré Saint-Louis, or the borough of Notre-Dame-de-Grâce, or Quebec's official flag (the Bourbon *fleur-de-lysée* comprising a cross), or the Crucifix hanging in the National Assembly, or the illuminated cross on the top of Mount Royal in Montreal are merely "historical" cultural artefacts with no religious connotations, for Muslims, Jews, Hindus, Sikhs, agnostics and atheists they are Christian (and more particularly, Roman Catholic) symbols.[51] Yet to frame the issue of re-naming streets and towns and removing ostentatious public crosses as one of reasonable accommodation means, contrary to the basic equality norm of the constitution, that only some people – those who do not share the cultural assumptions of the majority – have to explain and justify their cultural and religious preferences.

5. The Promise of Legal Pluralism

That the question of social diversity arises in the form of an inquiry into reasonable accommodation is because of the way in which issues of linguistic, cultural, religious, and ethnic difference are habitually conceived in contemporary constitutional law in liberal democratic States. Moreover, the predominant conception of constitutional law in these States is tributary to a usually unstated and unargued for, but nonetheless dominant, hypothesis about the idea, the scope and the purpose of law. That is, the claim advanced in this essay is that the ongoing debate about whether or not the concept of "reasonable accommodation" should be incorporated into the explicit constitution of a State is grounded in a particular view of law, the State, and of the meaning of the Rule of Law. This view, predominant among legal scholars in Western democracies, has five main tenets:

[50] This does not mean that every existing practice or cultural preference must be formally rejustified on a continuing basis. The quotidian following of the practice is its ongoing justification. Only when the universality of a practice is challenged by a claim to acknowledge a different practice reflecting a different cultural preference will it be necessary to formally justify both the basic practice, and to negotiate its relationship with the newly asserted cultural preference and practice.

[51] The Bouchard-Taylor Commission recommended that the crucifix be removed from the Assembly Chamber and placed in a hallway in a display explaining its origins and historical significance (recommendation G3). The day following release of the Report a motion by the Quebec Premier to reaffirm the place of the crucifix in the National Assembly was passed unanimously. *See* K. Dougherty, *We'll Keep Crucifix up, Charest Says*, The Gazette, 23 May 2008, at A-4.

1) Monism: the belief that law is formal and institutionalized such that a single legal order has a normative monopoly in a given territory
2) Centralism: the belief that law is exclusively the product of the political state
3) Positivism: the belief that there can be an *ex ante* hard criterion for distinguishing that which is law, from that which is not law
4) Prescriptivism: the belief that law is about externally-imposed rules and analogous normative statements
5) Chirographism: the belief that the optimal expression of law is text, not practice[52]

But there is another approach – legal pluralism – that contests each of these tenets and that is more open to acknowledging the plurality and fluidity of identity, and to relativizing the claims of those who would deploy the State as the vehicle of their domination. [53]

To take a legal pluralist approach is to display a disinclination to define categories or identity and to see any such categories as monolithic and necessarily comprised of definable traits. So, a pluralist would neither ask the long established Canadians of Chinese origin to pretend to be white, nor pretend that calling them a "visible minority" is a primary characterization of their place in Canadian life. Neither would a pluralist think of requiring a pale-skinned Muslim woman who has emigrated from Ireland to wear a headscarf if she wants to be a Muslim, nor conversely, of requiring her to "act white" because she "looks white." Finally, a pluralist approach enables us to ask about all the Canadians who may be marginalized in large cities, whether they migrated from Calcutta or Corner Brook, Guyana or the Gaspé.

Considering differences in the experiences of internal and external migrants in Canada underscores the point.[54] Do issues of social exclusion apply in the

[52] *See*, for an elaboration of these ideas in the context of law reform, R. A. Macdonald, *Unitary Law Re-form, Pluralistic Law Re-substance: Illuminating Legal Change*, 67 La. L. Rev. 1113 (2007).

[53] These claims about deep legal pluralism are developed in R.A. Macdonald and M.-M. Kleinhans, *What Is a* Critical *Legal Pluralism?*, 16 Canadian Journal of Law and Society 29 (1998); R.A. Macdonald, *Here, there and everywhere ... Theorizing Legal Pluralism; Theorizing Jacques Vanderlinden*, *in* N. Kasirer (Ed.), Mélanges Jacques Vanderlinden 381 (2006); R. A. Macdonald & D. Sandomierksi, *Against Nomopolies*, 57:4 Northern Ireland Legal Quarterly 610 (2007); R. A. Macdonald, *Non-chirographic Legal Pluralism*, Presented to the Joint Meeting of the Canadian Law and Society Association and the Law and Society Association, Montreal: 31 May 2008.

[54] Ultimately the pluralist perspective puts into question the centrality of the boundary drawing operated by the territorial claims of the political State. For a discussion of how pluralism relativizes the concept of citizenship and imagines, for example, a commonality in the legal status of internal and external migrants, *see* Macdonald (2005), *supra* note 36.

same way to Caribbean guest farm-workers in Quebec's eastern townships as to Newfoundlanders in Fort McMurray? Or equally to Bangladeshi immigrants in Toronto and to Gaspésiens in Montreal? Typically the internal migrant – the Newfoundlander and the Gaspésien – is afforded recognition as a full member of the political community, but receives no services meant to foster participation in the new socio-cultural community; typically the external immigrant – the Mexican farm-worker and the Bangladeshi – receives the services but is denied the recognition. To imagine that the issue is one of "reasonable accommodation" underscores the paradox. How ought a society to accommodate a displaced Gaspésien migrant? Does it even make sense to talk of adjustments Alberta makes in the tar sands as "reasonable accommodations" for those from Newfoundland? From these examples, one might well conclude that Canadians agree to a policy of "reasonable accommodation" in relation to something they don't recognize or don't like, while in other situations the same policy may not even be perceived as a "policy" or may be benignly labelled as a "labour market" inducement rather than an "accommodation."

The fundamental question is one of identity: how to foster positive not negative identity, for all, because that – rather than assimilation – is the basis of social inclusion. In the lens of legal pluralism, the State will not presume a single model of what being a citizen entails. More importantly, the world doesn't have to look the way the "wise people" of constitutional theory think it should.[55] Constitutional theorists are wont to imagine that the Rule of Law implies that a single universalizable, explicit norm can be derived for each issue of social policy. The role of the constitution is to formalize the norm and to specify the institution that has final authority to interpret the norm.[56] The legal pluralist, by contrast, recognizes and privileges the diverse and fluid implicit and inferential norms that guide and that are constituted by everyday interaction.[57] Even more to the point, the legal pluralist advocates

[55] It goes without saying that this is as true of constitutional theorists who hypothesize legal pluralism as it is of those who do not – with this difference. Fundamental to the pluralist hypothesis is that law is the result of a collaborative effort among citizens, and in so far as the legal order of the State is concerned, between citizens and officials. The idea of law as the collaborative articulation of shared purposes is developed at length in L. Fuller, The Morality of Law, Ch. V (2^{d}) (1969).

[56] Admittedly, some constitutional theorists accept that there are other legal orders besides that of the State, and are willing to apply the term "constitutional law" to artefacts of these legal orders as well. Nonetheless, the focus of constitutional law treatises remains exclusively the formal, textual constitution of the political State.

[57] R. A. Macdonald, *Pour la reconnaissance d'une normativité juridique implicite et 'inférentielle' [Towards the Recognition of Implicit and 'Inferential' Legal Normativity]*, 18:1 Sociologie et Sociétés 47 (1986).

an interpretive heterarchy in which multiple normative institutions each contribute to elaborating constitutional norms that privilege real choice about and mediate among multiple, fluid citizen identities.[58]

In this respect, the Report of the Bouchard-Taylor Commission is a model of a legal pluralist approach to social diversity and to legitimating religious, ethnic, and cultural heterogeneity in contemporary liberal-democratic States. Consider how its approach and recommendations exemplify the basic hypotheses of legal pluralism. Few recommendations target legislative action; indeed, the Commission pointedly declined to propose an explicit constitutional norm of "reasonable accommodation." This reluctance reflects a distancing from tenets of prescriptivism and chirographism. By contrast, many recommendations focus on local solutions, collecting, and disseminating best practices, and discouraging formal litigation of general principles in favour of empowering front-line institutions to develop and implement policies and procedures that meet the specific needs of the populations they serve. In directing attention to particular situation-specific practices the Report departs from tenets of monism and positivism. Still again, the Commission proposed that State organizations undertake an environmental scan of practices, artefacts, and protocols that carry implicit messages for members of cultural, ethnic, linguistic, and religious minorities of their inferior status. To acknowledge how the actions of the State exclude rather than include, subordinate rather than empower, and treat members of minorities as deviant rather than as integral parts of the social fabric is to reject the tenet of centralism. Finally, the Report sought to reconstruct and re-present the implicit values of Quebec society not as a cultural bulwark against the "other," but rather, in a manner that would align them as the foundation of the explicit aspirational "values of Quebec society as a pluralistic, democratic, egalitarian society."[59]

[58] R. A. Macdonald, *Les Veilles Gardes: hypothèses sur l'émergence des normes, l'internormativité et le désordre à travers une typologie des institutions normatives [The Old Guard: Hypotheses on the Emergence of Norms, Internormativity, and Disorder, Through A Typology of of Normative Institutions]*, *in* J.-G. Belley (Ed.), Le droit soluble: contributions québécoises à l'étude de l'internormativité [The Soluble Law: Quebec Contributions to the Study of Inter-Normativity] 233 (1996).

[59] The quotation is taken from sub-paragraph (d) of the mandate given to the Commission by the Quebec government. In arguing for such a reconstruction of "traditional values", the Report can be seen as a point by point refutation of the manner in which these implicit values were presented by the Code of Conduct of the Municipalité de Hérouxville. *See*, in particular, *Building the Future*, *supra* note 35, Part VII: An Evolving Quebec.

6. Conclusion

The essay has argued that the general approach of "multiculturalism" rather than "civic nationalism" is the only viable inclusive strategy for legitimating (rather than merely tolerating or accommodating) the heterogeneity of populations in contemporary liberal democracies.

Embedded in most negative reactions to ethno-cultural and religious diversity is the miscegenationist fear: acknowledging and accommodating difference is the first step towards a mongrelisation of a people. But the legal republican response to this fear – a thin conception of citizenship coupled with a strong "equal protection" constitutional norm – is inadequate. It leads directly to a conception of reasonable accommodation in which the failure of a legal rule or administrative practice to meet the needs of some particular group is restated as the willingness of the dominant culture to make an otherwise unwanted exception to its rules and practices to accommodate the specificity of immigrants, minorities and religious dissentients.

Much better is a conception of social diversity in which all citizens – including those that as members of the dominant group may not be aware that what they assume to be natural, necessary and desirable – will be required, when the need arises, to articulate and defend their cultural preferences. Much better is a conception of social diversity in which a legal rule or an administrative practice that is failing some group will be modified or adjusted so that the overall public policy objective at which it aims will be more fully realized across the country's entire population. This legal pluralist approach is, however, not without its own perils. Might it be that the mongrelisation of a people through a legitimation of ethno-cultural difference will simply produce another dominant mono-culture – an equally thick conception of ethno-cultural and religious homogeneity to which all subsequent immigrants must subscribe?

This risk is real.[60] But, for a society genuinely committed to the liberal democratic ideal, the legal republican alternative is worse. Reasonable accommodation is not what dominant groups offer to subordinated groups. Reasonable accommodation is not best conceived as an explicit constitutional norm that signals the toleration of ethnic, cultural, religious and cultural diversity.

The diversity of citizens is not an uncomfortable fact that must be accommodated. Rather the diversity of citizens and the acknowledgement of this diversity is the foundation upon which societies comprising heterogeneous

[60] That is, simply holding a legal pluralistic theory of law does not inoculate one against essentializing any of law, culture and identity. For the reasons set out in the sources cited *supra* note 23, however, we believe that explicitly recognizing the complexity of nature-nurture interplays, and attending to the impact of pluralism in our everyday lives are important prophylactics against even embarking on the quest for homogeneity.

populations are continuously being built. Explicit constitutional adjudication of diversity through claims of equality and counter-claims of reasonable accommodation denies the interactive, iterative and contingent character of all identities and all culture. For a legal pluralist, the implicit constitution is the medium is the message; its content is the audience is the subjects is the constituters is the message is the medium.

Part II

Transitional Constitutionalism

Bernd Rüthers*

The Functions of Law and Lawyers in Political and Social Transformation Processes

1. Introduction

Over the past century, Europe has experienced its fair share of political and social upheavals:

1) beginning with the Russian Revolution of October 1917;
2) continuing with the system changes brought about by WWI (in Germany, for instance, the Weimar Republic);
3) the dictatorships of Mussolini in Italy (1925) and Salazar in Portugal (1928/1933);
4) Hitler's power take-over in Germany (1933) and that of General Franco in Spain (1936);
5) the enormous system changes occurring in many if not all European countries due to World War II and its consequences; and
6) the new wave of fundamental system changes triggered by the collapse of the Soviet Union and the breakdown of the Warsaw Pact in 1989/1990 and affecting the entire "Eastern Bloc."

These political changes were often accompanied by military, economic, social, financial, and constitutional crises of almost catastrophic dimensions. I only need to hint at some of these transformations here.

* *Recht und Juristen in gesellschaftlichen und politischen Wandlungsprozessen* (translation from German by Marius Balan and Bogdan Iancu).

Bogdan Iancu (Ed.), The Law/Politics Distinction in Contemporary Public Law Adjudication, 117-132.

Nowadays, there is access to a wealth of information regarding the consequences of such changes to the law and lawyers of the respective countries. It is, therefore, all the more surprising that, for a very long time, these experiences have not been gathered, analyzed, and evaluated by legal history and doctrine. In fact, one can still notice nowadays a conspicuous reserve in grappling with these processes from a legal-theoretical perspective.

Germany has a rich experience in this sense. The German jurisprudence and legal system experienced, between 1919 and 1989, *six* different constitutions: that of the Second Empire, the Weimar Republic, the National-Socialist state, the post-war Occupation, the old Federal Republic, the German Democratic Republic (GDR), and the new Federal Republic, which in turn has been deeply transformed by the supranational legislation of the EC/EU. It is my belief that to this day, these events – in addition to the military, political, economic, and social changes accompanying them, have had profound influence on the German national and legal consciousness.

At least four of these changes – those of 1919, 1933, 1945/1949, and 1989/1990 – have affected the core values of the preexisting state forms and valid legal orders. Constitutional transformations of this magnitude do not only constitute *crises of the law,* they also affect *lawyers*, both individually and as a distinct professional class. A system change modifies previously uncontested juridical professions of faith and legal orthodoxies. Should lawyers wish to retain their public positions after a change of regime, they are expected to declare a new faith and show a minimal degree of loyalty to the new regime. Thus, they are frequently asked to pledge allegiance to new fundamental values – no wonder that the autobiography of a German jurist is titled: "Lawyer under Four Regimes."[1]

Reflecting on such periods demands from those involved in or affected by them considerable efforts, since he who wants to remember must swim upstream in two ways: against forgetfulness and against denial.

The past does not simply go away. It can be accepted or rejected but not "come to terms with" (*bewältigt*), as the rather unfortunate term "coming to terms with the past" (*Vergangenheitsbewältigung*)[2] would suggest. One is more likely to "confront" the past of *others*, very often self-righteously, from the Pharisaic vantage point of obstinately proclaiming the singular judiciousness of one's own position.

In what follows, I will open to critical scrutiny twelve hypotheses:

[1] F. Hartung, Jurist unter vier Reichen [A Jurist under Four Empires] (1971).

[2] One of the most commonly used terms in the German press and in political debates, it signifies a (self-)critical inquiry into the past and its overcoming (Translators' note).

First Hypothesis

Fundamental constitutional and political system changes produce legal effects reaching well beyond the surface level.

This means, among others:

1) a change in state ideology and in fundamental constitutional values, i.e. a complete overhaul of the entire legal order;
2) a change in or at least a revision of state and social leadership-the most radical examples in this respect are the "Law for the Reestablishment of the Civil Service" of April 1933 and the almost complete purge of lawyers holding office prior to 1945 in the Soviet Occupation Zone and the GDR;
3) change in the historical imaginary extending from national heroes to representations and categories of victims and all the way down to street name changes and new monuments commemorating prior "Resistance"; and
4) last, system changes produce law and lawyers crises, i.e., crises of trust in the legal system, and crises of identity in court leadership, administration, and academia still associated with the old regime.[3]

2. The Denied Interconnection Between Law and *Weltanschauung*

The analysis of legal transformations in totalitarian systems is particularly revealing. The perversion of the entire legal order under the National-Socialist and Socialist state in East Germany[4] has not yet been acknowledged and analyzed in its entirety, either as a matter of popular consciousness or as an object of academic study. Law school lectures deal with such matters predominantly as unfortunate professional mishaps or even brush over them in silence. In so doing, they face the risk of disregarding certain aspects of crucial importance:

[3] B. Rüthers, Ideologie und Recht im Systemwechsel. Ein Beitrag zur Ideologieanfälligkeit geistiger Berufe [Ideology and Law in System Change. A Contribution to the Study of the Ideological Susceptibility of the Intellectual Professions] (1992).

[4] The Socialist Unity Party of Germany (*Sozialistische Einheitspartei Deutschlands*), was formed in 1946 in the Soviet Occupation Zone through the forced merger of the Social Democrats and the Communists under the absolute control of the latter. The Communist Party was to retain this name in the GDR up until 1990 (Translators' note).

1) Once instituted, ideological systems produce effects that outlast the political systems to which they "belong." Depending on the system's duration and on the intensity with which those ideologies seize their contemporaries' minds and hearts, their repercussions are perpetuated even over generations; and
2) In the exceptional situation of legal renewal, be it *völkish*, socialist, or – closer to us – *European*, extremely important functional connections between law and its methods of reevaluation are more clearly revealed than in a normal situation. Such reevaluations take place in periods of normalcy as well but they remain often unnoticed. This holds true, for instance, with respect to the intense bond between the law and extra-juridical variables, such as axiological representations, dogmas, and articles of faith.

It is precisely in this "age of ideologies" (thus Karl Dietrich Bracher) that one often encounters the equally inciting and often suppressed problematic areas, as inciting and tense as it is occulting, of the interconnection between *law and metaphysics* or even between *law and ideology*. By the "metaphysical" foundation of the law I understand the inevitable subordination of the law to certain pre-established extra-juridical articles of faith.

Second Hypothesis

The politically established ideology/philosophy of a system determines the core contents of that particular legal order. It defines the "normative idea" which is typical to that system in a normal situation and the model of "justice" realized by the institutions of the State and, more specifically, by the judicature.

The ideal of justice realized in practice by the judicial organs is therefore not *a-temporal* and *abstract* but rather fitted to and oriented through the system's given ideology. The State does not carry into effect *the* one and only, timeless, "eternal justice" – does such justice exist? – but rather that of *its own system* (*Systemgerechtigkeit*) grounded in *its own metaphysics*.

Thus far I have touched upon legal sciences' vulnerability to ideology – a peculiar feature of the academic legal profession – as well as the special role played by lawyers in the systems of lawlessness (*Unrechtssysteme*) previously presented.

3. The Role of Lawyers during System Changes

The phrase "abominable lawyers" (*furchtbare Juristen*) appeared in German public discourse in 1978.[5] Since 1987, when it was incorporated into a book

[5] R. Hochhuth, *Schwierigkeiten, die wahre Geschichte zu erzählen [Difficulties in Telling the Truth]*, Die Zeit, 17 February 1978, at 41.

title,[6] the belief in the *particular* responsibility of the legal profession has been grounded in the public consciousness. Later on, when the judicial and prosecutorial practices of the GDR were brought to light fragmentarily, it seemed appropriate once again to condemn indiscriminately an entire professional body.

Due to the high number of colleagues in law schools, judges, prosecutors, civil servants, and members of the bar still active after 1945, the age of denial and silence regarding NS-lawlessness in the Federal Republic of Germany was almost "programmed." It lasted until the mid-1960s and till then the topic "law under National-Socialism" was an almost absolute taboo at many West German law schools such as Cologne, Bonn, Göttingen, Heidelberg, Munich. At best, optional lectures, which refrained from naming any colleagues with a previous National Socialist engagement, provided a popular alibi. Contrariwise, starting with the 1970s, the topic became ubiquitous and rose to the apex of academic attention, producing an overwhelming body of literature. If until 1970 touching on these matters had been *an evident career risk,* after 1970 it became quite obviously an *opportunity* for academic self-promotion and career-launching. Scholarly literature follows the laws of the academic market, pursuing opportunities and catering to personal vanities.

Lawyers also played an essential role in organizing and legitimating state lawlessness when the German Democratic Republic was established. They retained this stabilizing function, across the entire state apparatus, until the very end of the GDR.[7]

Attempts to compare systems which have programmatically adopted state lawlessness (*Unrecht*) and trampled on human rights in order to perpetuate their political domination are harshly criticized in Germany. This is why I must stress that my current reference to the analogous roles played by legal doctrine and the justice system in the political practices of both the National-Socialist State and the GDR does not rest on the assumption that these two systems were identical in their unjust domination. This thesis is false, be it only for the reason that the totalitarian ideologies underlying these two regimes were fundamentally different. Despite all its fundamental errors, Marxism-Leninism – regarded as a transcendental philosophy of history – cannot squarely be equated with the primitive racial biologism of the

[6] I. Müller, *Furchtbare Juristen. Die unbewältigte Vergangenheit unserer Justiz* [literally: *Abominable Lawyers. The Unconfronted Past of Our Justice System*; translated into English under the title *Hitler's Lawyers: The Courts of The Third Reich*, D. Lucas Schneider (Trans.) (1991)] (1987).

[7] Two very instructive studies afford insight into the infra-systemic conflicts between lawyers in the GDR: M. Hove, *Karl Polak – Parteijurist unter Ulbricht [Karl Polak-Party – lawyer under Ulbricht]*, Ius Commune / Sonderhefte – Studien zur Rechtsgeschichte 1949 (2002), and U.-J. Heuer, Im Streit – Ein Jurist in zwei deutschen Staaten (2002). For reviews of these works, *see, generally,* B. Rüthers, *Juristen unter wechselnden Verfassungen [Jurists under Changing Constitutions]*, 58 Juristenzeitung 82 (2003).

National-Socialist *Weltanschauung*. Nonetheless, in spite of these ideological differences, the ruling practices of totalitarian systems display surprisingly similar features.

Given the normative practices of the two dictatorships Germany has known in the 20th century, one must ask: Are lawyers more vulnerable to ideologies than other professionals? Are they professionally situated in a closer proximity to ideologies, so that they contamination is more readily possible? My answer must be a qualified and cautious "Yes."

4. Law as Normatively Solidified ("Coagulated") Politics

The essential mission of all legal professions consists of the *making* (Norm*setzung*) and the *application* (Rechts*anwendung*) of the law. The latter function is aimed at *transposing legal dispositions* (*Rechtsvorschrift*) into political and social reality. Any – I emphasize: any! – legal norm is geared by the adopting authority towards a certain political purpose (*politischer Gestaltungsziel*). The law is always (also) a means of configurating and directing various social and political domains in view of pre-existent, ideologically grounded beliefs (*Vorverständnisse*). From the standpoint of the norm-adopting authorities the essential function of the law is in fact the configurative one.

Third Hypothesis

All (!) legal norms are always a figment of the Lawgivers' *Weltanschauung* and legal policy in a normatively solidified form. The law constitutes, thus, a category characterized by profound political and ideological features. No legal norm is independent of *Weltanschauung* (or "axiologically free"). A "value-free" law would be essentially value-less.

5. On the Relation of the Legal Professions with Ideology-Proximity to Power

In applying legal norms, lawyers are bound by "law and justice" (*Gesetz und Recht*). This observation holds generally true for all legal orders. The German Basic Law makes specific provision in this sense with respect to the judiciary (Arts. 20(3) and 97(1)).[8] According to the GDR Constitution of 1968/1974,

[8] Art. 20 (3) reads: "The Legislature shall be bound by the constitutional order, the executive and the judiciary by law and justice (*Gesetz und Recht*)." Art. 97 (1): "Judges shall be independent and subject only to the law."

"socialist legality" represented – at least at the declaratory level – one of the fundamental principles of the socialist state (Arts. 19, 87, 90(1) and 97).[9]

Due to this constitutionally ordained law-bindingness, lawyers in public offices are "servants" to the normatively coagulated political instructions of the Lawgivers (*Normsetzer*). This is equally true in a state governed by the rule of law and in an unjust legal order. On closer and realistic examination, practical jurisprudence turns out to have an *affirmative function, conservative of the system* in *all* state-forms. Through its law-applying activity, practical jurisprudence transposes into reality the long-term, legally formulated, politics of the Lawgivers.

Whenever a system change occurs, the newly instituted political regime verifies whether the jurists inherited from the old regime are adequate for and capable of efficiently achieving the objectives pertaining to its desired "fundamental renewal of the law."

German lawyers are accustomed to such selection processes, having experienced them:

- after 1933, during the National-Socialist state;
- after 1945, during the very "flexible" "Denazification" processes in the various Allied Occupation Zones; and
- after 1990, during the reevaluation of judges and prosecutors from the former GDR.

Fourth Hypothesis

Lawyers live dangerously, due to the fact that, by virtue of their profession, they always exercise their functions in the proximity – even under the "spell" – of the existing momentary ruling ideology and power holders.

They are officers of the system and serve the dominating order of the moment, however defined, whether that order is "just" or "unjust," a Rule of Law state (*Rechtstaat*) or a state of lawlessness (*Unrechtsstaat*). This brings into prominence both the vulnerability to ideology characteristic of this profession and academic discipline and the special status enjoyed by lawyers under an unjust system.

Fifth Hypothesis

Fundamental changes to socio-political and constitutional systems bring about a peculiar literary genre in many disciplines. I would call it "transition literature."

---

9 The same wording can be found in the USSR Constitution, Art. 112.

Content-wise, this literature examines critically the demised legal order, with a view to emphasizing its weaknesses or abuses, while laying the foundation and legitimizing the new, purportedly "better" system. Transition literatures regularly display a pronounced autobiographical character. They appear at times of collective and subjective crises. Foundational legal values and professions of faith are then being redefined. Since, most commonly, the Lawgiver does not regulate in this respect immediately or – at best – does it generally and summarily, the old "inherited" laws must be reinterpreted, even misinterpreted. Guidelines and "assistance" to the courts, the administration, and the legal academia, are in this respect necessary. A slogan of timeless validity for such situations reads: "We rethink juridical concepts .... We are on the side of things to come."[10] Carl Schmitt, the "Crown Jurist" of the Third Reich, coined the catchphrase during the regime's initial, power-consolidation phase.[11]

Sixth Hypothesis

Primary agents in the process of rethinking entire legal orders under transition consist of:

- the writers of specialized doctrine by means of the dominant publica-tions and by virtue of their numerous contributions, produced with promptness and zeal, and profoundly regimented into the ranks of ideology and legal policy, and
- the leading decisions of all the courts but most particularly of the courts of last resort, which aim to amend the existing law.

Both professional categories often cooperate in a state of anticipatory obsequiousness towards the administrative or academic leadership. The line between the *seductive attraction* of the new system, on the one hand, and the *pressure* to conform exercised by it, on the other hand, is often hard to draw. The two are inextricably interlinked.

It is surprising that authors of the literary legitimization and glorification of the new state, its concept of law, its legal sources and normative concepts, are commonly well-known individuals of established professional reputation, often enough at the apex of their discipline. We are not dealing with mediocrity or with a negative selection of values but rather preponderantly with *professionally brilliant authors*. Matters evolved similarly in the two German states after 1945 and 1949 and in the GDR after 1989.

In 1967, in my first analysis of the (re)interpretation of the civil law under National-Socialism, I considered this "boundless interpretation" (*unbegrenzte*

[10] C. Schmitt, *Nationalsozialistisches Rechtsdenken*, 4 Deutsches Recht 225, at 229 (1934).
[11] B. Rüthers, Carl Schmitt im Dritten Reich [Carl Schmitt in the Third Reich] (1990).

Auslegung) a historically unique phenomenon: a small number of authors, usually renowned and influential, had "twisted" after 1933 the entire German legal order to turn it towards the National-Socialist program. On closer examination, nonetheless, I noticed that the selfsame process occurred after 1945. Anecdotally, we can also observe that, often enough, it is exactly the same *authors* who served the old regime that, after its demise, assumed the roles of harbingers and teachers of the new fundamental values of the diametrically opposed system. This is not uncommon even nowadays.

6. Interpretation or Mystification?[12] – Methodological Considerations as Constitutional Considerations

In the exceptional state of a system change, certain fundamental elements and functions of the law, legal science, and judicial practice become clearly visible. Such elements and functions are also present and active under a normal situation, but through the routine of daily recurrences they remain unnoticed and legal and political actors perform or observe them unconsciously.

Legal rules are precepts (*imperatives*) issued by the Lawgiver to law-applying organs (*Rechtsanwender*) in order to regulate given factual situations according to the former's conception. Especially in a democracy, these are the instruments of political realization and social configuration. Their normative content must not be influenced by the "tastes" and aspirations of those applying the law to substitute normative purposes with personal perceptions and representations of justice. This is the reason why the judiciary and the executive are bound by law. Those applying the law are its servants, not its masters. They are under duty of "thoughtful and rational obedience"[13] to the law. Legal interpretation is an *aliud*, if compared to literary, philosophical, or historical hermeneutics.

[12] Untranslatable word-play between *Auslegung* = "interpretation" (literally and etimologically *aus+legung,* to put out, in the sense of taking out the meaning of a text) and *Einlegung* = "mystification" (literally *ein+legung*, to put something in; the word means to insert but could also mean cheating, beguiling someone) (Translators' note).

[13] In original, "*dekender Gehorsam*" = "thoughtful obedience"; this phrase has been commonly used in post-war Germany in polemical contrast with the idea of discipline or unquestioning obedience to the orders of a superior characteristic of the authoritarian ethos of German political and state traditions. (Translators' note).

7. The Instruments of Extralegal Alteration of the Law

Seventh Hypothesis

The juridical linguistic and methodological instruments used to reinterpret the inherited ("old") legal order in the service of newly-instituted fundamental and objective legal policy values are:

1) the proclamation of a new "concept of law";
2) the construction of new "sources of law," in order to dislodge or alter "old" but still valid laws;
3) the reinterpretation of indeterminate legal concepts and of the so-called "general clauses" (terms and concepts not precisely formulated, empty linguistic formulas, with variable content, such as "good faith," "contra bonos mores" or "relevant ground");
4) the reinterpretation of fundamental legal concepts (e.g., "legal capacity"; "subjective right"; "contract"; "community"; "human dignity", marriage, family, "personality rights"; "fundamental rights"); and
5) the creation of new or competing interpretive methodologies.

These interpretive instruments and practices have been exhaustively described, particularly with respect to the system change of 1933.[14] In legal history the process is by no means new. On the contrary: all so-called substantive concepts, general clauses, and arguments deriving from the alleged "nature of the thing" (*Natur der Sache*) are formulated precisely in order to link the existing legal order with an *extralegal, ideologically-charged, axiological order*. They constitute nothing other than the "plug-in" of an extralegal ideology into juridical, normative validity. False labels aside, what we are facing in such cases is not interpretation (*Auslegung*) but mystification (*Einlegung*), i.e., concealed norm-making. To wit, this aspect constitutes the formal and legal-technical efficiency of such conceptual constructs and usages, regardless of how one views their contents from a political or ideological perspective.

For a long time jurists and others believed that, upon entry into force, a written legislative text would forever guarantee a stable and authoritative content. To an extent, this view is still shared – even nowadays. Perceptive observers such as Lorenz von Stein[15] and Oskar Bülow[16] noticed as early as the

[14] B. Rüthers, Die unbegrenzte Auslegung [Unbounded Interpretation] (1998) and *Entartetes* Recht – Rechtslehren und Kronjuristen im Dritten Reich [Degenerate Law-Law Professors and 'Crown Lawyers' under the Third Reich] 183-212 (1994).

[15] L. von Stein, Gegenwart und Zukunft der Rechts- und Staatswissenschaft Deutschlands [Present and Future of the German Science of Law and State] (1876).

[16] O. Bülow, *Gesetz und Richteramt [Statutory Law and the Judicial Function]*, 39(1) The American Journal of Legal History 71 (January 1995) (1885).

mid-19th century the fallacy behind the belief in a textually-institutive legal-normative content. Thus, Lorenz von Stein suggestively cautioned that: "all positive legal concepts are formally similar but content-wise they are social-legal concepts, depending for their meaning on a particular social order; they must be understood and taught as such."[17]

Another century had to pass before the social and political 'mobility' of normative contents could be fully grasped and – with great reservations – also taught in law faculties. Today, after the experiences of the successive European systemic transformations, the fact that legislative texts can never durably secure, upon the will of the historic law-maker, certain precisely determined contents and objectives has become a mater of common legal-theoretical knowledge. The characteristically hermeneutical thesis according to which a text is like music notes applies equally to legal texts: they rely and depend on the "musician's interpretation" in terms of his (pre)conceptions and temporal horizon. The reception theory, influential in literary studies, applies also to the law-applicant: the act of reading, i.e. interpreting the law, is not purely reproductive but to a considerable degree also productive, a creative act which confers meaning to a text (*Akt der Sinngebung*).[18]

This is a contemporary concern of the utmost relevance. Recent controversies surrounding the apposite meaning of fundamental legal notions such as: *human dignity*, *the protection of personality*, *family*, *marriage*, *private autonomy*, *discrimination*, etc., bear witness to the ever-present appositeness of the theme, even *outside* the realm of exceptional constitutional situations.

The considerable hesitations of the judicial practice, not only during different times and systems but, occasionally, in perfectly "normal" constitutional situations testify to this with spectacular and convincing forcefulness.

A look at the repeated phases of impetuous start, enthusiasm, and reverie, as depicted by the "transition literature" after 1933 and again after 1945 and 1949 in the Federal Republic and the GDR, respectively, compels us to delve into the more profound underlying causes of these phenomena. Reorientation-experts (*Wende-Experten*) active in all disciplines belong to the same people. Within each system – equally in rule of law and lawlessness states – one can find enthusiastic approval for the new order of powers and values, particularly in the system's initial phase. Could it be coincidental that two consecutive generations of exceptionally intellectually gifted criminal accomplices, belonging to the same people, dutifully served two totalitarian dictatorships? Were the individuals planning, organizing, and legitimatizing everything

---

[17] Stein, *supra* note 15, at 135.

[18] Partly for euphonic reasons (avoiding repetition) and largely in order to convey the accurate meaning of the original German text, the phrase "Akt der Sinngebung" was etymologically translated: "Sinngebung" means "interpretation" but also – if translated *ad literam* – "to give/confer meaning." (Translators note).

from total repression to mass-murder *inborn criminals* or hapless victims of ideological seduction? For now, this question will not be addressed.

Eighth Hypothesis

Questions of juridical methodology are simultaneously constitutional questions. The choice of an interpretive method determines the interpretive results, settling and dislodging the boundary between law-making and adjudication. Therefore, what is at stake is the separation of powers as instituted by the fundamental law.

Neither a solid reflection upon nor a critical evaluation of the methodological processes through which the law was perverted during the two German dictatorships has been undertaken so far. Both legal education and judicial practice – supreme courts included – display a rather surprising ignorance in this respect.

It is instructive to remember the political, economic, and social factors which played an active role in shaping the generations of lawyers at work around 1933 and 1945/1949 and later in the GDR (I will skip specific details here).

If my interpretation of problematic evolutions is accurate, system changes produce, especially among the young, a strong "inspiring effect" regimenting them into *changing the status quo ante* and building a *newer, "better" order*.

Phenomena such as the 1934 "Kiel-Kitzeberg Camp" of young National-Socialist academics or the meetings of ambitious young Marxists in 1951, during their internship at the Forst Zinna Administration Academy under the leadership of Karl Polak, as well as during the Babelsberg Conference in 1958, are eloquent examples of the strength and formative efficacy of this effect. Records in this sense by such participants as Franz Wieacker[19] (Kiel-Kitzeberg) and Bernhard Graefrath[20] (Forst Zinna) serve as evidence of enthusiasm. They testify to what degree the regimes' propagandas were capable of eliciting from an advancement-driven youth a sincere and zealous obedience to the system by promise of a brilliant career. Where this "inspiring effect" was insufficient to bring out the required ideological enthusiasm, both systems mobilized considerable resources to force compliance by nonconforming individuals in more or less subtle ways: exclusion, limitations of access to education, transfers to probationary positions, etc., so as to nudge back unto the right path the wavering and the deviationist. There are also sufficient accounts in this respect.

What is important for our topic is the comparative analysis of transition literatures (*Wendeliteraturen*) and of the "socialization cohorts"

[19] In 1 Deutsche Rechtswissenschaft 76 (1936).
[20] In 5 Neue Justiz 550 (1951).

(*Sozialisationskohorten*) which give rise to them. Closer examination reveals that transition literatures are produced not by isolated scholars but rather by groups of authors intensely related to one another. "Fortuitous" socialization cohorts, arising spontaneously at the beginnings of a new order, become communities of belief and action pursuing very concrete common historiographic and legal policy objectives. They aim at directing, even at obstructing, the collective memory, at the remembrance and forgetting of questionable aspects of the past. Socialization cohorts can thus become exclusivist and cohesive societies intent on "cosmeticizing" history and biographies.

An old Westphalian proverb says: "One never lies as much as before the wedding, during the funeral, and after a hunting trip." *Mutatis mutandis*, one can notice that one rarely encounters distortions and misinterpretations of history as brazen as those concocted by socialization cohorts in their post-transition literatures. Numerous examples of autobiographies, festschrifts, inaugural lectures, and obituaries validate this thesis empirically.

Ninth Hypothesis

The existence in the field of transition literatures of groups of authors sharing the same ideological bent is widely attested. Communities of common belief and pressure groups arise out of "socialization cohorts," whose membership appears at first to be random. It must be noted that usually such groups have very concrete aims with respect to history and legal policy. They aim to successfully direct – and more often than not to falsify – the collective memory.

The various motivations animating the authors of transition literature cover a very wide scope. Profound convictions, cold calculations of career opportunities, as well as atonement for past ideological deviations can equally stimulate enthusiastic acceptance of and justification for a newly-constituted state order. Bombastic stylistic exaggerations and ideological overzealousness appear whenever authors seek to dissimulate the previous stands into the joy of a new profession of faith and to demonstrate their credibility and their ideological loyalty to the new regime. These factors, together with the combined effects of incentives and pressures, influence group members in terms of perception, decision, and leeway for action. Membership in such a cohort and acceptance of its code of conduct trigger among the young a strong "absorption effect" providing individuals with a feeling of social acceptance and security, especially when the group can readily reap the favors of the potentates.

Contrariwise, exclusion from such a cohort signifies isolation, loss of solidarity, and danger of sanctions. The so-called "silence spiral" (*Schweigespirale*), a term put forth by communication sciences, reverts – in this case- into a “writing spiral” (*Schreibespirale*). Under dictatorships, those who start howling with the wolves of the new age will find it quite difficult to leave the pack.

8. On the Question of Guilt and Juridical Professional Morality – Individual Responsibility under the Seductive Attraction and Pressure of the Spirit of the Times and of Socialization Cohorts

Tenth Hypothesis

It is extremely difficult to pass judgment on the individual morality or the guilty involvement of various members of the “public” intellectual professions or even on the actions of entire professional categories in times of state lawlessness. Wholesale characterizations of entire professional groups as “abominable lawyers” or – respectively – “law-abiding jurists” ignore the backgrounds of complex constraints and circumstances, especially in the case of totalitarian systems.

It is safe to assume that the generations of lawyers of 1910, 1930, 1950, and 1970, i.e., Weimar Republic, Third Reich, Federal Republic, and the GDR, which exerted on the young professionals a strong “absorption effect,” consisted on the average of morally comparable human types. Nonetheless, their destinies and the conditions under which they practiced their profession could not have been more different.

It follows that system changes are extremely favorable to bending and disappointing justice-related hopes and expectations. This applies equally to both the victims and the perpetrators of a regime.

Experience shows that criminal law is a tool of limited applicability and efficiency in the struggle with the heritage of past states of lawlessness (*Unrechtstaaten*). By the same token, one cannot simply give it up completely. Questions of personal involvement, guilt, and individual criminal liability cover only a portion of the large problem area that needs charting after the collapse of a totalitarian regime. Faced with the question of integrating into such a system or not, the individual does not commonly have free choice, either judging from an external standpoint or regarding his liberty *in foro interno*. Due to his social milieu, professional education, family status, and social and economic circumstances, one’s decisional leeway is restricted in many respects. Bertold Brecht’s warning to those born after World War II (*Nachgeborenen*) should also be heeded in this context, as in all human societies – and our own is most likely no exception – the martyr quotient is still well under 1‰. This is no generalized excuse or justification for all those who allowed themselves to be accessories to public villainy, especially if their criminal character emerged in the form of public acts. However, one must take into account that belonging to a certain generation, i.e., membership in a "socialization cohort," which shares common political, social, and economic experiences, can exercise considerable pressure on the individual.

In toto, one should remark:

Eleventh Hypothesis

Lawyers affect the configuration and application of an existing political system decisively. Consequently, an exceptional responsibility devolves upon them, individually and as a professional group. They cannot avoid confronting this fact by invoking the vulnerability to ideology of other public professions.

In general, lawyers are neither more vulnerable nor more "abominable" than the representatives of other intellectual professions. However, in the case of a system change they face considerable, special 1 risks, due to their professional proximity to the power apparatus.

References to the "seductive attraction" and pressure exercised by socialization cohorts are not meant to obfuscate individual responsibility for one's teachings, writings or deeds. The responsibility for co-authorship (*Mittun*) in severe lawlessness is incumbent upon the individual.

Consequently, what conclusions can be drawn for the future from this retrospective analysis?

Twelfth (and Last) Hypothesis

There is much that lawyers can learn from history and most particularly from the history of system changes. As Cicero famously phrased it: "*Historia magistra vitae est.*"[21]

I am aware that my position cannot easily be squared with today's theory of history and yet I ask my reader to take into consideration that I do *not* claim that just anyone *could* or *would* (want to) learn from history. Such a possibility would require capacity and willingness to accept history as an experience. I believe however that nowadays' quite fashionable thesis that history cannot teach us anything is theoretical aberration.[22] Even a child

[21] "History is the teacher of life." And so also, in Deuteronomy (The Bible, Old Testament, King James Version): 32:7: "Remember the days of old, consider the years of many generations: ask thy father, and he will shew thee; thy elders, and they will tell thee."

[22] *See*, thus, for numerous references in this respect, A. Lübbe, *Aus der Geschichte lernen? [Can We Learn from History?]*, 7 Rechtshistorisches Journal 417 (1988). *Also see*, B. Rüthers, *Aus der Geschichte lernen? – eine Erwiderung [Can We Learn from History? – A Response]*, 8 Rechtshistorisches Journal 381 (1989) and H.-U. Wehler, Aus der Geschichte lernen? (1988).

who burns himself accidentally on a hot stove knows better than to make such preposterous claims. Of course, history does not teach us what to do in a concrete situation. It does, however, indicate what *should better not be done.*

The topic of my chapter was "Law and lawyers under the seductions and pressures of changing political systems." I tried to show that a comparative analysis of the structures called forth by system changes can both broaden our cognitive horizon and deepen our understanding of the dramatic processes involving jurists at times of political changes. This methodology has proven its usefulness in the field of comparative law. Comparisons lie at the source of any scientific endeavor. *A prohibition on making comparisons is a concealed ban on thinking.*

Lawyers could also learn from the history of their discipline a measure of modesty and skepticism towards pretenses of objectivity and absolute "justice" (*Gerechtigkeit*), both as a yardstick of their own decisions and for judging bygone times.

The moral arrogance of those born after the fact or those blessed with the "right" place of birth is equally improper, as it testifies to either self-delusion or hypocrisy. Above all, we should strive to create the general conditions that do not allow for such disasters to reoccur. In this sense Odo Marquard admonition that: "He who avoids exceptional situations proves wisdom" is relevant, since even the (very experienced in terms of re-orientations) poet Bertold Brecht knew that happy is the land that has no need for heroes.

ANDRÁS SAJÓ

Socialist Law Unaccounted

The functions of law and lawyers in political and social transformation processes are bounded historically and contextually. Bernd Rüthers considers three German socio-legal transformations and claims that there is a unifying theme originating in structural features of German society and politics. He does not claim that the model is applicable outside Germany. Here I would like to test his hypothesis in the post-communist context, especially with reference to Hungary.

Let us rely on Professor Rüthers' fundamental thesis: "A system change disrupts the preexisting juridical professions of faith and the legal orthodoxies deemed valid and followed by lawyers up to that moment." In other words, the system change affects lawyers as a professional order not only in their existence, but also in their professional reasoning and political-ideological loyalties. According Professor Bernd Rüthers' reconstruction, reflections on the past play a crucial role in this process. "Confrontation with the past" (*Vergangenheitsbewältigung*) is one of the specific forms of handling the past. It is not very common: in Germany, a long period of denial and silence followed the collapse of Nazi Germany and that of the GDR, and the discussion of professional responsibility was a taboo for very long periods of time. A partial denial continues even today in Central Europe and in former Soviet states.

Professor Rüthers emphasizes that lawyers played indeed a prominent role in operating and legitimating systems of injustice. Contrary to Germany, in some communist satellite states, especially in Hungary, and even in Poland, notwithstanding the "role [of law and lawyers] in establishing, organizing, and legitimating state lawlessness," such lawlessness was a limited one, at least in the last decades. The legal profession cannot be held more responsible for it than other participants in the exercise of power. True, at the time of taking over state power and/or consolidating it after violent popular resistance, law and lawyers were instrumental in mass injustice. But in more consolidated periods the injustice was primarily structural and certain concessions were

BOGDAN IANCU (ED.), The Law/Politics Distinction in Contemporary Public Law Adjudication, 133-136.

granted to the public, at least in Hungary. For example, the private exercise of religion was not persecuted or informally sanctioned, partly, of course, because the churches were sufficiently controlled by the secret service. Lawyers were not excessively involved in Hungary in the organization and maintenance of the repressive political system, primarily because the importance of law was reduced and other forms of social control prevailed. In late socialism, in some countries there was simply no need for mass violation of human rights. Extra-legal control and supervision, and the network of personal dependencies were sufficient for the social control serving communist party domination.

As to the ideological, system-legitimating role of communist law and its preachers, it is true that the legal ideology was part of the Marxist-Leninist propaganda. However, it did not play a central role, exactly because of the remnants of legal nihilism in Marxism and the strongly instrumentalist socialist concept of law. The specific legal 'contribution' of the communist legal ideology was expressed in the concept of "socialist legality," which served the primitive bureaucratic coordination needs of the socialist state organization. It reflected the fear of the communist leadership that one day excessive, unchecked brutality may turn against them. Of course, such legality did not provide protection against the powers of the secret police and forces of oppression, although in principle the higher one stood in power, the more protected the person was in matters of surveillance. The *nomenklatura* system meant that the privileges of the elite were protected. Such protection did not originate in the observance of the law, but quite often in the violation of it: secret police action depended on authorization, though not that of an independent judge but of higher party organs. This was the situation that had to be faced after the collapse of communism.

"Whenever a system-change occurs, the newly-instituted political regime verifies, on its own initiative, whether the jurists inherited from the old regime are adequate for and disposed towards the efficient achievement of objectives pertaining to the desired fundamental renewal of the law," writes Rüthers. The former socialist countries followed different ideological patterns and formally abjured all the injustice and illegality of the past. Yet, in reality, path dependence and contingencies of the emerging legal market prevailed.

The ideological difference is generally demonstrated by reference to the opposite positions of the Czech and Hungarian Constitutional Courts. The Czech Court insisted on the needs of justice in the handling of those responsible for the crimes of the past and allowed for lustration, while the Hungarian Court insisted that the transition should be a rule of law governed process.

Irrespective of ideology, when it came to the judiciary and lawyers in general, the exigencies of the day prevailed. In the early days of the transition, depending on the nature of the transition – which was, e.g., politically more radical in Czechoslovakia, and much less so in Romania –, political pressure resulted in some resignations. Nevertheless, most of the mobility within the profession was market-driven: many former prosecutors, judges, and policemen with a legal degree opted for the more lucrative private sector. If there was any need for self-justification this was indeed in line with Rüthers' thesis: the profession referred to "thoughtful and rational obedience" and blamed the law which they had to serve.

The legal elites continued to function and the demand for change ended up in a limited generational change. The institutional structures survived and quickly started to shape the administration of justice according to their organizational interests, relying on rule of law ideologies, e.g., independence of the judiciary. In a few cases, for instance in Bulgaria and Georgia, this attitude created tensions. In these countries internal and international forces insisted on more radical changes many years after the transition and the inherited judiciary rejected these attempts in the name of judicial independence.

The fundamental difference between the GDR and the other countries in the East was that outside Germany there was no one to replace the legal establishment and, by the time a new generation of lawyers was available, the old guard had fully consolidated itself. Of course, this precluded soul-searching and enabled the survival of old instrumentalism. The attempts to face the past were increasingly party-politics-motivated. In Hungary, the limited vetting affected a few judges only, partly because the lawyers collaborating with the communist regime did it in an informal way or the control was simply the control of the communist party. Further, in Hungary personality rights concerns were an important obstacle to more serious public accountability. In some countries there was no serious attempt to face the problems of the past for more than a decade, while secret police file leaks in the press continued to undermine the credibility of the whole issue of accountability for the past. Apparently, in most countries the communist secret services succeeded to survive, even if under democratic-parliamentary control. In some instances their influence on the government is visible – to the detriment of the rule of law.

Ironically, at least in Hungary, the area where there was a systematic attempt to undo the legal injustice of the past concerned people sentenced for war crimes after World War II. Following a decision of the Constitutional Court, ordinary courts accepted requests for retrial on grounds that the convictions of Hungarian officers were in violation of standards of the rule of law. These considerations applied to generals loyal to the Hungarian Nazi government, who had run away with the German Army and were in hiding after the war, and who had been convicted *in contumaciam* during communist times. In this regard, there seem to be important and understudied parallels with the Federal Republic (see, e.g., the cases against the lawyers who participated in the sentencing of von Dohnanyi and others).[1]

[1] Hans von Dohnanyi (1902-1945) was a lawyer, member of the German underground

resistance. Accused of participation in the July 20 plot to assassinate Hitler, he was interned in the Sachsenhausen concentration camp in 1944 and, subsequent to a summary trial by a drumhead SS court-martial, sentenced to death and executed in the last days of the war (on the 8th or the 9th of April 1945). The presidents of the SS kangaroo court would later be tried in the Federal Republic for aiding and abetting murder and, after various judicial tribulations, finally acquitted by the Supreme Court in 1956, on the grounds that the SS court had been constituted and functioned in accordance with the law then in force and so the accused had not "perverted the course of justice." The Federal Supreme Court distanced itself from the "Dohnanyi Decision" in 1995 (on the occasion of the former GDR-related perversion of justice trials). In 2002, on the 100 year anniversary of Dohnanyi's birth, the incumbent president of the Court officially expressed regret over the 1956 decision. (Editor's Note).

ALEXANDER SOMEK*

Idealization, De-Politicization and Economic Due Process: System Transition in the European Union

1. The New Boat

One of the topics of this volume is the role of law in periods of system transition. In a sense, it evokes the pedagogical setup of the immediate post-Reagan era. Countries where authoritarian or totalitarian regimes have recently been overthrown are seen as engaged in a dialogue with countries that had made a transition to democracy earlier. In this process, the former countries find themselves confronted with the expectation of having to catch up with a set of normative standards that have never been defined by them. In fact, the standards are believed to be characteristic of civilized nations. It is understood that for the purpose of transition a break needs to be made from a regime where the law used to serve as a mere façade and where major decisions were arrived at by the party nomenclature. The law was considered to be an expedient tool for the attainment of political goals. Human rights existed only on paper. There was no protection from illegal detainment or no judicial safeguard against inhumane or degrading treatment. The transition is supposed to re-establish politics within legal constraints. An independent

* The paper was first presented at a workshop on the role of law in periods of system transition, which was held at the New College Europe in Bucharest. I would like to thank Bogdan Iancu for putting together a truly exciting event. The paper was written while I was a fellow in the Institute for Advanced Study in Berlin. During my stay, I benefited greatly from discussions with Petra Dobner, Dieter Grimm, Bogdan Iancu, Martin Loughlin, Fritz W. Scharpf, Gunther Teubner and Rainer Wahl. As always, Mattias Kumm was my most serious critic. I would like to thank the University of Iowa College of Law for generously supporting of this project.

BOGDAN IANCU (ED.), The Law/Politics Distinction in Contemporary Public Law Adjudication, 137-167.

judiciary is to watch over their observance. No longer is the law to serve as a mere instrument for the attainment of political objectives, but to be respected as an end in itself.

Over the last few years, the situation of the dialogue has changed, at any rate, in certain respects. Not only is the formerly leading pedagogical nation no longer in the position to educate others credibly about the protection of human rights[1] and the rule of law,[2] the meeting ground has altered, too. The formerly existing geopolitical line dividing burdened and assisting countries has more or less disappeared or, under an alternative description, shifted farther towards the East. In many instances, both types of countries now belong to a larger unit that is widely assumed to be more than an international organization and less than a state.

Membership of the European Union changes everything. Intriguingly, in this new situation – which one might have expected to amount to the triumph of constitutional democracy, the rule of law, and human rights – it begins to dawn slowly upon the countries concerned that they may now jointly be standing at the threshold of yet another transition. For the new Member States, this may come as no small surprise. Nevertheless, if my observations below are correct, it may well turn out that, even from their perspective, with the accession to the European Union the original transition may eventually be superseded by another.

More precisely, I would like to point out, in what follows, that the European Union does not leave unaffected the ideals that it purports to serve. Through its operation these ideas are remarkably articulated. In an important respect, the law – constitutional law – is involved in this transformation. Three processes, in particular, merit consideration.

To begin with, constitutional language has become increasingly used not to constitute legal processes, but rather for the purpose of refurbishing existing arrangements. I shall refer to this transformation as *idealization*. It changes the nature of a constitution from establishing and limiting powers of collective agency[3] to putting the best possible face on what already exists. The phenomenon is not unprecedented in European constitutional history. Bonaparte used constitutional form in order to gloss over a break with the

[1] *See* Physicians for Human Rights, *Broken Laws, Broken Lives*, on people who endured torture at the hands of US personnel in Iraq, Afghanistan, and Guantánamo Bay (http://brokenlives.info).

[2] *See*, regarding an International Court of Justice finding of a violation of the Consular Convention by the United States and the United States' subsequent withdrawal from Convention's Optional Protocol Concerning the Compulsory Settlement of Disputes, F. L. Kirgis, *President Bush's Determination Regarding Mexican Nationals and Consular Convention Rights*, http://www.asil.org/insights061208.cfm.

[3] For a historically apt reconstruction of the concept of the constitution, *see* D. Grimm, *The Constitution in the Process of Denationalization*, 12 Constellations 447, at 452-453 (2005).

substance of constitutionalism.[4] Not that the Union is guilty of the latter, but the point of constitutionalization appears to be changing in its case as well.

This strategy is related to a second phenomenon that can be described as a process of creeping *de-politicization*. This affects the core of the European polity, namely, its position vis-à-vis democracy. Of the three phenomena sketched here, it is the one which has been concomitant to the growth of the European Community and Union since their inception. I will be taking it up, once more, simply because its effect becomes particularly pronounced in the face of a third process.

De-politicization needs to be seen as a background condition for the rise of a new *economic due process*. In the European context it is manifest in the claim that any legally created restriction on the pursuit of economic aims, regardless of whether it originates from public or private acts, requires a showing of its rational and proportionate pursuit of public interests.[5] The ascendancy of economic due process might trigger the most profound system transition in post-war Europe, that is, the transition from the co-existence of a variety of capitalisms to a more uniform and basically Anglo-American socio-economic system.[6]

I shall examine each of these processes in turn. Since the emergence of European economic due process is a more recent phenomenon, the analysis of the latter shall be more extensive than the discussion of the preceding topics on idealization and de-politicization.

2. Idealization: The Emergence of a Post-Constitutional Order

If anything, then the unspectacular breakdown of the European constitutional project revealed what it was supposed to be. The Lisbon Reform Treaty, regardless of whether it should ever have entered into force, amounts essentially to the Constitutional Treaty stripped of constitutional ornamentation. This suggests strongly that Ulrich Haltern was correct when he pointed out, already

---

4 *See* D. Grimm, Deutsche Verfassungsgeschichte 1776-1866 [German Constitutional History] 57 (1988).

5 For the original formulation of *substantive* economic due process in the context of the United States constitution, *see* Lawton v. Steele, 123 U.S. 623, at 661 (1887). For a more nuanced formulation of European economic due process, to which I shall return below, *see* AG Miguel Maduro's Opinion in Case C-438/05, The International Transport Workers' Federation & The Finish Seamen's Union v. Viking Line ABP & Ou Viking Line Eesti, 23 May 2007, at paras. 43, 48.

6 *See* M. Höpner & A. Schäfer, *A New Phase of European Integration: Organised Capitalism in Post-Ricardian Europe*, MPIfG Discussion Paper 07/4 at 21 (2007).

several years ago, that the constitutional project, then still restricted to the Fundamental Rights quarter, was basically a method of presenting a bleak technocratic project in a quaint disguise.[7]

The Lisbon Treaty ostensibly retreats from the ambition to create the aura of self-constitution. It is post-constitutional in both a straightforward and a cunning manner. On its face, it abstains from consolidating the authoritative legal texts – two treaties and a number of protocols – into one integrated whole. In what appears to be almost an act of defiance, the Union reciprocates the rejection of the Constitutional Treaty by asserting its peculiar pre-modern complexity. The abstention from grand gestures is indicative of the nature of a constitutional arrangement. It is easier to hide inconsistencies and tensions when provisions are spread over several documents. Cunningly, the Union thereby conceals what it proposes to reveal.

At the most elementary level, modern constitutions are exercises in mapping out existing powers. They can be understood as attempts to employ norms in order to render transparent the otherwise arcane practice of the State. Facilitating greater transparency and subjecting the exercise of powers to control are two dimensions of one remarkable strategy. In addressing norms to those already wielding power, for example a king, the power becomes reconstituted so that agents can be submitted to control. A king whose signature on a Bill of Parliament is countersigned by the minister is, even though relieved of all responsibility, no longer the same king who grudgingly conceded the constitution pursuant to which he now has to act. This is not to say that constitutions do not go beyond mapping out existing structures and vesting upon them the authority of higher law. Indeed, a constitution takes a king and constrains his power by confirming the rights of Parliament. A constitution bestows upon Parliament the right of legislative override in order to control an overconfident constitutional tribunal that relies overly on the artificial reason of the law. In a nutshell, constitutions establish countervailing forces in order to control agents and processes that already exist or whose presumptive pretense of supremacy needs to be subject to checks. Beyond introducing transparency, accountability and responsiveness (which are virtues of modern *administrative* law), they *create* responsibility for matters that would be experienced, were it not for constructions of agency, by the people as being beyond their control. Eventually, they introduce transparency not by illuminating machinations with a flashlight but by pushing responsible agents into the limelight of the political realm.

It is possible, however, to give even the more elementary mapping function of norms a scheming twist. Norms can be used to conceal matters. In the European post-constitutional situation, the Lisbon Reform Treaty provides

[7] *See* U. Haltern, *Pathos and Patina: The Failure and Promise of Constitutionalism in the European Union*, 11 Eur. L. J. 19 (2002).

ample evidence of this. Thereby, far from establishing new powers of agency, it even fails to render transparent what already exists.

First, the Reform Treaty deflects attention. It will be remembered that pre-existing provisions such as free movement, the clauses on the flag and the anthem, etc which suddenly became controversial, were pushed to the foreground by the Constitutional Treaty. The Reform Treaty leaves these buried in the framework of the existing treaty. As a result, the controversial issues are now in an obscured state.

Second, it is more than merely open to debate whether the Reform Treaty has made any progress with regards to social rights. Apart from the conditional clauses contained in the Charter and the reservations made by Poland and England, the Charter never claimed to do more than render explicit rights which already existed.[8] We simply cannot determine what surplus is to be expected from the Charter.[9]

Third, outside the purview of the Treaty remains the plethora of arrangements associated with "new governance."[10] From a constitutional perspective, it is to be regretted that the Treaty that might have been a constitution does not address a method of co-ordination that appears to elude classification according to the distinction between hard and soft law.[11] Generally, addressing the "hybridity" of social policy would have reintroduced an issue that is evidently on the hearts and minds of Europeans who treasure long-established European modes of dealing with the threat of social exclusion.

Fourth, what is most remarkable about the post-constitutional ordering is the ease with which it uses legal texts in order to idealize realities (the old "crit" slogan of "law as ideology" comes to mind here). When matters cannot be changed, they can still be cast in different light through the use of norms. It may be remembered, from Kelsen, that norms serve as a scheme of interpretation.[12] They invest events and structures with significance. From a legal point of view, x counts as y (an utterance as an oath, for example). Norms can be used, therefore, to idealize realities and thus to render social facts expressive of ideals or of something evil.[13]

---

[8] The observation has been also made by the ECJ. *See* Case C-540/03, European Parliament v. Council [2006] ECR I-5769.

[9] The ECJ has not infrequently appealed to the Charter in its jurisprudence, even though with caution. *See*, for example, Case C-131/03, R. J. Reynolds Tobacco Holdings v. Commission [2006] ECR I-7795.

[10] For a critical discussion, *see* C. Joerges, *Integration Through De-legalisation*, 33 Eur. L. Rev. 291 (2008).

[11] *See*, for example, D. M. Trubek, P. Cottrell & M. Nance, *'Soft Law', 'Hard Law' and EU Integration'*, *in* G. de Búrca & J. Scott (Eds.), Law and New Governance in the EU and the US 65 (2006).

[12] *See* H. Kelsen, Reine Rechtslehre [Pure Theory of Law] 3 (1960).

[13] We are all familiar with how this works in private law. The wealthy capitalist concludes an agreement with the penniless labourer. Evidently, such a situation is marked by unequal bargaining power. Nonetheless, through the lens of classical private law the situation is

Just like the Constitutional Treaty that preceded it, the Lisbon Reform Treaty allows the Union to claim to have resolved the democratic deficit. Article 8a (Article I-46 of the Draft Constitutional Treaty) proclaims merrily that the functioning of the Union is "founded on representative democracy" (Section 1) and that citizens are "directly represented" in the European Parliament (Section 2). Not that this is evidently untrue. However, it is not entirely true either. By glossing over the conflicting nature of existing realities it amounts to an idealization. Similarly, the European Parliament is always mentioned before the Council when addressing legislative proceedings. This is a nice symbolic gesture, which also conceals the fact that the European Parliament does not occupy the driving seat in the legislative process. Never mind that it is inconsistent with the "direct" representation of citizens of the European Union to have national parliaments in charge of exercising the subsidiarity early warning mechanism, which is laid down in a separate Protocol and mentioned in Article 8c(b) of the new EU Treaty. Why should the representatives of the Member States, that is, the members of the Council, not resolve the issue? Apparently, there is something amiss in European democracy, possibly even a disconnect between the Union and more credible modes of democratic representation. When push comes to shove, the true representatives, who have been the losers of the integration process,[14] are given a voice again. Never mind that the new people's initiative disenfranchises citizens from merely one or two Member States from "inviting" the Commission to submit a proposal for a Union Act (Article 8c) even when Union law, for example, as divined by the European Court of Justice, impacts selectively on their national traditions.[15] The Treaty idealizes and conceals when it proclaims that the European Parliament elects the President of the Commission (Article 9A), suggesting that he is the equivalent of a Prime Minister. Of course, the Commission President is effectively selected by the European Council and not by parties contending for power.

This is the "democratic life of the European Union" (a phrase that used to be an ornamental heading of the draft Constitutional Treaty). Apparently, its presentation involved denial and idealization. This may raise the suspicion that the political process of the European Union eludes constitutional form and maybe even, in order to be possible, needs to remain unfettered by constitutional discipline, a matter that has been beautifully hinted at by Dehousse[16]

presented as though it involved two agents who are both equally free. The economic inequality is immaterial to the application of the norm pursuant to which both actors ought to be counted as free and equal persons entering voluntarily into an agreement. The underlying social facts become neutralised, and rendered irrelevant, owing to the influence of normative idealisations.

[14] *See* J. H. H. Weiler, The Constitution of Europe 30-38 (1999).

[15] *See, e.g.*, Case C-147/03, Commission of the European Communities v. Republic of Austria [2005] ECR I-5969.

[16] R. Dehousse, *The Unmaking of a Constitution: Lessons from the European Referenda*, 13 Constellations 151, at 161 (2006).

> The price of this governance by consensus is known: an opaque system, barely legible, in which it is difficult to identify with precision those responsible for a decision – and thus to censure them if necessary.

There is much to this observation. Its intuitive appeal, however, should not blind us to the alternative suspicion that the ironical twists and turns of constitutional forms may even bespeak the absence of a political ordering of society, at any rate, in a manner in which we have come to conceive of it.

3. De-Politicization

The members of the European Parliament represent the peoples of Europe. So far, so good. As a representative institution, the European Parliament has grown increasingly powerful and influential in the European political process.[17] Nevertheless, it would be misleading to describe the European Union in terms of a parliamentary democracy. On the contrary, it is still more apt to describe the European Union as an organization whose success implies, and depends on, the reproduction of a democracy deficit.

The explanation is easily forthcoming.[18] From the perspective of offering meaningful political choices, elections to the European Parliament are more or less devoid of meaning. They are meaningless not because the peoples of Europe sense that the issues at stake in European policy-making are either overly technical or closer to the conduct of foreign affairs. What Europeans realize, rather, is that they cannot vote for a change. Elections are not decisive. Why should Europeans pay attention to developments that they suspect to be beyond their reach and, what is more, would be within their control only if they chose coarse avenues of protest, such as a referendum over a Treaty amendment?

Elections to the European Parliament do not offer European citizens the opportunity to vote for a change. In contrast to national politics, the competing parties fail to present different visions of the future of the European polity. There is nothing that voters can identify with. This matter is also the effect of an obvious constitutional deficiency. Political parties, if they were to form a coalition in the European Parliament, would not set the agenda of policy making of the European Union. Indeed, the agenda is set by the Commission in close collaboration with the European Council. Therefore, in the eyes of some of its citizens, the Union is perceived as if it were a spaceship traversing space-time oblivious to terrestrial life.[19] In the eyes of these very same citizens

[17] *See* B. Rittberger, Building Europe's Parliament: Democratic Representation Beyond the Nation State (2006).

[18] On the following, *see* M. Kumm, *Why Europeans Will Not Embrace Constitutional Patriotism* 6 I-CON 117, at 128-133 (2008).

[19] *Id.*, at 133.

the only available mode of opposition is some inchoate rejection of the Union itself. Dissatisfaction has an outlet when it becomes misdirected against "Europe." I wonder why European politicians are not more troubled by such a profound distortion.

Moreover, since legislative choices are arrived at with only minor and surprisingly rare opposition – it is not very vocal, at any rate – the overall political process becomes assimilated to the mindset of administration. The phenomenon that I would like to invite attention to is a variation of a Majonian theme. Majone pointed out that much of European risk-regulation is explicable in terms of the basically apolitical work of the European regulatory state.[20] European legislation, he claims, to a great extent, does not redistribute resources but effectively protects diffuse consumer interests by having businesses internalize costs. Of course, Majone's observation is debatable.[21] But the point is not whether or not Majone is indeed right and whether that technocratic legitimacy truly accrues to European regulation. Rather, Majone captures the de-politicizing spirit[22] with which policies are defined and pursued in the European Union. Instead of partisan contest and ideological conflict, the democratic element of the European policy making process purportedly materializes in "stakeholder participation" and the involvement of "civil society." Instead of offering mutually incompatible political programs a venue of contest, the process relies on variation and experimentation. The confidence that both lead to mutual learning suggests that the same overall paradigm is shared by all participants. Indeed, the constitution of the European Union is so strongly free market and competition-oriented that it is embedded in a very homogenous basic consensus concerning certain values. What one gets, therefore, is small-scale optimization instead of a debate over fundamental shifts. Instead of the contest between political leaders who imagine different futures of the Union, the visions of the European Union are defined in White Papers. They are prepared by expert groups in the wake of learned exchanges with representatives of the academe. The papers frequently propose the pursuit of incompatible objectives, such as increased competition and social inclusion, enhancing mobility and solidarity, enlargement and social cohesion. The overall process is deliberative, of course, beginning with meetings which prepare visionary perspectives all the way down to technical standard-setting in committees[23] or argumentative exchanges before the European Court of Justice.

---

[20] *See* G. Majone, *Europe's 'Democracy Deficit': A Question of Standards*, 4 Eur. L. J. 5 (1998).

[21] *See* C. Joerges & J. Neyer, *From Intergouvernmental Bargaining to Deliberative Processes: The Constitutionalisation of Comitology*, 3 Eur. L. J. 273-299 (1997).

[22] For a critique, which is, however, directed at a different target, *see* C. Mouffe, On the Political (2005).

[23] *See* C. Joerges & J. Neyer, *"Deliberative Supranationalism" Revisited*, 2006/20 EUI Working Paper LAW.

Overstating my point a bit, the European Union is a machine and not a body politic. It has internalized the ultimate goal of economic prosperity. This goal is growth, territorially and economically understood.[24] Its promotion is underpinned by an elementary neo-liberal consensus. Fancy talk about "governance without government" aside, Europe is not governed, but it is administered. The *bon mot* is Metternich's, of course. It was supposed to describe the Austrian situation prior to what was to become the 1848 revolution. Even though it would be more than reckless to compare Europe's current state to the situation of Europe during the Reaction period, there can be no doubt that the European Union does not have a political process comparable to those processes that could be observed for constitutional democracies before they became increasingly disempowered. What "new Europe" gets, as a result, from the European Union is a depoliticized version of democracy. It is not a single party regime, to be sure, but nonetheless very much its liberal administrative equivalent. With voter turnouts particularly low in some of the new Member States,[25] one might wonder whether the inherited distrust in political institutions, and its demobilizing thrust, is not likely to reinforce the already existing pattern of de-politicization.

4. Economic Due Process

4.1. The Extension of the Horizontal Effect

It is no secret that the European Court of Justice has employed the vocabulary of constitutional legality in order to attain integration objectives.[26] If one had to characterize its overall approach to the interpretation of Union law one would have to call it "pragmatist."[27] That is, adjudication serves to offer a trajectory for social reform. The law constrains only inasmuch as the path-dependence of judicial decision-making requires presenting new ideas in the idiom of pre-existing legal language.

In the case of the interpretative exposition of free movement provisions, the social reform agenda has been tied to the attainment of approximation objectives.[28] One can see the Court concerned with facilitating the smooth flow

---

[24] *See* S. P. Riekmann, Die kommissarische Neuordnung Europas: Das Dispositiv der Integration [The Commissarial New Order of Europe: The Mechanism of Integration] (1998).

[25] *See* R. S. Flickinger & D. T. Studlar, *One Europe, Many Electorates?: Models of Turnout in European Parliament Elections After 2004,* 40 Comparative Political Studies 383, at 385 (2007).

[26] For an attempt at a reconstruction, *see* A. Somek, Individualism: An Essay on the Authority of the European Union 228-244 (2008).

[27] *See* R. Dworkin, Law's Empire 151-164 (1986). I am adopting Dworkin's terminology without thereby suggesting that it is particularly well chosen.

[28] In fact, the reform objectives have been articulated quite clearly by AG Maduro, *supra* note

of transactions from one country to another. In this context, the preliminary reference procedure has increasingly come to serve as a vehicle for the judicial engineering of regulatory competition. The Court now offers economic activities the opportunity to benefit from less stringent regulations that are in force in a Member State different from the state where the activities are carried out. In *Centros*[29] and *Laval*[30] alike, the conduct of a business and the provision of services were effectively invested with the power to "import" some of their constitutive laws into the country of performance (the incorporation of the company in one case and the lower pay scheme in the other).

However, the selective importation of the more favorable regulatory regime, even though undoubtedly subservient to economic objectives, does not yet signify the decisive step toward the new economic due process that is the hallmark of the *Viking* decision.[31] The new economic due process reads the horizontal effect of fundamental freedoms, such as freedom of establishment, broadly and submits intervening action, for example, a blockade by a trade union, to the strict demands of proportionality.[32]

Since the *Walrave*[33] decision, it has been a well-established principle of Union law that free movement provisions apply not only to the exercise of public authority, but also to other rules aimed at regulating in a collective manner gainful employment. The extension, which originates first in the context of free movement of workers, does not allow the government of the Member State to evade its responsibility towards European workers by delegating the regulation of general terms of employment to a private or semi-private association. The most elementary idea underlying this extension is the old supranational argument from inequality of application. If the collective regulation of employment by social partners were not submitted to the same scrutiny as legislation, free movement rules would not apply equally to all countries.[34]

The horizontal effect of free movement provisions – intended as an exceptional extension of their *vertical* effect[35] – was thus developed in order to protect the interest of workers or job applicants.[36] The special cases

5, at para.35, as that of enabling "market participants throughout the Community to have equal opportunities to gain access to any part of the common market."

[29] *See* Case C-212/97, Centros Ltd v. Erhvervs- og Selskabsstyrelsen [1999] ECR I-1459.

[30] *See* Case C-341/05, Laval un Partneri Ltd, of 18 December 2007.

[31] *See* Case C-438/05, International Transport Workers Federation, Finnish Seaman's Union v Viking Line ABP, OÜ Viking Line Eesti of 11 December 2007.

[32] *See Viking*, *supra* note 31, at paras. 80-87.

[33] *See* Case C-36/74, Walrave and Koch [1974] ECR 1405.

[34] *See* Somek, *supra* note 26, at 206 & 213-215.

[35] This matter is even acknowledged by Maduro, *supra* note 5, at para. 36.

[36] This path of development is rendered obscure by AG Maduro in his remarkably scholastic account of the case law. In a manner reminiscent of nineteenth century *Begriffsjurisprudenz,* he uses disparate case law from free movement of workers and occasional cases from free movement of goods in order to arrive at the following general principle (*supra* note 5, at

addressing free movement of goods aside (French farmers' protest case[37] and *Schmidberger*),[38] the horizontal effect of free movement rules was supposed to give special force to the interest of workers. At least until *Agonese*[39] this has been the case. The same substantive thrust can be observed for the horizontal effect claimed for Article 141, from which, ever since *Defrenne*,[40] women (and men) were supposed to benefit directly. The Court severed the link with the interest of workers only in its most recent case law and extended, in an

para. 43): "[T]he rules on freedom of movement apply directly to any private action that is capable of effectively restricting others from exercising their right to freedom of movement." *Begriffsjurisprudenz* was notorious for reasoning deductively from insufficiently grounded premises. Maduro revives this practice. His opinion is also distinguished by its casual use of logic. For example, Maduro introduces the condition of effectiveness in order to limit the horizontal scope of application of free movement rules by likening the impact of private acts to the efficacy of state regulation. He concludes that so long as one strange shopkeeper in England refuses to sell Irish products he does not interfere with free movement of (Irish) goods; he would, however, if on the basis of a shared aversion of the Irish all other shopkeepers would do the same (*See id.*, para. 42). The construction is strange. Why should the interference with rights by one person depend on the existence of a number of similar acts by others, that may also only amount to interference if that one additional person acts as all the others do? For example, why should the existence of one hundred clever business people, whose combined acts cause the ruin of a person without a "wealth talent," make the act of the last person into an interference with the impoverished person's right to subsistence, assuming, for the sake of the argument, that there is such a right? It does not make any sense to approach the matter from that perspective. The only difference that the aggregate effect of the exercise of rights makes is that it gives the state a better reason to intervene in order to protect the rights of others, such as a hypothetical right to subsistence. Aggregate effects matter from the perspective of public policy, but never from the perspective of individual right holders. Arguably, what Maduro should have said is that, as soon as a situation arises where as a combined effect of a number of private acts an obstacle emerges that cannot be reasonably circumvented by the trader (*id.*, at para. 48), the state is under an obligation to do something about it. Hence, contrary to what is claimed bravely by Maduro, it is not by "implication" that the rules on freedom of movement apply directly to private persons as though they would become capable, as they march along with the crowd, of (collectively) interfering with freedom of movement. The only implication might be that at a certain *unspecified* point the state is under an obligation to do something about, say, the collective undertaking on the part of shopkeepers to thwart Irish industry and craftsmanship. According to Maduro, the state obligation consists of giving free movement horizontal effect. This is the gist of the argument. It is, however, inconclusive, for it is open to debate whether direct horizontal effect, that is, an obligation to sell Irish products, is also the least restrictive means vis-à-vis the private autonomy of shopkeepers who are to decide for themselves which variety of products they would like to offer to customers. If that freedom were completely cancelled, free movement would indeed be tyrannical.

[37] *See* Case C-265/95, Commission v. France [1997] ECR I-6959.

[38] *See* Case C-112/00, Eugen Schmidberger, Internationale Transporte und Planzüge v. Republik Österreich [2003] ECR I-5659. Both cases can be read as involving *Schutzpflichten* on the part of the state and can be thus distinguished from horizontal effect, narrowly understood.

[39] *See* C-281/98, Roman Angonese v. Cassa di Risparmio di Bolzano SpA [2000] ECR I-4139.

[40] *See* Case C-43/75, Gabrielle Defrenne v. Société anonyme belge de navigation aérienne Sabena [1976] ECR 455.

almost cynical reference to *Defrenne*, the horizontal effect of free movement provisions also to undertakings, by pointing out that these provisions apply in particular to all agreements intended to regulate paid labor.[41] This amounts to a stunningly formalistic *re-reading* of prior case law. All of a sudden, the *type of agreement* matters. It ignores an alternative rendition that would have focused on groups of persons whose interests have hitherto been deemed worthy of *special* protection.

4.2. The New Approach to Horizontal effect

The new approach is formulated, in *Viking*, in two different ways, one of which is narrow while the other is broad. Both are stated in one paragraph of the *Viking* opinion with the that what is formulated is one and the same idea.[42] However, it is plainly not.

According to the *narrow* formulation, non-state action, such as the blockade of a production site, come within the scope of the horizontal effect of a fundamental freedom (other than free movement of workers) when the action is "inextricably linked to" or "aimed at" the conclusion of a collective agreement.[43] This formulation is novel. It does not actually base horizontal effect on the idea of securing equal treatment in a supranational context of application.[44] On the contrary, it stretches the causal chain of interference to acts leading up to an agreement. Thus understood, even the narrow formulation stretches further than the original extension of horizontal effect to certain types of private party agreements.

The *broad* formulation takes its cue from case law affecting free movement of goods, which deals mainly with how demonstrations have interfered with that right.[45] In retrospect, the cases are presented as though they had introduced the principle of horizontal effect.[46] This is yet another instance of the Court's practice of creatively misreading its own jurisprudence, for the prior case law ostensibly affects the *state's* failure to protect the free flow of commercial traffic in Europe.[47] Even though the difference between the state's duty to

[41] *See Viking*, *supra* note 31, at para. 58.
[42] *Id.*, at para. 65.
[43] *Id.*, at paras. 36, 60.
[44] *See Walrave*, *supra* note 33.
[45] *See* Commission v. France, *supra* note 37, at para. 30; Schmidberger, *supra* note 38, at paras. 57 and 62. Both decisions are mentioned in *Viking*, *supra* note 31, at Para. 62.
[46] *See Viking*, *supra* note 31, at para. 62.
[47] Here is what the Court concluded in Commission v. France, *supra* note 37 at para. 66: "[I]t must be held that, by failing to adopt all necessary and proportionate measures in order to prevent the free movement of fruit and vegetables from being obstructed by actions by private individuals, the French Government has failed to fulfil its obligations under Article 30, in conjunction with Article 5, of the Treaty and under the common organizations of the markets in agricultural products." And here is what the Court said in Schmidberger, *supra* note 38, at

protect and horizontal effect may be imperceptible in certain instances,[48] it is noteworthy enough in both practice and principle. It affects the remedy.[49] Whereas horizontal effect would give rise to a remedy against another private party in an ordinary court of law – a tort claim, for example – a violation by the Member State of its obligation to protect a fundamental freedom pursuant to Article 5 EC Treaty against interference by private parties would give rise to a claim against the state. The remedy may indeed be a tort claim against the state that is based on the state's failure to comply with Community law.[50]

It is quite obvious why the latter solution is congruent with Union Law. If the potential violation – as in the case of demonstrations – comes about as an aggregate effect of private individual action, the remedy would be less effective if the affected party had to recover from a large group of non-associated individuals one by one. Indeed, the effectiveness of Union law counsels against horizontal effect in this type of case. If the state is the addressee of the obligation, it will be required to remove potential interferences whenever they arise. But assuming that the state is under this type of obligation, the obligation would have to be construed very narrowly from the outset, given that the state must not excessively interfere, in our case, with the freedom of association and the right to take collective action on the part of trade unions.

---

paras. 59-60: "Consequently, Articles 30 and 34 of the Treaty require the Member States not merely themselves to refrain from adopting measures or engaging in conduct liable to constitute an obstacle to trade but also, when read with Article 5 of the Treaty, to take all necessary and appropriate measures to ensure that that fundamental freedom is respected on their territory (*Commission v. France*, cited above, at para. 32). Article 5 of the Treaty requires the Member States to take all appropriate measures, whether general or particular, to ensure fulfilment of the obligations arising out of the Treaty and to refrain from any measures which could jeopardise the attainment of the objectives of that Treaty. [...] Having regard to the fundamental role assigned to the free movement of goods in the Community system, in particular for the proper functioning of the internal market, that obligation upon each Member State to ensure the free movement of products in its territory by taking the measures necessary and appropriate for the purposes of preventing any restriction due to the acts of individuals applies without the need to distinguish between cases where such acts affect the flow of imports or exports and those affecting merely the transit of goods." From the reference to Art. 5 EC Treaty and the language of the opinions emerges clearly enough that the Court is concerned with the obligation of Member States and not with horizontal effect.

[48] *See* M. Kumm, *Who Is Afraid of the Total Constitution?*, 7 German Law Journal 341, at 360-362 (2006).

[49] The matter is completely conflated in the AG Maduro's opinion who first (in para. 50) recognises a margin of discretion on the part of the Member States and then goes on (in para. 53) to claim that owing to the direct effect of purportedly horizontally effective Treaty provisions a claim against an other private party may in certain instances be based directly on the relevant Treaty provision.

[50] *See*, for that matter, Joined Cases C-6/90 and C-9/90 Francovich and Others v. Italian Republic [1991] ECR I-5357 Case C-224/01; Gerhard Köbler v. Republik Österreich [2003] ECR I-10239.

According to the broad formulation, which thus expands the focus to private acts more generally, the activity in question may be causally even farther removed from a collective agreement. The Court makes it explicitly clear only that protection from interference is available not only against "quasi-public organizations" or "associations exercising a regulatory task and having quasi-legislative powers."[51] If this broad formulation will be followed in subsequent judgments, any form of collective action by trade unions might count as an interference with the freedom to provide services. In *Viking*, the Court made it clear that freedom of establishment could be invoked against trade union acts seeking to pressure an undertaking into negotiating a collective agreement.[52] In fact, the Court counseled national courts to submit trade union action that counts as an exercise of the right to take collective action to a very stringent proportionality test. In the course of this test, trade union action is likened to regulation.[53] Hence, the Court expects trade unions to espouse stated objectives and to pursue them in a suitable and non-excessive way. Remarkably, the Court even suggested that "less restrictive" means would need to be exhausted first.[54] This is an unreasonable expectation, for it seeks to submit collective acts that are part of a struggle to a normative precept that has been developed for a context where those wielding sovereign rights are supposed to attain objectives in an unruffled and instrumentally fine-tuned way. Trade union action needs to be far cruder than bureaucratic rationality. In fact, it has to be excessive in order to attain its objective. It may well need to threaten to bring bankruptcy on an undertaking. Confronting trade union action with proportionality requirements destines it to lose out to business interests.

The conclusions that follow can scarcely be overstated. The right to establish businesses and to conclude agreements without being excessively burdened by the protective legislation or industrial relations at the place of business operation introduces substantive economic due process into a transnational setting, for it effectively shields freedom of contract from efforts to protect the interest of workers. The economic due process mentioned above was even pushed further by the AG preparing the opinion in the *Viking* case elaborating, even though unasked, the horizontal effect of free movement positions.[55] This

---

[51] *Viking*, *supra* note 31, at para. 64.

[52] *See Viking*, *supra* note 31, at para. 62: "This interpretation is also supported by the case-law on the Treaty provisions on he free movement of goods, from which it is apparent that restrictions may be the result of actions by individuals or groups rather than caused by the state [...]." In brackets follows a reference to Commission v. France and Schmidberger.

[53] For an apt critique, *see* C. Joerges & F. Rödl, *On De-formalisation in European Politics and Formalism in European Jurisprudence in Response to the "Social Deficit" of the European Integration Project: Reflections After the Judgements of the ECJ in* Viking *and* Laval, at 18 (2008, manuscript on file with the author).

[54] *See* Viking, *supra* note 31, at para. 88.

[55] *See* AG Maduro's opinion, *supra* note 5, at paras. 42-54.

elevates, via the principle of private autonomy, free entrepreneurship to the level of a universal right, which is likely to prevail over fundamental rights in case of collision.

4.3. Divided Economies in a Common Market

In *Laval*, the Court's jurisprudence had already taken for granted a certain model of the freedom to provide services.[56] It is a model that actually divides employees and their interests along national lines. It thereby reveals a commitment to the type of economic nationalism that is perfectly congruent with Ricardo's political ontology. Businesses are seen as competing against one another on the basis of their national comparative advantage, of which industrial relations and a system of social protection are considered to be an integral part. The new element introduced by the Court is that the setup now allows for aggressive regulatory invasions.

The overall anti-internationalist thrust[57] of the Court's approach comes to the fore in how the *Viking* Court came to pick and choose those trade union action goals that are actually admitted to the proportionality test. The Court readily takes the protection and improvement of seafarers' terms of employment into consideration.[58] What does not play a part, even though it occupied a prominent place in the acts of the International Transport Workers Federation,[59] is the establishment and strengthening of international solidarity.[60] The story underlying the *Viking* litigation strongly suggests that trade unions are actually capable of co-operating across national lines in order to avert social dumping.[61] The interest in strengthening trade union actions across national borders in spite of differentials in wealth and opportunities is not considered in the Court's assessment of the proportionality of trade union actions. This raises the suspicion that the Court does not take the right of collective action seriously. An analogy to freedom of expression may

[56] For a sketch, *see Laval*, *supra* note 30, at paras. 73-76.

[57] A particularly egregious example of this anti-internationalism is manifest in AG Maduro's opinion. Maduro suggests, in fact, that through internationally concerted action the stronger trade unions may extract from weaker counterparts concessions and thus rob the workforce of the latter of their comparative advantage. *See* AG Maduro, *supra* note 5, at 71. *See also* N. Reich, *Free Movement v. Social Rights in an Enlarged Union – the* Laval *and* Viking *Cases Before the ECJ*, 9 German Law Journal 125, at 135-136 (2008); C. Barnard, *Social Policy Revisited in the Light of the Constitutional Debate*, *in* C. Barnard (Ed.), The Fundamentals of EU Law Revisited: Assessing the Impact of the Constitutional Debate 109, at 151 (2006).

[58] *See Viking*, *supra* note 31, at para. 88.

[59] *Id.*, at paras. 8-15.

[60] *See* again, AG Maduro, *supra* note 5, at 71.

[61] *Id.*, at para. 12, where it appears as though the trade union in Estonia must have been ready to comply with the circular in which the International Federation asked them not to enter into negotiations with Laval.

elucidate the point. Freedom of expression would not be taken seriously where respecting its exercise was made conditional upon it serving certain, and not other, ends. Freedom of expression would not be safeguarded if, for example, it comprised communication with a political aim and not communication that appealed to the prurient interest. In our case, the elimination of international solidarity from the purview of legitimate objectives of trade union action is the equivalent of such a prudish attitude.

Anti-internationalism is also revealed in the overall image of the relationship between domestic and foreign workers that emerges from the relevant cases (*Laval, Viking* and most recently *Rüffert*).[62] With regard to the Posted Workers Directive,[63] the ECJ insists, above all, that substantive standards have not been harmonized.[64] The Directive is also said to envisage a narrowly defined set of regulatory strategies which may be used in particular in order to determine the minimum wage. While Article 3(1) of the Directive lays down regulatory standard cases, such as laws, regulations or universally applicable collective agreements, Article 3(8)(2) contains a special rule for the case where no collective agreement has been declared universally applicable. On its face, it offers Member States discretion[65] to base themselves, "if they so decide," on agreements which are, roughly speaking, de facto widely used in a geographical area for a certain industry of profession.[66] It makes sense to accord to Member States the discretion to select a standard, in whatever form, or to abstain from adopting one. Should the Member States decide to declare working conditions mandatory for service providers from another Member State, it is reasonable to expect them to apply the standard that is generally used for domestic firms as well, for this avoids raising the specter of discrimination; this explains why there is a requirement to select standards that are widely used in a particular sector. Should the Member States, however, decide to abstain from selecting such standards[67] they may do so for a number of good reasons. For example, they may choose to accept risks which relate to the competitiveness of domestic businesses or leave the determination of working conditions to the social partners whenever an established system of industrial relations would have them do so.

---

[62] *See* Case C-346/06, Dirk Rüffert v. Land Niedersachsen of 3 April 2008.

[63] *See* Directive 96/71/EC of the European Parliament and of the Council of 16 December 1996 concerning the posting of workers in the framework of the provision of services, OJ 1997 L18, at 1.

[64] In other words, the Directive does not harmonise the content of working conditions. *See Laval*, *supra* note 30, at paras. 60, 68.

[65] This is completely overlooked by Reich, *supra* note 57, at 143, who believes that such a decision by the Member States needs to be expressly taken.

[66] *See* P. Davies, *Posted Workers: Single Market or Protection of National Labour Law Systems*, 34 CML Rev 571, at 580-581 (1997).

[67] To repeat, the Directive offers this discretion since Article 3(8)(2) explicitly determines that "Member States may, if they so decide, base themselves on [...]."

The ECJ, by contrast, apparently misconstrues discretion as an obligation on the part of the Member States to declare collective agreements relevant for firms posting workers where, pursuant to domestic practice, no collective agreement is universally applicable in a geographical area and profession. This obligation is even so narrowly construed by the ECJ in both the *Laval* and the *Rüffert* case that wage determination on a case-by-case basis by strong unions,[68] or a collective agreement for public contracts only (instead of a geographical area or profession or industry),[69] and even statutory wage determination outside a general minimum wage statute appear to be pre-empted by Union law.[70]

The Court attributes to the Directive the pursuit of a social objective in a context defined by regulatory interaction. Unless the wages paid in accordance with the wage scale of the home state are relatively higher than minimum wages in the host state, the posted workers are supposed to benefit from the higher minimum wage that is universally guaranteed in the country of service.[71] The Court presents this guarantee as if it amounted to a social right. But the minimum wage introduces also a cap. Unless, of course, employers who are not exposed to collective actions by unions voluntarily agree to pay more than the local minimum wage, no action may be taken by a union of the host state in order to extract from employers higher compensation.[72] Hence, established industrial relation systems in which (strong) trade unions have the liberty to attempt to extract concessions that are more favorable for workers than statutory minimal standards are in principle deemed incompatible with Union law.[73] Incompatible with this strict construction of the Directive is also a combined action of the workforces of both countries in instances of transnational service provision. On the contrary, it is assumed that the wage has already been determined in the host state. The service providers enter only later. If matters were up for grabs when they arrived they would find themselves burdened with an unpredictable situation, which would make the conduct of business for them "less attractive" or "more difficult."[74]

At first glance, it may appear even fair not to allow trade unions attempts to move beyond a certain minimum wage as soon as foreign bidders enter the picture, for allowing them to do so might give rise to collusion with domestic competitors and hence, indeed, to protectionist effects. The interpretation by the ECJ is disturbing, nonetheless. When the provisions of the Directive are read in light of what is said in its preamble then they are to be construed

[68] *See Laval*, *supra* note 30, at paras. 69, 71. For a comment, *see* Joerges & Rödl, *supra* note 53, at 21-22.

[69] This is what Art. 3(8) of the Posted Workers Directive, narrowly construed, appears to require.

[70] *See Rüffert*, *supra* note 62, at paras. 24, 28.

[71] *See Laval*, *supra* note 30, at para. 76.

[72] *See Laval*, *supra* note 30, at paras. 81, 108.

[73] On the Swedish system, *see Laval*, *supra* note 30, at para. 24.

[74] *See Laval*, *supra* note 30, at para. 99, 110.

"without prejudice to the law of the Member States concerning collective actions to defend the interests of trades and professions."[75] Thus understood, it is a grave misunderstanding to read the provision on minimal wage such that the Swedish system of wage determination on a case-by-case basis comes out as contrary to Union law. The preamble suggests that where a conflict with established industrial relations arises, the Directive must yield. By contrast, the ECJ reverses the overall thrust of the Directive. The Directive's aim is to protect posted workers against wage discrimination and to protect locally settled workers against social dumping. While the latter aim is indeed explicitly recognized by the Court,[76] the first aim drops out of the picture. In a case where trade unions would be in the position to protect the interests of *both* posted and domestic workers the Court effectively ends up protecting the interest of the service provider to break into the market in compliance with a "nucleus of mandatory rules for minimum protection."[77] The vision of a divided economy comes to full fruition at this point. While posted workers receive the "nucleus," trade unions, in internal situations, would not encounter any constraints by Union law when it comes to extracting from employers greater concessions. The approach distinguishes between the interest of the domestic and the foreign labour force by assigning to the latter, in principle, a lower status, which is only compensated by the *company's* competitive advantage.[78] This is how what might have been a social guarantee becomes, in fact, a vehicle of market access.

4.4. The *Schmidberger* Trap and the Social Aims Catch

There might be objections that what I have proposed so far does not amount to a fair characterization of the ECJ's position. The ECJ readily recognizes the right to take collective actions and merely stresses the equal relevance of fundamental freedoms.[79] The manner, however, in which the Court goes about recognizing fundamental freedoms is remarkable, to say the least, for it absorbs fundamental rights adjudication into the holistic grasp of Union law.

The trap that is thereby created for national fundamental rights traditions has already been prepared in the *Schmidberger*[80] case. The underlying issue raised the question concerning whether the blocking of road traffic by environmental

[75] *See* Directive 96/71/EC, recital 22.
[76] *See Laval*, *supra* note 30, at paras.75, 103.
[77] *See Laval*, *supra* note 30, at paras.73-74.
[78] In *Laval*, *supra* note 30, at para. 74, the Court states that the nucleus of minimal protection exists in order to "ensure a climate of fair competition between national undertakings and undertakings which provide services transnationally [...]".
[79] *See Laval*, *supra* note 30, at paras. 90-96.
[80] *See* Schmidberger, *supra* note 38; Case C-36/02, Omega Spielhallen- und Automatenaufstellungs- GmbH v. Oberbürgermeisterin der Bundesstadt Bonn [2004] ECR I-9609.

groups and the local population illicitly interfered with the free movement of goods. Instead of recognizing that it was a valid public interest on the part of the Member State to maintain its own system and level of fundamental rights protection, the Court effectively disowned *national* traditions and replaced them with the common constitutional tradition of the Member States. The case was thus transformed into a matter that does not concern the potential collision between national constitutional law and Union law, but rather is presented as fully internal to Union law.[81] This transformation may be referred to as the *Schmidberger* trap. Once the trap has snapped, the Union standard of fundamental rights protection applies.

There may be objections that what I refer to, flippantly, as the *Schmidberger* trap is an indispensible satellite of the supremacy of Union law. Otherwise Union acts would be governed by national fundamental rights standards. The very purpose of introducing the Community standard into the case law since *Internationale Handelsgesellschaft*[82] has been to avoid subordinating Union law to *national* fundamental rights scrutiny. But the matter is clearly different in the *Schmidberger* type of case. The question is not whether legislative or administrative acts adopted by the Union are considered void or in any other manner repugnant in respect of national fundamental rights, but rather whether the disruptive application of a fundamental freedom should be discontinued out of the Union's respect for the diversity of national systems of fundamental rights protection. Of course, such respect would entail a different mode of application, for it would also reflect the different weight that is attributed to a right pursuant to the respective national tradition. While, for example, the right to strike is recognized in some constitutions,[83] it is absent in others. A differential resolution of the relevant issue would lend credibility to the merry promise contained in Article 6(3) EU Treaty, which states that the Union shall respect the national identities of its Member States. In what respect should such identity more plausibly materialize, and be more deserving of respect, than in the case of the protection of fundamental rights? Evidently, this is a question which affects the proportionality principle.

However, this approach was not adopted by the ECJ. As a consequence, national fundamental rights regimes have become leveled to one Union standard. Hence, Member States can no longer appeal to their very own bill of rights as offering a legitimate overriding reason of the public interest for

---

[81] *See* Schmidberger, *supra* note 38, at para. 71. In Omega, *supra* note 80, the Court wavered between absorbing the Member States' own fundamental rights standard (para. 34) and respecting legitimate differences with regard to the national level of protection (para. 38). Apparently, the matter was not settled among the judges themselves.

[82] *See* Case 11/70, Internationale Handelsgesellschaft v. Einfuhr- und Vorratsstelle für Getreide und Futtermittel, [1970] ECR 1125.

[83] For example, the Swedish constitution. *See Laval*, *supra* note 30, at para. 92.

the defense of interferences with fundamental freedoms. Whatever rights they may have laid down in their own constitutional instruments, they are ground into the "common constitutional tradition" which is part of Union law.

The *Schmidberger* trap is closely associated with a competence coup to which I shall return below. The important role that it plays in the most recent jurisprudence of the Court is further confirmed by another amazing transformation which I would like to refer to as the social aims catch. It affects the direction of justification in the relationship between fundamental rights and fundamental freedoms.

With almost identical wordings, the Court states in *Laval* and *Viking* that the activity of the Union extends to the social sphere.[84] The Court thus appropriates jurisdiction in matters affecting the interests of workers by invoking the aim pursued by the Union. It explicitly refers to Article 2 EC Treaty which considers promoting "a high level of employment and of social protection." The reference to the overarching objective is used to quell doubts about whether the Union does not ride roughshod over jurisdictional bounds when its law adversely affects the exercise of the right to strike and other forms of collective trade union action.

The move is not entirely novel. In a more restrictive form, the Court had introduced it earlier to claim the relevance of fundamental freedoms as a side constraint on Member state acts in areas where the Union officially lacks power to adopt harmonizing legislation.[85] It thus established jurisdiction in the area of negative integration, from which arose the usual asymmetry in the relationship between the powers of positive and negative integration. The latter takes precedence over the former.[86] The often invoked "scope of the application of the Treaty" is virtually boundless in the field of negative integration. The success of this move has pre-empted attempts to claim exemption from community competence on the ground that no jurisdiction had been conferred on it, for example, in certain social matters. The fundamental freedoms now apply to anything, subject to a noteworthy exemption,[87] that is a potential obstacle to intra-Community trade.[88]

---

[84] *See Laval*, *supra* note 30, at paras. 104-105; *Viking*, *supra* note 31, at paras. 78-79.

[85] *See, e.g.,* Case C-158/96, Raymond Kohll v. Union des caisses de maladie, [1998] ECR I-1931.

[86] For a more nuanced discussion of the matter, *see* G. Davies, *Can Selling Arrangements Be Harmonized?*, 30 Eur Law Rev. 370 (2005).

[87] *See* Cases C-267/91 and C-268/91, Criminal proceedings against Bernard Keck and Daniel Mithouard [1993] ECR I-6097.

[88] Ironically, the point about the potentially universal reach of negative integration was made so vigorously by AG Maduro in his opinion (*supra* note 5) that he inadvertently stumbled over a potential restriction. After stressing that there seems to be no reason why the fundamental freedoms should not be applied to measures affecting social policy while they undisputedly constrain measures regarding the protection of public health, the environment or the consumer (para. 25), he went on to examine whether a parallel exemption ought to be made as had been made in the *Albany* case (para. 26). The AG concluded that while the exemption from

Nonetheless, the introduction of the social policy trap is an even bolder step. The Court now refers to an aim, and not to the constraining effect of fundamental freedoms, in order to cast aside the jurisdictional bounds as they have been defined in the respective policy chapters of the Treaty. In addition, the Court thereby also conquers the field of countervailing considerations that offer resistance to negative integration. They are no longer reasons of the Member States, whom it took decades to develop their very own models of social capitalism. They become transferred into the Union's very own reasons, for they reflect the Union's very own "social purpose." In principle, therefore, the Member States' systems of social protection find themselves demoted to a level where they represent different modes with which the Union attains its own objectives in the context of a multilevel system.[89]

4.5. The Direction of Justification

It is to be expected that the Union's conquest of the social territory will not only come at the expense of the diverse national traditions of protecting social rights but also affect what I would like to refer to as the direction of justification. This was made clear by the Court in *Viking*:

> However, in *Schmidberger* and *Omega*, the Court held that the exercise of the fundamental rights at issue, that is, freedom of expression and freedom of assembly and respect for human dignity, respectively, does not fall outside the scope of the provisions of the Treaty and considered that such exercise must be reconciled with the requirements relating to rights protected under the Treaty and in accordance with the principle of proportionality [...]

The exercise of fundamental rights needs to be justified vis-à-vis fundamental freedoms and not the other way around. The situation would be manifestly different if the direction of justification were reversed. Then the question would have to be asked as to whether allowing companies effectively to undermine collective action by trade unions, even when exercising their right of establishment (*Viking*) or the freedom to provide services (*Laval*), would not fall below the level of social rights protection that needs to be guaranteed by any Member State. Business objectives would require sufficient weight to justify an interference with the interests of labor. Moreover, the means chosen would have to be least intrusive.

In constitutional terms, the resulting question for fundamental rights affects reverse proportionality (*Untermaßverbot*), that is, whether or not the

---

competition rules was necessary in order to facilitate the conclusion of collective agreements no adverse effect on industrial relations and social dialogue was to be expected from the application of fundamental freedoms (para. 27). In light of the outcome of the *Viking* case the argument would now actually favour a parallel exemption. Hence, there is reason to treat social policy differently form the protection of health or the protection of the environment.

[89] For a pertinent statement, *see* AG Maduro, *supra* note 5, at para. 59.

Union or the Member States have done *enough* to protect the interests of workers. Arguably, the Court held in *Laval* that in laying down the categories of workers' interests (*e.g.*, working time, remuneration, and paid vacations) comprising "the nucleus of mandatory rules for minimum protection," the Union comports with reverse proportionality. That the Member States lack the jurisdiction to go beyond this level of protection – for example, by allowing strong unions to negotiate minimum pay at the local level – is congruent with the *Schmidberger* trap and the social aims catch, respectively. The Union, at any rate in the context of free movement, ascribes to itself the power to occupy the field for the protection of fundamental rights whenever it acts in fulfillment of the demands of reverse proportionality.[90]

The application of reverse proportionality can be mirrored by the application of the proportionality principle vis-à-vis interference with fundamental freedoms. Union acts that interfere with transnational business operations can pass muster as long as they are required in order to give life to freedom of association. At this point, the asymmetry in the direction of justification kicks in. The more stringently the proportionality principle is applied vis-à-vis collective trade union action the more yielding becomes the requirement of reverse proportionality. In fact, reverse proportionality loses its force when it is effectively reduced to a mere refraction of the proportionality applied to interferences with fundamental freedoms. The purportedly pre-emptive Union standard for fundamental rights is then a by-product of what passes muster vis-à-vis the exercise of fundamental freedoms. Fundamental rights lose their bite. This is what happened in the *Rüffert* case. The level of protection became reduced to the minimum laid down in the Directive, for it is that which is deemed tolerable with regard to fundamental freedoms. The asymmetry in the relationship between fundamental freedoms and fundamental rights could scarcely be greater. The social aims catch thus effectively subordinates social rights to the pursuit of economic objectives.

4.6. The Jurisdictional Coup

In *Laval* the Court introduced an interpretation of the Directive on posted workers according to which a minimum wage determination that relies on the force of trade unions alone is inconsistent with the Directive. Such a system

[90] In a constitutional context, the application of reverse proportionality (*Untermaßverbot*) is usually very deferential with regard to the legislature. In the case of fundamental freedoms, the beneficiaries of deference, all of a sudden, are individual companies. They find themselves invested with ample power to decide. This power to decide becomes depoliticised, for while it makes sense to see a legislature under the positive obligation to protect the freedom of association on the level of its legislation, it is more than odd to imagine a similar duty to rest on private actors. Economic due process is liberating for corporations.

would not allow the service providing company to discern the national wage level, which it should be able to foresee in order to sustain its competitiveness.[91] This interpretation goes to the core of the autonomy enjoyed by trade unions in Sweden.[92] In a similar vein, the *Rüffert* case rules out stipulating a minimal wage in a statute that governs the provision of services only for the public sector.[93]

It should not come as a surprise that this development goes to the heart of how social policy has been organized, hitherto, in the European Union. It was based on what might be called the strategy of "domestication," in the dual sense of the term.[94] First, even after the amendments introduced by the Amsterdam and the Nice Treaty social policy has remained – when one examines the complex interplay of conferral and reservation of competence in Article 137 EC Treaty – largely a domestic affair. Second, social policy has been domesticated in the sense that the operation of services is in principle subject to the discipline of competition law (with broad exemptions, however, which were formulated in the *Albany* case[95] for supplemental pension insurance)[96] and generally bound to observe the lines drawn by fundamental freedoms.[97]

Since only matters of a non-commercial nature do not affect fundamental freedoms, as was made amply clear by the Irish abortion case, fundamental freedoms apply to any commercial activity having a cross-border aspect. Where does Union competence come to an end, then?

The stop that is usually invoked and that promises, at first glance, to be a true winner has not worked well in the past. What I have in mind are explicit exemptions from Community jurisdiction, such as Article 137(5) EC Treaty. This paragraph states explicitly that the provisions of Article 137 shall not apply to pay, the right of association, the right to strike or the right to impose lock-outs.

The assumption underlying this strategy of jurisdictional containment is, hence, that fundamental freedoms do not apply to matters for which the Community has no jurisdiction. But in this simple form the argument does not work. As I tried to point out above, it is not evident why a jurisdictional restraint on positive integration, such as Article 137(5) EC Treaty, should automatically also translate into a stop for negative integration. Even worse,

91 *See Laval, supra* note 30, at para. 110.

92 *See* Joerges & Rödl, at 20-21.

93 *See Rüffert, supra* note 62, at paras. 26, 39.

94 On the following, *see* F. W. Scharpf, *The European Social Model: Coping with the Challenges of Diversity*, 40 Journal of Common Market Studies 645 (2002).

95 *See* Case C-67/96, Albany International BV v. Stichting Bedrijfspensioenfonds Textielindustrie [1999] ECR I-5751.

96 In *Viking, supra* note 31, at paras. 50, 53, the Court pointed out that the *Albany* exemption cannot be transferred to the context of free movement for the mere fact that the "circumstances" are "different." This statement does not reflect a serious effort at an explanation.

97 *See*, with rich references to the prior case law, *Laval, supra* note 30, at para. 87.

in the past, similar stops have not worked for positive integration either. In those areas where the Community promises to attain, in the course of harmonization, a "high level of protection," the ECJ had already found a way of working around explicit exemptions from Community competence. The story associated with tobacco advertisement and product regulations is the case in point. It does not have to be retold here.[98]

Even though the creeping extension of Community competence cannot be accounted for without taking a separate constituent power into account and is hence, inexplicable in terms of an *exercise* of conferred powers,[99] one might expect the Member States to fare better in matters falling outside the protection of health, worker safety, consumer protection, and the environment. Indeed, the stop argument can be given a stronger appeal when it is viewed from a different angle. Article 137(5) excludes the regulation of strikes and lockouts. Assuming that, as was the case in *Laval* and *Viking*, free movement rights were applied in a manner that affected the matters mentioned in Article 137(5), the removal of obstacles on the basis of the four freedoms triggers harmonization competence via Articles 14 and 95 of the EC Treaty. When it comes to strikes and lockouts, the Union all of a sudden simultaneously seems to possess and not to possess harmonization competence. This is clearly an impasse. Whoever adheres to the wording of the Treaty will expect Article 137(5) – the *lex specialis* – to prevail. Consequently, the Union cannot have harmonization competence in this area. By implication, however, the application of fundamental freedoms does not extend to this field. The reason is straightforward. The Union has harmonization competence partly because this power is needed to clean up the mess resulting from the application of fundamental freedoms. Even though the Union may have clean-up power without the power to make inroads into national legal systems, it would be more than questionable to attribute to the Union the power to create the mess without seeing it also invested with the power to tidy things up. If the application of fundamental freedoms could be extended to matters where the Union lacks powers of positive integration the asymmetry in the relation of negative and positive integration would actually result in a deregulatory downward spiral. The Union would thus drift into the direction of a neo-liberal social model. This problem is concealed in the *Laval* and *Viking* cases, for the ECJ reads the Directive as though the Union legislature had already spoken on the issue of collective action.

I conclude, therefore, that Article 137(5), if read in conjunction with Articles 14 and 95, effectively excludes the application of fundamental freedoms to matters which have been explicitly exempted from Community jurisdiction. Hence, what the Court should have said in *Laval* and *Viking* is that freedom to provide services and freedom of establishment do not apply to situations affecting trade union's rights to take collective action. What is more,

[98] *See* Somek, *supra* note 26, at 111-137.

[99] Or so I argue in Somek, *supra* note 26.

if one were to maintain a doctrine of parallelism with regard to fundamental freedoms and powers conferred by the Treaty, the inroads made by the Court in national systems of social protection would be flat-out unconstitutional, for they would conflict with what has been set out in Article 137(4), which states that the provision of this Article shall not prevent any Member State from maintaining or introducing more stringent protective measures compatible with this Treaty.

If the above argument is correct, we cannot but conclude that the ECJ decided two major cases in a manner which is contrary to the wording of the Treaty. One may wonder whether this type of "reasoning" is consistent with the task of the preliminary reference procedure, which is to assist national courts in cases of Treaty *interpretation*. In fact, if the Court does not engage in Treaty interpretation, its pronouncements raise the specter of nullity. Cunningly, the Court purported to engage in Treaty interpretation by inferring competence from a mere task. But the latter claim is patently absurd, for it effectively renders superfluous all specific and detailed attribution of jurisdiction in the later chapters of the Treaty. The Court went on, however, to undermine the autonomy of national systems of social protection and social rights, in this case concerning how Finland guarantees the right to strike, by submitting them to the scrutiny of a highly fragmentary Union social constitution.[100]

5. The Core of System Transition

The concern obviously raised by the triad of idealization, de-politicization and economic due process is that the Union, in order to attain market integration objectives, appears to be breaking away from its commitment to the rule of law. As the discussion has shown, the pursuit of market integration objectives is taking precedence over the constraints set by Treaty law; or, at any rate, over standards of their methodologically sound elaboration. The ECJ arrives at a new doctrine of horizontal effect with the purport to elaborate prior cases, but what it really does is to indulge in abstractions that are in no manner warranted by a contextual reading of these cases. The new doctrine is potentially oblivious to the difference between the direct horizontal application of fundamental freedoms to conduct by private parties and the failure on the part of the Member State to act on behalf of their protection. The ECJ treats action by trade unions as being on the same level with the exercise of sovereign rights, by submitting

[100]For an apt observation, *see* C. Joerges & F. Rödl, *Von der Entformalisierung europäischer Politik und dem Formalismus europäischer Rechtsprechung im Umgang mit dem „sozialen Defizit" des Integrationsprojekts, Ein Beitrag aus Anlass der Urteile des EuGH in den Rechtssachen Viking und Laval [About the De-formalization of European Politics and the Formalism of European Adjudication in Relation to the 'Social Deficit' of the Integration Project-A Contribution regarding the Result of the ECJ Decisions in* Viking *and* Laval*]*, ZERP-Diskussionspapier 2/2008 at 17.

both to stringent requirements of proportionality. The ECJ ignores the wording of the Posted Workers Directive and has no qualms about construing it *contra legem*. The ECJ comes up with inventive legal designs in order to augment the Union's room for maneuver, such as the *Schmidberger* trap, the social aims catch and the competence coup. Apparently, the Court expects to get away with sloppy reasoning and the stretching of premises simply because it has the power to declare what the law is. But what it produces, instead, places the rule of law in jeopardy.

This is a hazardous gamble. The demise of the rule of law would mark, undoubtedly, a development that is both surprising and disquieting. The Union's core claim to legitimacy might have been, at any rate at the outset, the idea that Europe was to emerge as a legal community (*Rechtsgemeinschaft*). According to Walter Hallstein, the "majesty of law" was supposed to accomplish what war and bloodshed were unable to achieve for centuries.[101] Yet, the development may not be so surprising, after all, for it can be argued that with the launch of the internal market agenda, the original emphasis on legality became superseded by a penchant for economic rationality.[102] Gradually, the commitment to legality was replaced with the observance of an economic superlaw. It would be congruent with this development to see central components of legal form, such as *stare decisis*, turned into an empty vessel for the attainment of economic aims. Instead of constraining the future with regard to what has been decided in the past, the invocation of law conceals the discontinuity implicated in ever more volatile strategies of social re-engineering.

---

[101] *See* W. Hallstein, Der unvollendete Bundesstaat. Europäische Erfahrungen und Erkenntnisse [The Incomplete Federation-European Experiences and Insights] 33 (1969): "Die Gemeinschaft ist eine *Schöpfung des Rechts*. Das ist das entscheidend Neue, was sie gegenüber früheren Versuchen auszeichnet, Europa zu einigen. Nicht Gewalt, nicht Unterwerfung ist als Mittel eingesetzt, sondern eine geistige, eine kulturelle Kraft, das Recht. Die Majestät des Rechts soll schaffen, was Blut und Eisen in Jahrhunderten nicht vermochten. Denn nur die selbstgewollte Einheit hat Aussicht auf Bestand, und Rechtsgleichheit und- einheit sind untrennbar miteinander verbunden. Keine Rechtsordnung ohne Gleichheit vor dem Gesetz, Gleichheit aber bedeutet Einheit. Auf dieser Einsicht beruht der Vertrag von Rom, und darum schafft er eine Friedensordnung par excellence." [The Community is a *legal creation*. This is the decisive novelty from earlier attempts to unite Europe. Europe came about not through power, by submission, but through a spiritual and cultural force, the law. The majesty of the law must accomplish what centuries of blood and steel could not. After all, only voluntary unity has prospects of continuity, and legal equality and legal unity are inextricably conjoined. No legal order without equality before the law – and equality implies unity. This understanding is the basis of the Treaty of Rome and because of this it creates a framework for peace *par excellence*.]

[102] *See* C. Joerges, *Economic Law, the Nation-State and the Maastricht Treaty*, *in* R. Dehousse (Ed.), Europe after Maastricht: An Ever Closer Union? 29 (1994). *See also*, Joerges & Rödl, *supra* note 53, at 7. For the claim that with the cases that have been under consideration here the European integration project is about to enter even a "post-Ricardian" age, *see* Höpner & Schäfer, *supra* note 6, at 8-9.

The matter can be given a far less grim outlook, however, when taking into account that the use of law as an instrument for the attainment of socially valuable objectives is itself part of a defensible or, at any rate, debatable jurisprudential creed, which is usually associated with American legal realism. In his *opus magnum*, Dworkin reconstructed its core under the name of "pragmatism."[103] From the perspective of pragmatism, thus understood, legal rules and standards are valuable – or "valid" – inasmuch as they either render government action predictable or serve any other worthy purpose. The value of predictability is not absolute. It can be overridden by other considerations of public policy. Such an override may be justified, in particular, when a modification of rules promises to be a better means of attaining specific aims than a rule that is currently in place.

As an approach to adjudication and regulation, pragmatism is defensible on its own terms as long as the engineering agency, be it a Commission or a Court, pursues worthy objectives through rational means. Since pragmatism does not espouse faith in formal values, such as the pedigree of legal enactments from their relevant sources, its claim to legitimacy depends entirely on the substance of its policies. Predictability features as one substantive value among others. Even though not absolute, it may be achieved in different ways. In the case of the ECJ, the overall neoliberal drift inherent in its jurisprudence allows one even to anticipate, within limits, various moves and turns that would remain completely unpredictable were one to rely on precedent and existing doctrine alone. The basic question would then be whether the Court's jurisprudence pursues worthy aims with adequate means.

In a way, the new economic due process may appear to be desirable for new Member States, for it opens the door for them to benefit from comparative competitive advantage.[104] Nonetheless, the respective leveling down ("social dumping"), which is to be expected from the disempowerment of trade unions, is of questionable political merit, to say the least. It is part of a shift in the integration process whereby "organized economies are no longer [considered as] equally valid production regimes."[105] Rather, the very existence of differences between and among systems of socially sustainable capitalism is taken to present obstacles to market integration. The Union pushes the Member States towards reforming their economies along the lines of universal economic liberalization. Even outside the Court's jurisprudence, institutional differences are increasingly perceived to be obstacles to competition.[106] This is new. So long as neither the Commission nor the Court targeted the institutions

[103]*See* Dworkin, *supra* note 27, at 151-164.

[104]Accordingly, the Member States were very much split in these cases along the "old" and "new" divide. *See* B. Bercusson, *The Trade Union Movement and the European Union: Judgement Day*, 13 ELJ 279 (2007).

[105]Höpner & Schäfer, *supra* note 6, at 8.

[106]*See id.*

of organized economies, such as an established system of industrial relations, the competition between and among Member States may have reinforced the respective differences provided that those produced relative strengths.

This shift may signal the adoption of commendable public policy. Determining whether this is indeed the case would require, however, a political choice. The ECJ is not the type of institution to which one would primarily entrust this choice. Indeed, one would not even do so provisionally, for the decisions by the ECJ affecting Treaty interpretation are officially subject to reversal only through Treaty amendment. Owing to the heterogeneity of national interests, it is highly unlikely that these amendments will come to pass.[107] But even if they should, it still remains unclear whether the Court would be responsive to constraints signaled by Treaty language. At this point, it is important to take into account what happened to the authority of constitutional law in the European Union. As I tried to point out above, owing to the prevalence of *idealization*, constitutional amendments have been transformed into means of refurbishing, rather than of constraining existing relations of power. Moreover, the European political process does not offer the forum where the peoples of Europe could debate and select the economic and social model relevant to their future. The *de-politicization* of decision-making renders such a debate impossible. Hence, the triad of idealization, de-politicization and economic due process gives rise to a syndrome of disempowerment that may well become explosive in the long term,[108] at any rate in the case where the European economy should experience a downward slope.

If the overall quality of political objectives is cast into doubt, then the rule of law can no longer be said to be in good shape, pragmatically understood. As pointed out above, from a pragmatist perspective everything hinges on the substantive soundness of objectives and the rationality of the means to pursue them. Given that this decisive question cannot be settled by acceptable means, even from that point of view, the rule of law has already taken a turn for the worse in the European Union.

[107] The matter has been rightly pointed out by F. W. Scharpf, *Reflections on Multilevel Legitimacy*, 07/3 MPIfG Working Paper at 11-12 (2007).

[108] On the unfeasibility of attempting to unify different aspirations and institutional models of Welfare capitalism in Europe, *see* F. W. Scharpf, *Notes Towards a Theory of Multilevel Governing in Europe*, 00/5 MPIfG Discussion Paper at 22 (2000).

6. Conclusion: Farewell Monnet?

Any critical legal analysis, unless belonging to the genre of critical legal studies proper,[109] is expected to conclude with suggestions for improvement. Hence, I would like to sketch, in conclusion, three options, the sequence of which betrays the author's diffident penchant for utopianism.

In my opinion, a mild reply to economic due process would employ the preliminary reference procedure in order to challenge the precedential authority of questionable rulings.[110] This strategy would avoid challenging the Court decisions head on and thus work around the disruptive effect involved in raising the specter of nullity. In its most provocative form, nonetheless, the strategy would confront the ECJ with its own reasoning and have national judges ask whether the ruling, even though relevant for the parties, relied on too shaky foundations in order to establish a general rule. In milder form, the ECJ could simply be encouraged to distinguish cases on factual grounds.

In recommending that this strategy be chosen, I do not want to deny that Court documents issued with the purport to be preliminary rulings can be null and void. In fact, with regard to the cases at hand, the respective claim can be made for reasons internal to European Union law and, hence, on a basis different from the *Solange*-logic that has come to pervade the relationship between Highest Courts in the multilevel system.[111] The manipulation of existing law in the spirit of dogmatic pragmatism is not a sound basis for the creation of legal norms. For pragmatic reasons, nonetheless, it may be preferable to refer specific questions to the ECJ by signaling that disregard of preliminary rulings might be the option that national courts may want to resort to, should the ECJ fail to address their concerns adequately.

Alternatively, the Member States themselves may decide to adopt a political opt-out mechanism that is also to be applied to rulings by the ECJ. A proposal to this effect has been made by Fritz Scharpf.[112] Its relative modesty suggests pessimism as regards political mobilization at the Union level. According to Scharpf, an opt-out strategy would help Member States to defend concerns

[109]*See* M. Fischl, *The Question that Killed Critical Legal Studies*, 17 Law & Soc. Inquiry 779 (1993).

[110]Of course, the questions regarding precedent would have to be officially addressed as questions of Treaty interpretation. But it cannot be denied that early on the ECJ established a system of precedent. *See* Case 283/81, CILFIT and Lanificio di Gavardo SpA v. Ministry of Health [1982] ECR 3415, at paras. 13-14.

Conceivably, there is one even milder reply. It would permit the offending Member States to pay off damages to the firms that were allegedly harmed by them. The illegality of their behaviour would stem from failing to protect the interest of transnational service providers. I do not want to entertain this possibility here.

[111]*See* Case 45036/98, Bosphorus Hava Yollari Turizm ve Ticaret Anonim Sirketi v. Ireland [2005] ECHR 440.

[112]*See* Scharpf, *supra* note 107, at 16.

that reflect peculiarities of their very own situation in the European Union (the Austrian system of University admission is a case in point). Individual Member States should be granted an exemption, however, only if they find the support of a certain number of others. The prospect of an opt-out later "might facilitate agreement in the Council on new EU legislation and thus strengthen the political modes of EU policy-making."[113]

Even though I find this proposal attractive, I wonder whether it would not open the door to enduring and profound fragmentation. Alternatively, one may want to consider not an opt-out but a full legislative override by the Council. It seems to be the only way to end the arrogation of prerogative power by the ECJ with regard to Treaty interpretation, which according to seventeenth century Republican theory would have struck one as "tyrannical," anyway.[114] The Council of the European Union would be the appropriate institution to address the concerns raised by the ECJ's ill-founded endorsement of economic due process. The relevant questions cut deeply into Europe's political economy. Hence, a decision by a simple majority (of fourteen) may not be enough to quell doubts by the new Member States about the old guard ripping them of their comparative advantage. Hence, some supermajority, for example 17 states, may be adequate to the task. Introducing at least the override of Court decisions into the primary law of the Union is a matter of great exigency, in particular if the first strategy fails to have any effect. Hence, the Member States may in this case want to rely on the root operating system of European Union law, that is, public international law, in order to introduce the override rule *qua* abrogating regional customary law. In fact, responding to the Court's arrogation of authority by creating new law is the only manner of preventing acquiescence with its rulings to count as authoritative treaty interpretation through subsequent practice by contracting parties.[115]

Finally, the emerging crisis may also be indicative of the fact that the Monnet model of European integration has finally run its course.[116] From the outset, this model was not supposed to be maintained forever. The experience with the constitutional treaty has taught that constitutionalization from above creates recalcitrance by European peoples. Conversely, the disgraceful failure of European governments to lend amended supranational arrangements the semblance of a constitution leaves an opportunity for the

[113] *Id.*, at 16.

[114] *See* Q. Skinner, Liberty before Liberalism 70 (1998): "[…] [I]f you live under any form of government that allows for the exercise of prerogative or discretionary powers outside the law, you will already be living as a slave."

[115] *See* Art. 31(3)(b), Vienna Convention on the Law of Treaties, United Nations Treaty Series, vol. 1155, at 331.

[116] *See* Höpner & Schäfer, *supra* note 6, at 23, arguing that "integration by stealth" has reached its limits.

peoples of Europe to re-appropriate constitutional ideas for themselves. The pursuit of the Community method is creating a dangerous impasse. Adopting a real constitution may be the only way out.

Adam Czarnota

On Post-Communist Transformation, Structural Corruption and Dealing with the Past as a Constitutional Process

1.

The subject of this chapter is one of the most controversial topics that arise in post-dictatorships and is usually referred to as transitional justice or dealing with the past. This problem cannot be reduced to dealing with the remnants or legacies of former communist regimes. This year, the post-communist world will celebrate the twentieth anniversary of the roundtable talks that started the process of transfer of power and triggered all the subsequent changes. It is worthwhile to look at transitional justice not from the narrow perspective of criminal law or criminology but as a constitutional process for the new polity whose mode of operation is the rule of law.

In the Western legal tradition, law was not a tool for dealing with historical justice. It was a well-designed tool for coping with injustice on a smaller scale. At the same time, the concept of historical justice was also present in Western culture but was conceptually separated from normal justice. This distinction is represented by the two different goddesses that were responsible for justice in antiquity. In ancient Greece, they were known as *Dike* and *Themis* and, in ancient Rome, *Nemesis* and *Justitia*.

The first dealt with the historical and/or divine dimension of justice, quite often referred to as providence or fate. The realisation of this dimension of justice was left in God's hands. It appears that the criteria for this type of justice were perceived as different from those applied and developed by human reason. The realisation of this type of justice was left to other times, usually outside human time. It related to the apocalyptic character of total justice.

Bogdan Iancu (Ed.), The Law/Politics Distinction in Contemporary Public Law Adjudication, 169-185.

Nemesis was presented as the goddess of justice and revenge, a personification of wrath and punishment. This is beautifully presented in the fascinating engraving, *Nemesis*, by Albrecht Dürer.

Themis and *Justitia* were goddesses of the human dimension of justice. In their administration of justice, they were more understanding of and softer towards human errors. They are usually presented as blind. On the one hand, this shows a commitment to the main principle of human justice, namely the impartial application of law. At the same time, however, that blindness shows the limitations of justice embodied in human legal systems. These limitations are due to the limitations of human knowledge. How can we do justice when our knowledge about events and especially past events is limited? That is why human legal systems contain so many principles that limit justice temporally, such as statutes of limitations, the presumption of innocence, and non-retroactivity. But this is only part of the issue. Another aspect is the apocalyptic character of the type of justice exemplified by *Nemesis* and *Dike*. Until our time, there was no attempt to find a legal approach to the process of political and social change. That was a matter of fate and divine retribution. The demand for legal redress for the communist past is based on a refusal to accept blind fate.

It appears to me that, in discussions on the extremely complicated problem of dealing with the past, the line is still drawn between those who adhere to the limited concept of human justice – as represented by *Justitia* and *Themis* – and those who look at it from the point of view of historical justice – Justice with a capital J – based on principles that are considered universal in time and space and should be implemented regardless of the social cost.

In this chapter, I argue that 'dealing with the past' is based on a combination of two perspectives and that the process of building bridges between these two perspectives requires a new approach in legal thinking and, more importantly, institution building. The combination of two different strategies and institutions is needed in order to deal with the wrongs of the past. The traditional legal approach is not satisfactory, and we can observe the creation of a new type of quasi-judicial institution. The problem of 'transitional justice' or 'dealing with the past' is about the future of the societies concerned. The problem of coming to terms with the communist past is a constitutive matter for post-communist societies. It is also a constitutional problem for the new post-communist systems, and different approaches to the problem have had an impact on the form and structure of new regimes in the region.

The problem of dealing with the past is unfortunately not only theoretical, notwithstanding the fact that it is fascinating to theoreticians. The interrelations between dealing with the past and theories of regime change, between the rule of law and constitutionalism, can and should be discussed together.

Each society that has undergone a regime transition has faced the problem of transitional justice, particularly societies in transition from dictatorial to democratic regimes. However, since even in those transitions the main problem was how to deal with mass violation of human rights, the issue was mainly one of criminal law. The problems faced in the case of the South African transition from apartheid are more complicated, since the problems that have to be dealt with relate to the beneficiaries of the regime and the redistribution of property rights as well as gross violations of human rights.

It is true that a universal problem faced by all societies in transition from authoritarian rule is how to build a democratic culture that respects human rights. In this context, the problem of dealing with the past as a constitutional process for all societies in transition from authoritarian rule is a universal one. The specificity of 'dealing with the past' in post-communist societies is the enormous complexity of the problem, due to the peculiarity of the communist system. One of the most visible legacies of that peculiarity is the need to cope with the problem at the same time as rebuilding the entire institutional setting.

From a practical point of view, dealing with the past can be divided into four parts:

1) relations between the new and old regimes;
2) the problem of decommunisation and lustration;
3) the problem of retributive justice for crimes committed under the old regime;
4) the problem of restitution of property after communism.

The specific type of communism and specific form of exit from communism determined the relationship between the old and new regimes and the policies for 'dealing with the past'.[1]

Apart from Romania, the transfer of power in other former communist Central and Eastern European states was peaceful and was accomplished through negotiations. Old communist elites who were still in control of the state apparatus decided to co-opt representatives of the previously illegal opposition. The two most spectacular roundtable talks took place in Poland, which established the model, and then in Hungary. Other countries at least tried to follow the established pattern. The very fact that negotiations took place between representatives of communist ruling elites and representatives of the opposition provided the former with the legitimacy that had been denied to them from the beginning of the regimes. At the same time, roundtable talks

[1] *See* the very illuminating book by Pavel Câmpeanu, Ceauşescu. Lata odliczane wstecz (2004) (original Romanian title: Ceauşescu, anii numărătorii inverse (2002)), in which this distinguished Romanian sociologist shows the connection between the installation and dismantling of certain types of communist regimes.

morally compromised representatives of the former opposition who took part in negotiations. In other words, communist elites acquired some social capital at the expense of the opposition due to the negotiations.

In the process of the negotiations, the communist elites naturally tried to guarantee themselves impunity and immunity, as well as the best positions in the new regimes. At the unique historical moment when the negotiations took place, nobody thought that communism would collapse so quickly, and oppositional elites were therefore ready to strike a deal. The roundtable talks established a breaking point between the old communist and new post-communist regimes. In other words, the agreements achieved in the roundtable talks established a basis for legal continuity between the regimes, with consequences for the new legal and political order. Symbolically, as stated in the constitutional amendments, the new law-governed state was born as a legitimate child of the communist regime that had been unlawfully installed. Old communist regimes that had operated with no regard for the law thus posthumously received the legitimacy denied to them since 1944.

The new post-communist regimes tried to address the problem of continuity and at the same time emphasise the lack of continuity by adopting, with rather limited results, a policy of drawing a 'thick line' between the present and the past, as it was described by the first non-communist prime minister in post-communist Central and Eastern Europe, Tadeusz Mazowiecki. The idea was to involve all citizens in the process of building a new political and social order after communism and, at the same time, to stress that it would be a new political and social structure, not simply a continuation of the former regime.

It should be stressed that different countries adopted different approaches to the past and that they did so inconsistently and with varying results. It is probably possible to make some generalisations based on the type of exit from communism. The later the exit took place and the less organised the opposition, the more radical the rhetoric, though not necessarily the policies. Nevertheless, in all countries the new ruling elite faced the issue of doing justice to the past. The question that nearly all societies asked themselves was whether it was better to a draw a thick line under the past and forget it or to face up to the wrongdoings of the past.

This is an important moral question, and the answer has been different in different societies. To a great extent, the answer actually given depended on the balance of political forces within the political elite. In each post-communist society, the answer was usually mixed, meaning that some policies were adopted to cope with at least some elements of the difficult past.

The issue is not what type of strategy was adopted to deal with the past but what legal strategy. Law represents authority and law is authority. Law can authoritatively condemn or authoritatively vindicate. Law is not a stranger to the issue of dealing with the past, since its very essence relates to experiences from the past and the correction of past wrongdoing. Law as a system of norms and institutions is a mechanism for systematic remembrance and forgetting. During the two-thousand-year history of the Western legal tradition, a very impressive arsenal of techniques has been developed in order to remember but also forget (statutes of limitation, *nullum crimen, nulla poena sine lege*, etc.) What is important is the fact that law possesses authority and that both remembering and forgetting are approved by the authority of law. This means that individuals and groups can remember and not forgive but that it is impossible to start a new legal action.

This particular characteristic of law, namely its authority, plays an important role in all possible strategies for dealing with the past. What is important is the approach that is adopted by the law. I will deal with this issue in the second part of this chapter.

After regime change due to the loss of war or negotiations, new elites always face the same problem: what to do with the wrongdoings of the past? The question is not so dramatic when the collapse of regimes is due to revolution or defeat by an external power. The outcome in this situation is always a condemnation of the past and the imposition of the victors' justice. Usually, criminal law is used in order to show the criminal character of the former regime and show trials play an educational role for the new political and social community.

More complex problems in relation to dealing with the past are faced by the new political elites when regime change is achieved through negotiations. On the one hand, the old power is being recognised as a partner and is usually interested in granting itself general amnesty for past wrongdoing. On the other hand, there is pressure for justice and revenge from below and from some factions within the new political elites. The legal strategies adopted are never perfect, but we can evaluate them from the perspective of their contribution to new normative values.

In all post-communist countries, there is always a combination of retributive justice (criminal trials, lustration and decommunisation) and restorative justice (restitution of property, usually referred to as reprivatisation, and rehabilitation of victims). Surprisingly, I do not know of any political or legal strategy that focused on the creation of a public discussion about the operating mechanism of communist regimes and the involvement of all citizens in sustaining that regime; in other words, a strategy that focused not only on revenge and stigmatisation but also on public truth telling and reconciliation: a real coming to terms with the past by the entire society by overcoming the key divisions within society. An interesting question concerns why there was not a single attempt to stimulate a public debate about the involvement of citizens in the operation of communist regimes. The only attempt of this kind in the post-communist world of Central and Eastern Europe was the *Enquête Kommission* in the Federal Republic of Germany.[2]

[2] *See* A. James McAdams, Judging the Past in Unified Germany 88-123 (2001).

There is no doubt that those who committed crimes under the former regimes should face the law and also punishment. At the same time, criminal law cannot play the role of public truth telling and reconciliation. Mark Osiel, the American socio-legal scholar, wrote a book in which he tried to show, on the basis of the Argentinean example, that criminal show trials (not in the Stalinist sense but in accordance with the rule of law, publicity notwithstanding) are able to implant liberal values in society, especially with regard to the observance of human rights.[3] He follows the theory of Emile Durkheim that, in modern societies based mainly on organic solidarity (division of labour), the function of the criminal law is the reinstatement of basic accepted values in society.

I have doubts about this, as there are limits to what criminal law and criminal procedure can achieve, and this is not such a bad thing. Opening up the procedure would also open space to abuse the law. Even Osiel admits at one point that criminal law plays a limited role.

Communist regimes were based on controlling society not only through the party cells in all factories and organisational units but also through permanent surveillance by the secret police and its collaborators. The extent of the control was not the same in every country in the communist camp. Some societies were under more relaxed surveillance, but the so-called 'problem of the files' nevertheless exists. The legal strategies adopted by the relevant countries vary. The most radical was the strategy adopted in the former DDR, where every person, and not only citizens, has a right to see his or her own files, with the names of the secret collaborators not being deleted. From the media, we have learnt about the personal tragedies involving brothers spying on brothers and husbands on wives. It is true that such a strategy clears the atmosphere, but I do not think that it stimulates public discussion about the mechanisms of the past and our involvement in sustaining the regime. It still has a private character, as it involves a private citizen having access to his or her file through the Gauck Commission. In an interview given to the Polish weekly magazine *Wprost*, Joachim Gauck said that 'there is only one way to finish the problem with the files', meaning the way adopted by Germany. This might stop the use of files in political battles and for short-term political gains, but it does not have healing potential for an entire society.

Other countries, such as Poland, adopted a middle-of-the-road approach. This approach is based on the sequestration of the archival records of the secret services in the Institute for National Remembrance. Every citizen has a right to apply for access to his or her file, but the decision is taken on the basis of whether the applicant was victimised. Only applicants recognised as victims of the regime are granted access to their files. At the same time, 'victim' status is very broad and plays the role of positive lustration. Again, this is a private approach that excludes national debate. Pseudo-debate exists in the form of typical journalistic sensationalism.

---

3 *See* M. Osiel, Law and Collective Memory (1997).

Other legal strategies, such as decommunisation and lustration, also play a very limited role in societies dealing with the past. I can understand the security reasons behind the lustration of state officials, but generally the entire process of lustration has failed everywhere. It has been used mainly in political battles and for political gains. Lustration and decommunisation also play a role in curtailing discourse on the operation of the communist system. Instead of encouraging a serious societal discussion, lustration limits the discourse by selecting a few scapegoats. Of course, the level of responsibility of the members of the *Politburo* was higher than that of members of the Communist Party, but if we think about facing the difficult past 'in the service of life', all levels of responsibility and operation must be the object of societal discussion. The question remains whether this is possible in case of the former communist countries. In some parts of the world there were attempts to do precisely this, via the establishment of so-called truth commissions, such as the comprehensive process of facing its difficult past undertaken by South African society in the institutional form of the Truth and Reconciliation Commission.

It appears that the unwillingness to adopt the strategy of public debate in order to deal with the past in post-communist societies is related to the character of communist society. The communist system was characterised by moral compromise and changes of role from perpetrator to victim and back to perpetrator. A lack of clear moral borders, changes of role and moral compromises engaged in by all but a few righteous persons all create a situation in which dealing with the past in the form of public cleansing cannot be carried out by the generation that grew up during communist times.

This does not mean that it cannot be attempted by creating a new type of legal institution that accommodates elements of both *Justitia* and *Nemesis*. Only in such a way is it possible to deal with the past as a constitutional process. Restricting the confrontation of the past to traditional legal mechanisms, based mainly on criminal law and retributive justice, is not a good approach. There is a need for a new type of quasi-judicial institution.

2.

The Polish sociologist Zdzisław Krasnodębski has formulated a thesis about two transformations. He claims that two transformations – one open and transparent, the other hidden – actually took place in Poland.

The open and transparent one was the transformation of the institutional structures of the communist state into the formal institutions of parliamentary democracy. The second parallel transformation – the hidden one – was the process of local modification and concretisation of the new institutions of the state and market economy and their rules to work in the interests of the transformed communist elites and co-opted segments of former oppositional elites.[4] Earlier and in a different way, specifically in relation to political life, another Polish sociologist, Andrzej Rychard, formulated a thesis about two levels or scenes of conducting politics in post-communist Poland.[5]

I accept the thesis that there were and continue to be two dimensions to social life. The standard criticism of such a broad thesis is that transformation is only a partly controlled process, that it is rather a spontaneous process and that the spontaneous dimension creates side-effects that later figure as the phenomena that Krasnodębski classifies as a hidden transformation. Potential critics presenting such a position could be partly right. Post-communist transformation is a spontaneous process, but only partly. It is enough to control crucial strategic points in order to have an influence on nearly the entire process of transformation. That does not mean, of course, that someone or some centre is able to control *all* elements of transformations but, as noted above, it is enough to have an influence on the outcome of transformation. Such a position has nothing to do with a 'conspiratorial vision of history' but rightly stresses the possibility of constructing social reality after communism. Everybody who studies the matrix of communist societies and states knows that there was a similar dichotomy present during state socialism: visible and invisible dimensions of life. Invisible factors were more important than visible ones. The entire system was constructed around that double structure. Institutions known from communist history had their façade and their real content. It is difficult to argue why such a double structure would not survive the transfer of power.

I support the thesis as articulated by Krasnodębski that there were and continue to be two dimensions to transformation. The next logical step is to identify that hidden dimension of transformation. From a common sense approach, all processes and mechanisms that are not open and transparent are hidden. The hidden dimension of the post-communist transformation has a different meaning. It relates to the creation of a network of groups with vested interests that used the formal, open institutions to promote and pursue those interests. It means that the hidden dimension of the transformation is in symbiosis with its open dimension and that legally formal and *prima facie* open institutions become in time dependent for their functioning on the hidden elements of the transformation. It means that these two dimensions became functionally interdependent on each other in fulfilling their respective functions. In other words, the hidden structure of the transformation became structural and constitutive for the entire process.

---

4 Z. Krasnodębski, *Postkomunizm – życie po życiu [Postcommunism – Life after Life]*, Rzeczpospolita, 8 May 2004.

5 A. Rychard, *Polityka i społeczeństwo w Polsce: ewolucja porządku instytucjonalnego' [Politics and Society in Poland: Evolution of the Institutional Order]*, *in* E. Mokrzycki, A. Rychard & A. Zybertowicz (Eds.), Utracona dynamika? O niedojrzałości polskiej demokracji [Lost Dynamism? On the Immaturity of the Polish Democracy] 147 (2002).

The transformation was officially about the creation of new democratic institutions that would be open and transparent in their operation. It was the popular belief and conviction that these institutions would establish a framework for an open public space after communism. The operation of new institutions would be based on certain transparent legal rules that would work in an impersonal way. Expectations were very high but were also based on realism. The main arguments used in the discussions within the political ruling class after 1989 were opposed to experimentation and the choice of a 'third way'. The new ruling elites chose to transplant institutions and recipes from developed free-market liberal democracies in the West. Free-market economics, human rights, the rule of law and democracy were the order of the day. The only perceived problem was that the cooks were not properly trained and did not know what ingredients should be used in order to prepare the menu. Understanding these ideas was rather simple and was connected to the belief and conviction that, after an initial period of introduction of institutional change, there would be a healthy system with a strong and open public space for discussion and strong but controlled state institutions that would be able to implement and guarantee the rule of law, justice and the realisation of the public good and, moreover, that the operation of the state institutions would be based on formal rationality as described by Max Weber. This blueprint was not implemented. The question, therefore, is: what went wrong? Why does such a dark picture emerge from popular consciousness as well as from the sophisticated analysis of social scientists such as sociologists, political scientists, and academic lawyers dealing with the operation of legal system?[6]

3.

In searching for the answer to this question, social scientists look back to the beginning of transformation as the source of future problems and dissatisfaction. They differ, however, on when to locate the beginning of the transformation. Some claim that it started in 1989 with the transfer of power from the communists, and a minority claims that it started much earlier, at the beginning of the 1980s, with the introduction of martial law in Poland by General Jaruzelski's government.

Without empirical evidence, we cannot solve this problem at the moment. However, it is not that important from our point of view. What is important

[6] *See*, for instance, J. Hausner & M. Marody (Eds.), Jakość rządzenia: Polska bliżej Unii Europejskiej? [The Quality of Governing. Poland Closer to the European Union?] (2000); Mokrzycki *et al.*, *supra* note 5; M. Jarosz, Władza, przywileje, korupcja [Power, Privilege, Corruption] (2004); J. Mariański (Ed.), Kondycja moralna społeczeństwa polskiego [The Moral Condition of Polish society] (2002); Z. Krasnodębski, Demokracja peryferii [Peripheral Democracy] (2003).

is that there is a general consensus among social scientists that something went wrong with the transformation process and that the outcome of this is a problem with the functioning of state institutions.

The problem with the transformation is that it was and is not restricted to politics but that it also includes the economy and all other areas of life. Most important from the point of view of its effects have been the connections between politics and the economy. The political class chose the wrong model of economic transformation. The same model for the transformation of property relations was implemented in all former communist countries.

We can solve the problem of who was responsible for the adoption and implementation of this model. There are two positions. Some claim that it was Western agents and forces interested in realising their interests in the countries that were joining the world market.[7] The second position is that the political class in post-communist countries is responsible and that it was interested in this model rather than another model of change in the system of property rights.[8] The collapse of the Iron Curtain opened up all the countries of the former COMECON to global market forces, but this did not predetermine their choice of economic policy.

Again, it is not my intention to solve this problem. More important is the outcome of the adopted model of economic change. One effect is a hybrid economic system in which one part functions according to the classic model of the free market, while another part still operates according to the old communist system of hand-steering the economy.

The same hybrid system functions at the level of the state. The state functions on the basis of contradictory principles and is essentially dysfunctional. Different types of rationalities regulate the functioning of different parts of the state. At the most general level, the state still performs the functions of the owner, is involved in governance of the economic units and is also involved in the redistribution of wealth. On the other hand, the state itself has created different types of funds (or special economic agencies) in order to limit its own involvement in economic decision making and processes. Jadwiga Staniszkis, in my opinion the most interesting commentator on the post-communist transformation, has written about the commercialisation of the state's economic assets, including the commercialisation of its traditional functions. This commercialisation process does not mean that the state is free

[7] D. Wincenty, *Transformacja, prywatyzacja i czołowi aktorzy [Transformation, Privatisation and the Main Actors]*, 13 Studia Polityczne (2002); J. R. Wedel, Collision and Collusion. The Strange Case of Western Aid to Eastern Europe (2001).

[8] *See* A. Zybertowicz, W uścisku tajnych służb: upadek komunizmu i układ postnomenklaturowy [In the Hug of the Secret Services: The Collapse of Communism and the Post-Nomenklatura System] (1993); A. Zybertowicz, *Demokracja jako fasada: przypadek III R.P [Democracy as Façade. The Third Polish Republic Case]*, *in* Mokrzycki *et al.*, *supra* note 5, at 173-216; J. Staniszkis, Postkomunizm. Próba opisu [Postcommunism. An Attempt at Description] (2001).

from economic responsibilities. On the contrary, what changed is that formally commercialised state economic assets have fallen prey to the politically dominant group. In other words, commercialisation is connected to political capitalism, a system in which political position translates easily and without any restriction not only into the extraction of economic rents but also into a dominant economic position.

Contradictions in the economic and political system have an impact on the social fabric and are reinforced again by society. After fifteen years of transformation, it is justifiable to say that the system of change did not achieve the expected aims. Instead, a system based on different types of rationality is being created. Observers from outside can easily see a façade that is composed of institutions that, from a distance, look like typical institutions of Western free-market liberal democracy. From within, it is possible to observe the operation of the hidden dimensions of the transformation.

The different rationalities and hidden dimensions of the entire system translate to the legal system as well. It might be more appropriate to say that the legal system itself reflects that double character of the transformation and is deeply anchored in systemic contradictions.[9] Law plays the role of a regulator of the transformation process in the economy and a tool that provides a framework for planning and controlling these processes.

4.

Legal scholars usually look at legal texts. Only a small fraction (including legal sociologists) are interested in the *functioning* of the legal system. This raises a methodological problem with respect to finding the right approach to the hidden dimensions of the operation of law. This is due to the dominant role of legal positivism as a paradigm for law and also for thinking about law. What captures the interest of lawyers are existing legal principles, norms and rules: not the substance or functioning of law but only positive law.

After World War II, Professor Gustav Radbruch formulated his famous thesis that legal positivism disarmed German lawyers in the face of Nazism. This severe criticism of legal positivism was made by a former Weimar Republic minister of justice and law professor who for many years had been a prominent legal positivist in Germany.

The dominant type of legal theory under communism was simplistic legal positivism with a thin Marxist sauce. Marxist philosophy provided a sort of superficial rhetoric but was not taken seriously by either legal academia or the legal profession. Vulgar legal positivism was functional and instrumental

[9] *See* examples regarding the privatisation law in Poland, *in* C. Kosikowski, *Prawne aspekty prywatyzacji w Polsce [Legal Aspects of Privatisation in Poland)*, *in* M. Jarosz (Ed.), Pułapki prywatyzacji [Traps of Privatisation] 41 (2003).

to justifying any new type of regulation. There was no questioning of the 'holders of power'. Acceptance of any command of the sovereign was the rule. The entire legal system, including legal education, was based on this communist version of vulgar legal positivism. There were a few individual lawyers representing a non-conformist approach, but they were outside the system of the institutions of justice. In the process of implementing the lustration law in Poland, we learnt how broadly and deeply the legal profession had been infiltrated by the secret services and how many judges, prosecutors and members of the bar had collaborated with the secret services (although this contravened official professional ethics). Such a legal profession does not guarantee the autonomy of law.

Did something change after the collapse of communism? On the surface it looks like it did, since one of the first constitutional amendments was the introduction of the concept of the 'democratic law-governed state' and the implementation of a bill of rights guaranteeing liberties that had been suppressed during communism. The implication is that freedom and democracy will flourish when the holder of political power, the government, is governed by law and citizens have guarantees relating to the enjoyment of their rights. After fifteen years of transformation, it is possible to say that the entire ideology of the post-communist transformation can be reduced to a few keywords, such as: democracy, the rule of law, rights and – later – one big keyword that, if it did not replace at least overshadowed the former three, namely the market economy. This combination is what created the problem in practice. The rule of law means that law plays a particular role in society by providing a framework for actions and acting as a medium for communication. To play such a role as a basis for expected rational behaviour, law has to be relatively stable and relatively autonomous from politics and the economy.

There were structural obstacles to the implementation of the autonomy of law, which were of a different nature than the above-mentioned character of the legal profession. Post-communist transformation requires changes in the institutional framework of state and society. The economic changes – the process of building the market – is carried out by the holder of political power. Decisions about the commercialisation and privatisation of state assets are taken by the government. This should not sound alarming, as the same occurs in the process of privatisation in market economies. In fact, it is not the same, as in market economies even the most radical privatisation decisions are taken and conducted by the government in a market environment. The market and its institutions operate as relatively autonomous domains in relation to politics. In the former communist countries, market institutions were created from scratch by political decision. The market is still not an autonomous institution. Law played a crucial role in the creation of the market institutions. Due to the character of the transformation itself, there was no room for law as an autonomous system. Law has been an expression of the will of the sovereign with almost no limitations.

So far, so good. If the law of the transformation process was an expression of political will and the legal profession inherited from the communist system a vulgar form of legal positivism, the implementation of the law adopted by the holder of political power should go smoothly. Nothing could be more wrong. Since the beginning of the transformation, there have been complains about the operation of the courts, the public administration and, later, local government. Twenty years after the transition began, the situation is, at least according to public opinion, worse not better.

One factor that we should take into account is that the main element of the transformation that really caused rapid changes in social institutions and the fabric of society consisted of economic changes, especially changes in the distribution of property rights.

The creation of the market economy promised in the so-called Balcerowicz plan had a profound impact on society. This was not only an economic impact but a moral one as well. Implementation of the plan opened up opportunities to become rich quickly and acquire property rights in former state assets. Members of the new political class created laws that established criteria for the commercialisation and privatisation of state-owned assets. The implementation of those laws was subsequently in the hands of the state administration, dependent on its political masters.

The law created by the legislators (parliaments) was of poor normative quality. It did not reflect the rules of a high standard of legislation, and this was only partly due to the huge legislative necessities, namely the need to regulate whole areas of social life under relentless pressures. It is true that the parliaments in all the countries in transition from communism were exceptionally creative and that the number of new statutes adopted was huge. However, the other cause of 'bad law' consisted of vested interests on the part of the ruling class in terms of realising particular interests of their political base and/or certain other groups. One example is Lew Rywin, who proposed a system of regulations on media ownership on behalf of the 'power-holding group' that would have given the Agora Group a dominant position on the market. Rywin's corrupt offer probably represents only the tip of a huge iceberg. The investigation conducted by the special parliamentary commission made public other interesting and not understandable facts, such as the fact that the prime minister at the time knew about the offer and did not inform the minister of justice, the president of the republic also knew about it and did nothing and other less important public officeholders were also aware and did nothing. This also confirmed that the institutions of the state are not oriented towards and not acting in the service of the public good in the difficult process of transformation. People holding the highest public offices advance the interests of their own political support group. This is more than clientelism.[10] Clientelism could work in the public interest when the political system in post-communist countries becomes so crowded with interest groups that they hinder the development of the entire system.[11] András Sajó, the distinguished Hungarian scholar, wrote in relation to post-communist Eastern European countries in transformation that "political corruption is not just about corruption of the public/private sphere, or about bribery in government offices and parties; it constitutes a series of events dictated by the needs of the political structures. It is political in the sense that it is the political structure itself that enables and requires practices that became a structural (constitutive) phenomenon of society."[12] This thesis successfully captures the peculiarities of corruption in the post-communist countries.

Due to the above-mentioned legislative pressures and vested interests, the legislators are in the process of creating bad law. This bad law is full of inconsistencies and contradictions. At the same time, it is very complicated and allows the interested parties and groups to interpret it to their advantage. Another characteristic is the delegation of regulation. The justification given for the delegation of regulation to particular ministers relates to the needs of transformation, but in practice this discretionary delegation is used to advance the realisation of parties' interests under the so-called 'bounty law'. At the same time, governance by means of the discretionary powers of the relevant ministers destabilises the law. So far, all political parties use the existing regulations in a rather loose manner for the realisation of their particular interests while paying lip service to the rule of law.

5.

So far, I have established that the post-communist transformation has a double character, in the sense that it has visible and hidden aspects, and that political corruption is different from the traditional blurred border between the public and private spheres.[13] In addition, as I have mentioned, the law serves a

[10] For an historical overview of the phenomenon of clientelism, *see* A. Mączak, Klientela. Nieformalny system władzy w Polsce i w Europie XVI-XVIII w. [Clientelism. Informal Systems of Power in Poland and Europe from the XVIth to the XVIIIth Century] (1994).

[11] *See* the very insightful paper by A. Zybertowicz, *Anty Rozwojowe Grupy Interesow. Zarys analizy [Anti-developmental Interests Groups. Outline of the Analysis]*, presented to the Polish Sociological Association's Annual Conference, Poznań 2004 (on file with the author).

[12] A. Sajó, *From Corruption to Extortion: Conceptualization of Post-Communist Corruption*, 40 Crime, Law & Social Change 171 (2003).

[13] On the rule of law in Central and Eastern Europe after 1989, *see* A. Czarnota, M. Krygier & W. Sadurski (Eds.), Rethinking the Rule of Law after Communism (2005); and W. Sadurski, A. Czarnota & M. Krygier, Spreading Democracy and the Rule of Law? The Impact of EU

function in the system of structural corruption. The claim that the law is bad law and that is in the background or an outcome of corruption are propositions that can be easily supported.

The question remains: what is the relationship between the law-governed democratic state or the concept of the rule of law and the structural corruption in post-communist states? The rule of law is about transparency, accountability and predictability. The element of predictability is a necessary foundation for rationality. Rationality on the other hand is a necessary precondition for a free-market capitalist economy according to Max Weber. It seems to me that rule of law in post-communist states acts as a façade that masks the structural corruption of the state. After fifteen years of double transformation in which the rule of law played the role of a façade some of the states have arrived at the point where this double role has started to reproduce itself. In such cases, we face a new type of situation in which the system, with a façade and the institutions behind it, is reproducing itself.

Just after the transfer of power in 1989, the new ruling elites agreed on the implementation of the rule of law – understood in a formal, positivistic way and reduced to the concept of legality and the rule of legal texts – in the countries in question. This implementation was signalled by constitutional changes that spelled out that the state was from now on a 'democratic law-governed state' as well as some institutional changes necessary for the implementation of the rule of law. The most important of those changes was the introduction of the independence of the judiciary. In Poland, the National Council of the Judiciary was established as an independent self-governing body. The main function of this body was to safeguard the independent position of the judiciary. In a material sense, the salaries of the judges went up, but not by that much. In effect, independence and irremovability were granted to a professional group that in the communist past had been totally dependent on political power. The former Chief Justice of the Supreme Court of Poland, Professor Strzembosz, believed that the judiciary would clean itself of compromised judges but without pressure being put on the entire profession. This did not happen, and compromised judges are still in their positions. The judges gain institutional and material safeguards and benefits in order to guarantee the independence of judiciary, but they never learn about judicial accountability. One of the social preconditions of the rule of law, independence of the judiciary, was introduced too early in the process of transformation, with serious consequences for the rule of law. This means that the entire court system in Poland is not efficient in general, but it is especially inefficient as far as corruption is concerned. In a number of cases, the statute of limitation already applies and the cases cannot be continued.

In a recent press interview, the Commissioner for Human Rights expressed an opinion broadly shared by the public, namely that 'the judiciary is without ethos'. The outcome of this is a boycott of the celebrations marking the twenty-fifth anniversary of the establishment of the office of the Commissioner for Human Rights by the President of the Constitutional Tribunal and the Chief Justice of the Supreme Court.

Another dimension is corruption among judges. The respectable daily Polish newspaper *Rzeczpospolita* has made public information about the connections between judges and criminals. The cases of one judge from Toruń, who gave a favourable verdict in a criminal case for economic advantage, and a judge from Lublin received especially broad coverage. In both cases, the procedure for the removal of the judges took a long time. In the beginning of 2005, the media made public the scope of corruption within the judiciary in Olsztyn, the capital of one of the north-eastern provinces.

Until the introduction of the lustration law, the number of judges who collaborated with the secret services was unknown. After 1999, the numbers are still not known, but the names of members of the judiciary who returned positive lustration declarations were published in the governmental gazette *Monitor Polski*. Since the Polish lustration law only penalises lies told in the context of the lustration process, they still occupy their position. Attempts to remove them on the basis of a breach of the judicial oath, by means of a disciplinary procedure, have met with vigorous resistance from the profession.

It is possible to mention many other examples of corrupt behaviour by the legal profession and reflect on the causes of such behaviour. It seems to me that the premature introduction of the 'democratic law-governed state' played a crucial role in institutionalisation of the double character of the transformation.

The constitutional provision on the 'democratic law-governed state' was interpreted, by the legal profession, in a narrow positivistic way in accordance with the principle of legality. This narrow interpretation blocked the flexibility necessary for steering the process of transformation but also blocked any possibility of interpreting legal norms from the point of view of their merits or a substantive concept of justice, not to mention the crucial issue of transitional justice. The premature and narrow interpretation of the 'democratic law-governed state' principle allows old networks to smoothly adapt to the new reality and, in some cases, to control it. In other words, the rule of law has played a role in the creation of the double character of the transformation. It gives legitimacy to the new regime, while at the same time its narrow interpretation allows the new institutions and rules to be abused by the hidden networks of interests. One of the latest examples of this concerns the Polish Supreme Court, which adopted a motion stating that judges who had extended the decrees of martial law during communism were obliged 'by law' to do so. This motion, which was adopted in December 2007, now appears in the official book of binding legal principles of the Supreme Court. It shows that new law and 'new' judges provided legitimacy, at least of a formal-legal kind, to actions that could be recognised as illegal (since the relevant decrees were illegally adopted).

The noble principles that were supposed to regulate the operation of the political system were turned into their opposite. The case of the post-communist state in which the actual functioning of the rule of law is completely contrary to normative expectations probably cannot be treated as universally valid, but it is nevertheless worthy of study.

The effect of the double transformation is a peculiar system in which we have ritualistic politics at the level of state institutions, with a democratic façade and a very narrow public sphere controlled by networks of powers. Law plays a role in both cases by safeguarding networks of vested interest as well as by petrifying the ritualistic character of politics and public discourses.

6.

Law is a mechanism for systematic remembering and forgetting and, in dealing with the past, should always be in the service of life to ensure a better present and future. The best way to do this is to deal with the past as part of a constitutional process. As the moral and political philosopher Hanna Fenichel Pitkin says: constitutions are not only something that we *have* but they are also what we *are* and more importantly something that we *do*. By *do* she refers to "the action or activity of constituting – that is, of founding, framing and shaping something anew."[14] Facing and dealing with a difficult past from a legal perspective is part of 'what we do' – reshaping ourselves and our societies.

[14] H. F. Pitkin, *The Idea of a Constitution*, 37 Journal of Legal Education 168 (1987).

Bogdan Iancu*

Constitutionalism in Perpetual Transition: The Case of Romania

1. Post-Accession Constitutionalism-Early Apprehensions

For a very long time after the adoption of the 1991 Constitution, neither public debates nor political disputes were framed in the language and logic of constitutionality or constitutionalism. The local "Guardian of the Constitution" was relegated to a marginal, almost irrelevant position. Justly so, considering that the only major public appearance by the Romanian Constitutional Court for more than a decade had been an early decision legitimatizing the candidacy of the incumbent president for a third consecutive mandate.

It appears therefore surprising that, over the last three years, many public and political debates have suddenly started to be carried out within constitutional parameters. The Constitutional Court began to render decisions with high political stakes, invalidating for instance crucial judicial reform legislation,[1] important provisions of both Houses' Standing Orders,[2] and the

* Versions of this argument have been presented at the *Wissenschaftskolleg zu Berlin* (Thursday Colloquium, December 2007) and the Central European University (Visiting Scholar doctoral seminar lecture, February 2008). I thank all participants for comments and discussions. I thank the *Wissenschaftskolleg* librarians for superb research support and the Central European University for a visiting research grant.

[1] Decizia nr. 375/6 iulie 2005 referitoare la sesizările de neconstituţionalitate a Legii privind reforma în domeniile proprietăţii şi justiţiei, precum şi unele măsuri adiacente (M.Of. nr. 591/08 iulie 2005).

[2] Decizia nr. 601/14 noiembrie 2005 privind constituţionalitatea dispoziţiilor Regulamentului Senatului (M.Of. nr. 1022/17 noiembrie 2005) and DCC 602/14 noiembrie 2005 privind constituţionalitatea dispoziţiilor Regulamentului Camerei Deputaţilor (M. Of. nr. 1027/18 noiembrie 2005).

Bogdan Iancu (Ed.), The Law/Politics Distinction in Contemporary Public Law Adjudication, 187-211.

Law on Access to Personal Files and the Disclosure of the Communist Political Police.[3] The Court has now become a constitutional actor of imposing stature, whose positions are an important part of the larger political equation and can no longer be ignored.

This tide of newfangled judicial activism tracked the acceleration and final stages of pre-accession reforms and arguably reached its peak (in terms of both importance and number of interventions) after the entry into force of the Accession Treaty on 1 January 2007. It coincided with a protracted political-constitutional crisis, which reflects the present and more general crisis of the justice system, for instance within the field of anti-corruption measures.[4] The backsliding of anti-corruption reforms can partly be imputed to the distorted dynamics characteristic of Western-imposed anti-corruption campaigns. Nonetheless, some of the local features, such as consistent manipulation of the rule of law by almost all the institutional actors involved in order to avoid substantive tackling of some cases and issues, cannot be solely attributed to failed policy strategies.

These developments are unsettling. In Romania, the transition to liberal constitutional democracy was publicly presented after the collapse of state socialism as a "return to Europe" and comparisons were ubiquitously made with the modernization process in the nineteenth century. Legal processes of democratic transition in Eastern Europe have always been processes of legislative and institutional "Westernization" and the general opinion, at least among the locals, was that rule-of-law reforms would now be easier and faster. A renewed measure of optimism, especially once the Enlargement gathered pace, seemed indeed justified. Through their "return to Europe" journey, the junior enlargees were to benefit from the benevolent but stern mentorship of the EU Commission and its "political conditionality" *acquis* requirements to nudge them gradually unto a clearly landmarked path to constitutional civility. Accession to the Union was foreseen as the successful completion of constitutionalization.

By the same token, whether a return has taken place, to what Europe has the East returned, and what could be the further implications for the constitutional state, are questions that do not relate only to parochial concerns and eccentricities.[5] The failure of the recent didactic process would also shed legitimate doubts on the future of European constitutionalism itself.

---

[3] Decizia nr. 51/ 31 ianuarie 2008 (M.Of. nr. 95/6 februarie 2008).

[4] This crisis is documented by the disgruntled (and yet ever more deferent in tone) progress reports of the Commission within the framework of the Cooperation and Verification Mechanism. *See* COM (2008) 62 final/2 of 14.2.2008 and COM (2008) 494 final of 23.7.2008, *available at* http://ec.europa.eu/dgs/secretariat_general/cvm/index_en.htm. *See also*, for a detailed and more openly critical view, the report of EU expert Willem de Pauw, *available at* http://www.economist.com/media/pdf/romaniacorruption.pdf (last visited 6 December 2008).

[5] Even though I refer primarily to Romanian developments, a larger case can however be made regarding the impact of the Enlargement on the former communist jurisdictions. *See generally*,

2. Overnight Modernization: Comparative Note on Constitutional Neophytes, Legal Transplants, and Value Systems

In 1870, at the beginning of the modernization reforms, the new ruler of the Romanian Principalities, German Prince Carol of Hohenzollern-Sigmaringen wrote with disdain and disbelief to the *Allgemeine Zeitung* in Augsburg:

> These people, who have for the most part completed their social and political education abroad, totally forgetting the circumstances of their homeland, seek nothing else than to apply here, clad in fantastic-utopian forms, the ideas with which they have been nourished there, without ever considering whether they will fit these realities or not. Thus, this unfortunate country, which had always been subjected to the most cumbersome yoke, has passed all of a sudden from brutal despotism to the most liberal Constitution. In light of all my experiences, I believe this to be a misfortune so much the greater as Romanians do not possess the virtues that are required by a quasi-republican form of government.[6]

Carol was referring to the adoption of the 1866 Constitution, a slightly adapted transplant of the 1831 Belgian liberal model, and to the local liberal elite, which had mandated its adoption. Although harsh, this wholesale indictment of overnight modernization and modernizers was supported by the facts. The disparity between the adopted modern Western practices and the antiquated realities of his new adoptive country must have appeared grotesque to the prince.

To wit, well into the third and fourth decades of the nineteenth century, the administration of justice in the Romanian Principalities of Moldova and Wallachia had followed a Medieval-Oriental pattern. "Enlightened despotism" reforms undertaken in the course of the late eighteenth-century by the princes Constantin Mavrocordat and Alexandru Ipsilanti had sought to remedy some of the worst deficiencies, by introducing court records, mandatory public trials, *res judicata* for judgments more than a century older, and a ban on the sub-delegation of jurisdiction. Some timid attempts to introduce salaried judgeships independent of the chief county administrators were also made.

These earlier reforms were defensive in nature, short-lived, and largely nominal.[7] Nineteenth-century records attest extraordinary trials held in the

---

W. Sadurski, A. Czarnota & M. Krygier (Eds.), Spreading Democracy and the Rule of Law: The Impact of EU Enlargement on the Rule of Law, Democracy, and Constitutionalism in Post-communist Legal Orders (2006).

6 M. Oroveanu, Istoria dreptului românesc şi evoluţia instituţiilor constituţionale [The History of Romanian Law and the Evolution of Constitutional Institutions] 266 (1992). Unless otherwise indicated, the translations are mine.

7 The Calimach Code of 1817, although decisively influenced by the Austrian Civil Code, was redacted in the traditional medieval form of a "pravilă." I am grateful to Professor Daniel Barbu for bringing to my notice the "defensive" character of the early legal modernization

country by the princes themselves. As late as 1827, the situation was still such that a memorandum by Prince Barbu Ştirbey to the Russian consulate drew attention to the system of "legal theft" through which judicial functions were delegated by the higher nobles to their subordinates.[8] The differentiation between judicial, executive, and administrative functions was for the most part practically unknown until 1864.[9]

A contemporaneous source, the *Dissertation* by Constatin Moroiu reveals that, as of 1827, out of the twelve judges in the newly founded judicial departments, no more than four showed up regularly at the sessions. This is not surprising, as the salaries they received were, according to an account, mere "alms."[10] They sought compensation apparently, since, as a critic noted: "judges have law books written on parchment sheets which they twist and turn, just as they wish, to squeeze the money out."[11] Sometimes the "*ispravniks*" (county administrative officers which served as de facto common pleas trial judges) would imprison both plaintiff and defendant, without discrimination, to collect the jail fee from both.[12]

In 1829, the Russian General Mircovici had to ask the *Divan* (Privy Council) of Moldavia to hold sessions in the public building and "not in their houses, as they are accustomed."[13] At about the same time, in Wallachia, another Russian administrator, Ignaty Iakovenko, recounted that one of the noblemen exercising judicial attributions, the Great Hatman, not only held trials at his house but had a private jail there as well. Well into the first half of the century, it was still the custom for those charged with a crime to be brought in heavy irons and neck shackles before the *Divan* and for those seeking redress to first kneel and kiss the hands of the prince (this latter custom was discontinued

processes in the Romanian principalities. *See,* on "defensive modernization," H.-A. Wehler, Deutsche Geselleschaftsgeschichte (Vol.I) – Vom Feudalismus des Alten Reiches bis zur defensiven Modernisierung der Reformära: 1700-1815 [German Social History (Vol.I) – From the Feudalism of the Old Empire to the Defensive Modernization of the Reform Age: 1700-1815].

[8] V. A. Georgescu & P. Strihan, Judecata domnească în Ţara Românească şi Moldova, 1611-1831 [Princely Justice in Wallachia and Moldavia] vol. II, at 161. *See also*, I. Ceterchi (Ed.), Istoria dreptului românesc [The History of Romanian Law] Three Vols., (1980-1987), esp. Vols. II and III.

[9] The Organic Statutes, enactments of constitutional status passed at the behest of the Russian Administrations of the principalities of Moldova and Wallachia during the Russian Protectorate following the Treaty of Adrianople of 1829, included (at the declaratory level) separation of powers principles. For instance, the provision of Article 212 of the Organic Statute for Wallachia, which read: "The separation of two branches of the Government, the gubernatorial and judicial powers, being of the highest necessity for the uprightness of judgments and for the safeguard of justice, will from now on, in all ways, be maintained."

[10] Georgescu & Strihan, *supra* note 8, at 179.

[11] *Id.*, at 170.

[12] *Id.*, at 161, n. 2.

[13] *Id.*, at 177.

only in 1835). Legislation, such as it existed, was unconsolidated. Some newer codifications, as the Calimach Code, since promulgated in Greek, could not be applied in the country.

The magistrates were advised in circulars and decrees to follow always "the virtues of the Heavenly Judge": prudence, kindness, moderation, patience, and evenhandedness. They did not seem to have duly followed the advice, since, as an insight into how the regular trial took place, various princely decrees repeatedly forbade slander, curses, and beatings during the trials. For instance, a reiterated decree provided for caning for those who dared hit a judge, but hastened to add that punishment would only follow if the party rather than the judge had struck the first blow.[14]

As late as October 1944, while serving as a barrister in a dispute between the town of Botoşani and the monastery of St. Nicholas-Popăuţi, Mihail Kogălniceanu, who would shortly thereafter assert himself as one of the main architects of modern Romania, barely managed to obtain leave for a public trial. His successful plea in that particular case would earn him six months of mandatory seclusion in a monastery.[15]

All these matters had begun to irritate in no small measure the young intellectuals returning from their studies abroad animated, as was said at the time, by "the ghost of French disobedience."[16] Yet, the local reality was so remote from their foreign experiences that the language they used seemed alien to the locals: tellingly, they would soon be called *bonjourists*. Conversely, the pretentious mongrel Romanian-French jargon in which they expressed pleas for reform was in part justified by the fact that their native tongue could not fully support, lexically speaking, the new concepts these reformers were seeking to advance.

Nonetheless, by the beginning of the next century, the country was to have a relatively well-functioning modern constitutional and legal system. What Carol had failed to take into account was the cultural impact, namely the locals' "neophyte zeal" to identify with the new system, adopted with mimetic enthusiasm bordering sometimes on self-forgetfulness.[17] Transplants of legal

---

[14] *Id.*, at 180.

[15] *Id.*, at 184.

[16] *Cf.* I. Stanomir, Limbaj şi drept: evoluţia vocabularului constituţional până la 1866 [Language and Law: The Evolution of the Constitutional Vocabulary Until 1866] (2002), Dr. Jur. Dissertation, on file with the Faculty of Law Library of the University of Bucharest.

[17] The metaphor of "neophyte zeal" is used by Constantin and Dinu C. Giurescu in their canonical History of the Romanians to explain why the Romanization of Dacia, conquered by Emperor Trajanus in 106 AD and abandoned by Aurelian after 271 AD, was, albeit so brief, so successful. Romanians are the only Eastern European people who speak a Latin language, in spite of the relatively short duration of the Roman colonization and, moreover, in spite of the fact that the majority of the colonists settled by the Empire in the new province were not even "genuine" Romans. They came overwhelmingly from outside the Italian Peninsula, mostly from

norms are also transplants of values, and constitutional norms or norms of constitutional relevance make in this respect, for obvious reasons, the most taxing demands on legal transfers. It surprising to see how fast the local political and legal system internalized the inner logic of the borrowed institutions. When, in the wake of a failed 1870 pro-republican plot, juries acquitted the revolutionists, attempts were made to abolish the recently introduced jury system, parliamentary debates on the matter referred to the British traditions of the jury system (a bulwark against tyranny, best protection of the subject against despotism, etc.). No references were made to similar medieval local precedents and institutions and, what is of the essence, irrespective of the position on this particular matter, all debaters were situated within the newly transplanted paradigm. Nor was the process purely a one-way road. In 1912, the High Court of Cassation asserted in the course of an ordinary trial, in the absence of express textual authorization in the 1866 constitution, authority to review incidentally the constitutionality of legislation. The decision was very favorably received in France, where two prominent public law authorities of the time, Berthélemy and Jèze promptly reported it in the *Revue du Droit public*.[18]

All this is not to deny that for a long time social realities trailed behind the adopted constitutional-political system. Modernization was, in Romanian and arguably more generally in Eastern European context, a late and incomplete process, halted abruptly in its course by authoritarian dictatorship, fascism, WWII, and state socialism.[19] However, even when discounted by the social effectiveness of legal measures, it is still nothing short of wondrous that a modern legal and functional constitutional system could replace a medieval structure in the span of two generations. In hindsight, the general picture and main contrast presented by the nineteenth-century reforms is that of clarity of purpose and direction, rendered by the local desire and aptitude to emulate a clear normative model, perceived as civilizing and therefore worthy of emulation.

the Oriental provinces of the Empire. The thesis of the two historians is that it was precisely the desire of these provincials to emulate the flourishing civilization of the metropolis, to prove themselves as worthy citizens of the Empire, which determined the success of Romanization. *See* C. C. & D. C. Giurescu, Istoria românilor [History of the Romanians] 98 (1971).

[18] Curtea de Casaţie, hotărârea din 16 martie 1912, partea a 4-a, p.29. *See* comment in H. Berthélemy & G.Jèze, Pouvoir et devoir des tribunaux en général et des tribunaux roumains en particulier de vérifier la constitutionalité des lois à l'occasion des procès portés devant eux [The Purview and Duty of the Judiciary and in Particular of the Romanian Judiciary to Verify the Constitutionality of Legislation in the Course of Ordinary Litigation], RDP 148 (1912).

[19] The current impact of these contradictions is well-captured by András Sajó as "post-communist pre-modernity." A. Sajó, *Becoming "Europeans": The Impact of the EU "Constitutionalism" on Post-Communist Pre-Modernity*, *in* Sadurski et al., *supra* note 5, at 175.

3. Post-Communist Pre-Accession Constitutionalism – Communities of Fate

3.1. Constitutionalization I: The Founding Fathers

Romanian post-communist transition was marked by a violent uprising, followed by a long period of social convulsions and rule by well-consolidated post-communist elites. This context rendered impossible a public debate on the totalitarian past.[20] Since the legitimacy of the Communist period was left unquestioned at the level of constituent discourse, a return to the pre-Communist liberal constitution of 1923 or even a larger public discussion on the legitimacy, purposes, and functions of the new constitution remained the passing concerns of a marginal minority. The drafting debates were monopolized by the field "experts" (existing public law professors, who made a clumsy but swift ideological about-face from the Marxist-Leninist theory of state to the now more lucrative doctrines of the bourgeois rule of law) and the interests of the party in power, the National Salvation Front (an ideologically loose but politically well-consolidated aggregation of interest groups perpetuating the ruling elites).[21]

Hence, constitution-making in 1991 represented a mixture of status-quo entrenchment and "bricolage."[22] The momentary power concerns determined the essential structural features. Among these, the most important arrangements, still relevant nowadays, are:

[20] "Confrontation with the past" has been a marginal matter other than at the level of elite discourse. The Romanian Law on Access to Personal Files and the Disclosure of the Communist Political Police was passed a full decade after the change, in 1999 and inoperable in fact until 2005, when the files were transferred from the custody of the SRI (Romanian Intelligence Service) into that of the CNSAS (National Council for Studying the Former Securitate Archives).

[21] The debates can be consulted in Geneza Constituției României 1991: Lucrările Adunării Constituante [The Genesis of the Romanian Constitution: The Proceedings of the Constituent Assembly] (1998). *See also* A. Iorgovan, Odiseea elaborării Constituției- fapte şi documente, oameni şi caractere; cronică şi explicații, dezvăluiri şi meditații [The Odyssey of Drafting the Constitution: Deeds and Documents, Individuals and Characters; Chronicle and Explanation, Unraveling and Meditation] (1998).

[22] *See.* M. Tushnet, *The Possibilities of Comparative Constitutional Law*, 108 Yale L. J. 1225 (1999). In Tushnet's taxonomy, the general attitude towards foreign law in constitutional adjudication (and constitution-making) can be categorized along three ideal-typical categories, functionalism, expressivism, and bricolage. Whereas functionalism and expressivism reflect coherent constitutional-legal worldviews, bricolage is a sort of unprincipled and playful legal ad-hocery. A bricoleur, in *forma mentis* a primitive, simply "makes do" with whatever tools he has at hand.

1) a popularly elected President with vaguely formulated attributions (a combination which provides simultaneously a strong basis for legitimacy and easy deflection of responsibility);

2) an exceedingly cumbersome legislative process contrasting with constitutional authority for the Government to take, on a plea of necessity, provisional measures of legislative effect by decree – "emergency ordinance" (ensuring an ornamental and inefficient legislative process, easily by-passed through prerogative law-making by the executive); and

3) a very rigid amendment process, requiring both extraordinary concurrent majorities – two-thirds in both Houses and, in case of a divergence, three-fourths in joint plenary session – and a referendum ratification of amendments (to safeguard in perpetuity the initial arrangement).[23]

Some power-allocating arrangements, for instance the provision in Article 143 requiring as a condition of appointment to the Constitutional Court 18 years of experience in the legal academe or practice, merged the gate-keeping and status quo political interests of the moment with a professional-corporatist generational interest of the "experts."

Obversely, the aspects that were not of immediate political interest were left to improvisation. Title II, Chapter 2 of the Constitution (Fundamental Rights and Freedoms), for instance, is a dilettante compilation of classical liberal rights, sometimes generously qualified with limitation clauses, provisos, and redundancies;[24] some aspirational-melancholic remnants of state-socialism[25]; and occasional touches of paternalism (for instance, the State and public authorities "shelter" the right to private property and the right to privacy). The Romanian Ombudsman ("Advocate of the People") is also, for instance, the product of constituent contingency. The Ombudsman appeared somewhat awkwardly and vaguely in the 1991 text, as a probable consequence of an inarticulate desire to follow also "the Scandinavian model." The institution was not established until 1997 due to lack of political interest to pass the necessary implementing legislation, and was shrouded in quasi-obscurity thereafter. Yet, on occasion of the 2003 so-called "Euro-amendments," the term of office for the Advocate of the People was extended by one year and the Ombudsman was given new and more confusing attributions.[26]

[23] In Europe, only the Spanish Constitution provides for a more cumbersome amendment process.

[24] For instance, free speech does not protect for instance, "the defamation of the nation or country"; freedom of conscience, in constitutionally ecumenical spirit, includes an obligation for the denominations to renounce "any forms, means, acts or actions" of enmity in interfaith relations (Arts. 29-30).

[25] The state is for instance under an obligation to ensure the right to a decent standard of life and the right to health care (Arts. 33 & 43).

[26] The Advocate can raise both *objections* regarding the constitutionality of statutes *ex ante*

The further away from the Founding, the more detrimental this strong generational self-preference of the Romanian Founding Fathers becomes. When the political conditions which determined the choice of specific constitutional arrangements obtained, for instance the large, decisive, parliamentary majorities of the 90's and the first part of this decade, the constitution was irrelevant. Until recently, the division of power and the procedures provided for in the fundamental law could be substituted by political domination. As such conditions no longer apply, the constitution becomes politically relevant but, unable to fulfill its stabilizing legal functions, it is transformed into an additional political battle-ground.

3.2. Constitutionalization II: The Extended Family

The next wave of constitutionalization was brought about by the needs of the "political conditionality" *acquis* adoption. Most of these latter-day changes, irrelevant to the population, passed totally unobserved, through the conveyor belt of the legislative process or, more commonly, of governmental ordinances. The preexisting local view of the rule of law as a space of continuous negotiation coincided perfectly with the instrumentalism entailed by the bureaucratic, top-down checklists of the Commission and a broad social and political consensus that whatever was required had to be fulfilled unconditionally. At any rate, the requirement to pass vast amounts of legislation, as such, was in essence perceived as unproblematic, since communism and the vagaries of transition had provided enough evidence that law on the books could turn out to be practically irrelevant.

Having been called upon to determine the constitutionality of Emergency Ordinance 31/2002 regarding the prohibition of organizations and symbols with a fascist, racist and xenophobic character and forbidding the promotion of the cult of persons guilty of crimes against peace and humanity,[27] the Constitutional Court expressed a general feeling. The restriction on the

(abstract review), according to Art. 146(a) and, according to Art. 146(d), an *exception of unconstitutionality* in *ex post* concrete review regarding the constitutionality of specific provisions in laws and ordinances in the course of ordinary litigation. The essential idea behind the institution of concrete review is not to "purify" the system of unconstitutional elements. This purification results incidentally from the defense of concrete fundamental rights by a party who raises the exception and should therefore dispose over the procedure; the Ombudsman is not party to the litigation. *See, generally*, C. L. Popescu, *Avocatul Poporului ca titular al dreptului de sesizare a Curții Constituționale potrivit Constituției revizuite* [*The Attributions of the Obudsman to File Applications for Judicial Review to the Constitutional Court in Light of the Revised Constitution*], 6 Dreptul 54 (2004).

[27] Ordonanță de urgență nr. 31 din 13 martie 2002 privind interzicerea organizațiilor și simbolurilor cu caracter fascist, rasist sau xenofob și a promovării cultului persoanelor vinovate de săvârșirea unor infracțiuni contra păcii și omenirii, M. Of. nr. 214 din 28 martie 2002.

fundamental right to free speech by emergency decree rather than statute and the constitutional requirement of "emergency" were duly met, since they "corresponded to the requirement of the European Union in the field," which had to be "urgently" implemented in order to secure accession, a governmental and national priority.[28]

A better indicator of the general mood came however in 2003, when Romanians turned out to the polls very reluctantly – having been called to validate the so-called "Euro-amendments" to the 1991 Constitution. The duration of the referendum had to be extended at the last minute through emergency ordinance, in order to meet the quorum necessary to validate it. In the end, 55.7% of the registered voters turned out at the poll but 89.7% of them voted in favor of the amendments. The population was naturally uninterested in the substance of constitutional provisions which they had not been meaningfully consulted or informed about and which they perceived as being of only indirect and rudimentary instrumental concern.

However, not all the Euro-changes could follow this ritualistic course, since not all the problems on the ground could be reduced to and quantified purely in terms of legislative and constitutional output quotas. Two areas perceived to be in need of structural changes stood out from the very beginning of the accession process: the combating of corruption and the reform of the judiciary. Both of these phenomena posed onerous perception and conceptual problems from the onset. The exact law/politics configuration of the judiciary reflects always, even in a mature democracy, a careful and negotiated trade-off between the opposed potential dangers of direct political manipulation and – respectively – insulation of corporatist rent-seeking interests from change; how the line is drawn depends on a constellation of factors.[29] In Romanian, and perhaps more generally Eastern European context, this problematic was aggravated, on the one hand, by the self-interested manipulation of the principle of judicial independence by the professional-corporatist interests and, on the other, by the

[28] Decizia nr. 67 din 3 februarie 2005, M. Of. nr. 146 din 18 februarie 2005. In this argument, as one can notice, the constitutional requirement of "emergency" as a condition for justifying an exception to the ordinary legislative process and the necessity of justifying limitations on fundamental rights are presented as implying in terms of fundamental law adjudication the same psychopathological stringency that desires have in the daily life of overexcited individuals: "When I truly want something, then it is absolutely necessary and I will stop at nothing to fulfill my wishes!" The Ordinance may or may not have been deemed constitutional. The argument (or lack thereof) is problematic here.

[29] *Cf.* for instance R. Badinter & S. Breyer (Eds.), Judges in a Democracy – An International Conversation (6-The Judge Confronts Himself as Judge) 275 ff. (2004) and sources cited on this matter in the Introduction.

incapacity of the Commission, perhaps due to its own bureaucratic cognitive limitations,[30] to advance a clear, principled model of reform.[31]

Moreover, the various requirements, benchmarks, suggestions, up to now, have often contradicted each other. In terms of judicial reforms, the Commission seems to want everything at once. Much like a character in a classic Romanian fairy-tale, a nobleman who ordered a villager's daughter to come to his manor "neither dressed nor undressed, neither riding nor walking, neither on the highway nor about it,"[32] the Commission set for the Superior Council of the Magistracy (the Romanian High Council of the Judiciary) simultaneous benchmarks of capacity and accountability, independence and responsibility, efficiency and transparency. The local situation does not allow for this cornucopia of virtues, however. The Council (and the judiciary as such) can either be rendered more politically accountable by legislatively subordinating it, to a certain extent, to the Ministry of Justice, at the risk of political manipulation or – conversely- it can preserve its autonomous position, at the risk of a certain degree of corporatism and unaccountability. Between these two ends, many shades and policy consequences exist on the spectrum, but any choice tilts the balance in one specific direction: accountability comes at the price of independence, political independence, at the price of autonomy.[33]

---

[30] If one accepts Giandomenico Majone's well-known and influential thesis that the "nature" of the European state – nature best represented by the Commission – is economic regulation based on the "independent agency" (governance) model inaugurated by the American regulatory commissions, the predilection of the Commission for political neutrality and neutralizations can perhaps be better understood. *See* G. Majone, Regulating Europe (1996).

[31] *See,* for a the discussion of the 'mythical' character of the Commission's 'political conditionality' requirements, in the context of the Bulgarian judicial independence reforms, D. Smilov, *EU Enlargement and the Constitutional Principle of Judicial Independence, in* W. Sadurski, A. Czarnota & M. Krygier (Eds.), Spreading Democracy and the Rule of Law: The Impact of EU Enlargement on the Rule of Law, Democracy, and Constitutionalism in Post-communist Legal Orders 313 (2006). On the complexities of judicial independence reforms, especially Western reform campaigns, S. Holmes, *Judicial Independence as Ambiguous Reality and Insidious Illusion, in* R. Dworkin (Ed.), From Liberal Values to Democratic Transition: Essays in Honor of János Kis 3 (2004).

[32] The story goes further that, as she came to the lord's manor riding a he-goat, and thus, the goat being short, with her feet dangling on the ground ("neither walking nor riding"), as the goat trotted about in zigzags ("neither on, neither about the highway"), and as she was dressed in a fishermen's net ("neither dressed nor undressed"), the local lord, "astounded by her cleverness" and "being he a bachelor," immediately wedded her in marriage. The Accession parallels are in no need of further elaboration.

[33] *I.e.,* insofar as constitutionally possible to make such legislative changes, which means by now in the Romanian context almost impossible. As a constitution-making task, the institutional matter can be approached in various ways, for instance by factoring a number of distinct political institutions and representative of professional bodies into the equation (*see for instance* the South African Constitution, Art. 178-Judicial Service Commission). It is also possible to not over-specify the attributions in the constitutional text (the Spanish case, Art. 122 of the

The issue of corruption, crusading against which has been a popular post-communist panacea, is fraught with difficulties of its own, insofar as the term often serves as an undefined proxy (misnomer, metaphor, or synecdoche) for a wide range of distinct phenomena and grievances.[34] As the system as such was seemingly perceived to be corrupt, the solution, from the perspective of the Commission, could only be located wholly "outside" of it. It would now appear to be the case that, if proselytizing strategies are dominated by a monomaniac concern that the missions would "go native," the whole project of evangelizing "savages" may be doomed from the start.[35] Within the area of combating high-level corruption, for instance, the Commission supported two political neutral institutions: an autonomous anti-corruption prosecutor's office (the National Anticorruption Directorate) and an independent agency for vetting all public servants' asset declarations, conflicts of interests, and incompatibilities (the National Integrity Agency). A long tradition of entrusting broad administrative and regulatory mandates to independent agencies could have cautioned a measure of skepticism and parsimony in making use of neutral 'governance' mechanisms in order to solve complex systemic problems. Numerous examples existed, after all, with respect to the ways in which such institutions could fail to fulfill their mandate by under- or over-reaching ("ossification"; "tunnel effect") or could be absorbed by the sub-systems they are called to regulate ("capture").[36]

Constitution), so that a certain leeway and political readjustment is possible. The composition of the Romanian Superior Magistracy Council (overwhelmingly elected members of the judiciary and prosecutors) and its main attributions with respect to appointments, promotions, and disciplinary actions are determined by the Constitution. In all these respects, only the Italian *Consiglio Superiore della Magistratura* enjoys a larger degree of constitutionally protected autonomy and insulation from political change. Moreover, so far, the relatively timid legislative efforts to curb the Council's primary attributions and practices – inasmuch as constitutionally possible – or to alter its current composition have been invalidated by the Constitutional Court. In DCC 375/2005 (*supra* note 1), the Court invalidated, for instance, a legislative provision would asked newly-elected members to the Council positions of leadership in the court system or in the prosecutor's offices to relinquish the leadership position upon election or lose their Council nomination. The Court invalidated, arguing that the Constitution implicitly requires prosecutors and judges elected to the Council to preserve their active exercise of their professions (and so also, apparently, their active positions of power), lest they should become pure administrators. A provision requiring sitting judges reaching the general statutory pension age to fully retire from judicial office was invalidated on equality grounds.

[34] *See* A. Sajó, *Corruption, Clientelism, and the Future of the Constitutional State in Eastern Europe*, 7 E. Eur. Const. Rev. 37 (1998). *See also, generally*, A. Czarnota & M. Krygier, *After Postcommunist: The Next Phase*, 2 Annu. Rev. Law Soc. Sci. 299 (2006).

[35] *See* A. Sajó's *Universal Rights, Missionaries, Converts, and Local Savages*, 6 E. Eur. Const. Rev. 44 (1997). András Sajó's observations regarding wholesale one-size-fits-all human rights exports in the 90's apply surprisingly well, *mutatis mutandis*, to the "human rights, democracy, and rule of law" accession process-related exports a decade later.

[36] The classical regulatory pathology argument is M. H. Bernstein, Regulating Business by Independent Commission (1955). These pathologies are primarily related to institutional design

More relevant for our purposes, recourse to independent agencies is very often an admission of foundational uncertainty and indecision. This measure of indecision and uncertainty could be condoned temporarily and tolerated by the system for a variety of reasons; in our case not necessarily all related to the external accession pressures. For instance, new "politically independent" institutions entail political appointments, a bounty that can be distributed equidistantly ("neutrally") across the political spectrum every four or five years. Moreover, since the rationale and responsibility for creating the institution can be 'exported' to Brussels, this represents perfectly democratic spoils and political patronage, with virtually no electoral risks attached. Yet the systemic tolerance that applies to the establishment of such an institution will not necessarily obtain in terms of its actual subsequent performance. A judgment can still be reserved with respect to the integrity commission[37] but the continuous misadventures of the independent prosecutor's office already serve as cautionary tale and a good basis for an early prediction. As the Commission itself did not fail to notice in its progress reports, none of the major corruption indictments reached trial on the merits, as judges invariably returned the major files on various procedural dilatory rationales or referred to the Constitutional Court diverse unconstitutionality exceptions; the Constitutional Court occasionally obliged, invalidating various pieces of anti-corruption legislation.[38]

and therefore not restricted to the area primarily described by Bernstein, social and economic regulation.

[37] The integrity agency was very recently established, after much procrastination and relentless Commission pressures. Perhaps symptomatic, the website of the newly-established agency supports an e-poll survey on whether it had been opportune to establish it at all; one third of those taking this poll said "no" http://www.integritate.eu/?pollvote=9 (last visited 9 December 2008).

[38] *See* the first Cooperation and Verification Report of 27 June 2007 (Report from the Commission to the European Parliament and the Council on Romania's progress on accompanying measures following Accession, COM (2007) 378 final, *available at* http://ec.europa.eu/dgs/secretariat_general/cvm/docs/romania_report_20070627_en.pdf). Here, a measure of impatience is joined with confusion and precatory-hortatory ethical admonitions. For instance, at page 16 of the report, the courts are chastised for lenient and suspended sentences in corruption cases, that is, for not understanding "their essential role in the effort to curb corruption in Romania." One paragraph down, the Commission understands that references to the Constitutional Court are "procedurally correct" but deplores "the tendency of the courts to refer cases to a higher level of jurisdiction instead of dealing with them at a lower level." Yet, the Constitutional Court is not just a higher but also a different level of jurisdiction; within the logic of the system, ordinary courts are not fully authorized to pass judgment on matters of constitutionality and are therefore under a qualified duty to refer exceptions up to the Constitutional Court. What is procedurally correct happens to be substantively and systemically "correct" as well, at least from the operational standpoint of the system, whatever incidental deleterious consequences these actions may have. *But see* de Pauw, *supra* note 4, understanding that it cannot be announced as a legal duty of a court (one may add, at least in the absence of sentencing guidelines) to render harsher corruption sentences.

A certain degree of underperformance of the reform process was to be expected. When one seeks to remedy systemic structural deficiencies of such magnitude and complexity under pressure, one encounters, firstly, overtaxing perception difficulties. Problems have to be reduced to manageable conceptual paradigms – "corruption"; "judicial independence"; "judicial accountability", etc., which could be then translated into institutional design and policy imperatives. A subsequent matter is finding the "objective" "uncorrupted" or "incorruptible" – access points. Last but most important are related issues of synopticism and simultaneity. Namely, the reformers are faced with the perplexing cartographic implications of "drawing a map of the [reforms] on a scale of 1 to 1" while anticipating reactive changes in the scenery.[39] For instance, high-level corruption prosecutions require not only an independent prosecutor's office but also a well-functioning judicial system, presupposing a judiciary which is at the same time politically independent, impartial, professional, and accountable. The problems related to underperformance and abuse of discretion by the High Judicial Council, in turn, represent faithfully the state of the judiciary, a state of facts which itself has multifarious causes and interrelations (the system of legal education is a perhaps more remote but crucial one). No easy solution presents itself, especially as the vested interests within the respective areas have already insulated themselves with the help of various rule of law-derived slogans ("judicial independence"; "separation of powers"; "university autonomy"). Since systems have the capacity to reproduce, even the hope of generational change is of doubtful benefit. Whatever reforms are to be made under these terms could only be the long-run products of contextual empathy, chiseling at the margins, and Weberian political ethics of "strong and slow boring of hard boards." The formalistic missionarism of the Commission and the conspicuous lack of a catechism manual reinforced, for the most part, some local contradictions.

4. Post-Accession Post-Postcommunist Constitutionalism: The Living Tree

While it is true that the term "post-communism" loses its descriptive and conceptual grip on facts the further one moves away from the collapse of state socialism, this primarily means that the related problems of post-communism become yet one more (relevant but not determinant) set of factors to be taken into account, another generation of contradictions.[40]

[39] U. Eco, *On the Impossibility of Drawing a Map of the Empire on a Scale of 1 to 1*, *in* How to Travel with a Salmon & Other Essays 95 (1995).

[40] *See*, on the waning conceptual strength of the term "post-communist," Czarnota & Krygier, *supra* note 31 and A. Sajó, *Pluralism in Post-Communist Law*, 44(1-2) Acta Juridica Hungarica 1 (2003).

From the standpoint of European constitutionalism, these successive generations of tensions have now been internalized and have become, as it were, an equal component of the "common constitutional traditions of the Member States." It is of general interest therefore to see how common traditions are defined by their local keepers, an interest all the more actual ever since European law has also become a matter of constitutional concern for some of its new Members.[41]

The two examples that follow are important not in terms of the particular results reached by the Court but with respect to the methodological consistency and sophistication of the reasoning.

4.1. Human Dignity-Retributive and Repressive Implications

The definitions of the crimes of insult (Article 205) and defamation (Article 206) in the Romanian Criminal Code date back to the original draft of the code, as it was passed in the vintage socialist edification year of 1968. Article 207 provides for a defense of truth in defamation cases "where the statement or allegation was made in order to protect a legitimate interest." This defense is qualified and – of course – it applies only to factual statements.[42] Moreover, courts have construed the requirement of a "legitimate interest" limitatively and in a circular manner, as being coextensive with the degree of factual accuracy of the information provided by the press. Local trial courts interpreted the provisions restrictively, imposing occasionally on journalists generous prison sentences and the attached secondary penalty of disqualification from the

[41] *See,* on how Central and Eastern European Constitutional Courts have started to voice "Solange"-type constitutional reservations with respect to Europe-related domestic legislation (and the paradox entailed by the circumstance that the courts of the new enlargees claim to defend fundamental rights and the rule of law against "Europe," which had been presented – before the Accession – as a civilizer in this respect), W. Sadurski, *"Solange, Chapter 3"– Constitutional Court in Central Europe-Democracy-European Union*, 14(1) Eur. L. J. 1 (2008) and A. Sajó, *Learning Co-operative Constitutionalism the Hard Way: the Hungarian Constitutional Court Shying Away from EU Supremacy*, 2(3) Zeitschrift für Europa- und Staatswissenschaften 351 (2004). The Romanian Constitutional Court took an early and even bolder if perhaps less sophisticated position, asserting competence to review the conformity of implementing competition legislation (state aid to small and medium-sized enterprises in the beer industry) with Art. 87(3) in the EC Treaty. *See* Decizia nr 59 din 17 ianuarie 2007 (M. Of. Nr. 98 din 8 februarie 2007). It is some ground for a measure of apprehensive optimism that the decision was harshly criticized, *see* S. E. Tănăsescu, *Libera concurență [Free Competition-Case Comment]*, 5 Curierul Judiciar 1 (2007).

[42] A Romanian observer notes that the defense of truth has been turned by trial and appellate courts into a requirement of *probatio diabolica*, cf. S. Răduleţu, *Libertatea de exprimare şi limitele ei-Comentarii ale art. 30 din Constituţia României [Freedom of Expression and Its Limits-Comments on Article 30 of the Romanian Constitution]*, 5 Curierul Judiciar 81, at 87 (2007).

exercise of civil rights, large damage awards, and temporary prohibitions on practicing the profession as security measures. As a consequence, Romania lost a number of cases before the European Court of Human Rights, on the ground of Article 10 (freedom of expression) infringements.[43]

Early applications to the Court by way of exceptions of unconstitutionality, raised by defendants in the course of defamation trials, argued that the definitions of the crimes in the two articles and the restrictive nature of the defense instituted an irrebuttable presumption of guilt and thus infringed on the fundamental right to freedom of expression. These complaints were addressed by the Court with the blunt observation that every right entails correlative obligations and that, at any rate, it was within the political purview of the Lawmaker to decriminalize, should the legislative branch so desire: "The lawmaker alone should decide whether insult should or not be decriminalized. If the legislative branch decides in favor of incrimination, one cannot maintain that the [Criminal Code] provision infringes on the Constitution."[44]

When, in 2006, the lawmaker exercised this unfettered freedom of decision and abrogated the provisions, a number of plaintiffs raised exceptions of unconstitutionality on various grounds, arguing primarily that their constitutionally protected dignity rights had been infringed and that a "legislative void" had been created by decriminalization.[45] It should be noted that, if these acts are not incriminated, civil redress will still be available in tort law, under the general tortious liability provision of Article 998 in the Civil Code.[46] All trial court judges referring these exceptions recommended, in line with the previous decisions, that the exceptions should not be admitted.

[43] *See, e.g*, Dalban v.România [GC], Judgment of 28 September 1999, ECHR 1999-VI and Cumpănă and Mazăre v. România [GC], Judgment of 17 December 2004, (2005) 41 EHRR 14.

[44] Decizia nr. 200/1999 (M. Of. Nr. 58 din 8 februarie 2000) and Decizia nr. 40 din 7 februarie 2002 (M. Of. 243 din 10 aprilie 2002). The Court seems to adhere to the Marxian understanding of human rights according to which any fundamental right is accompanied by an equal and correlative duty of the right-holder (I have the right to work and the duty to work..). See, in this respect, Decizia 108/1995 (M. Of. Nr. 9 din 17 ianuarie 1995), on an exception of unconstitutionality regarding the application of Art. 325 in the Criminal Code (Distribution of obscene materials). On that occasion, the Court took the opportunity to declare that the alleged conflict between morality and art is "a false [constitutional] problem," given that what is of interest "are not the means utilized by the artist but the object as such, the work of art" and the work of art could never be "offensive to human dignity by excessive vulgarity, lubricity, and prurient nature. Such creations cannot be called works of art but rather, just as our criminal legislation defines them, materials of obscene character." The Romanian artist has, in short, a clear constitutional right and duty to create pretty art.

[45] When the articles were abrogated, the provisions had been already amended to eliminate the prison penalty and both crimes carried only criminal fine penalties.

[46] "Every act of man that causes damage to another obliges him by whose fault it happened to remedy it."

However, the Court reversed its decision and decreed that the Lawmaker, who in 1999 was constitutionally free to do as it pleased, was now, in early January 2007, under a constitutional obligation to re-incriminate: "The Court cannot agree with the opinion [of the referring judges] that the abrogation of Arts. 205, 206, and 207 in the Criminal Code is the option of the legislator as a matter of penal policy and that, consequently, the exception would be without merit … The legislative leeway that Parliament has in such cases can only be exercised by regulating the conditions of incrimination for antisocial acts that infringe upon the values guaranteed by the Constitution."[47]

The reasoning appears to rest on three main arguments. Firstly, the Court observed that Article 30 (Freedom of expression) entailed limitation clauses and that among these limitations was "the dignity … of a person"; the Court noted also that dignity, as proclaimed by Article 1 of the Constitution, was a "supreme value."[48] Supreme values trump all subordinate ones. Secondly, the Court pointed out that Article 30 imposed a criminalization duty on the legislator since, as it was clearly stated in Section 8 of that Article: "Indictable offences of the press shall be established by law." The Court summated the first two rationales, in a sociologically-inclined passage, worth citing at length: "Should such deeds not be discouraged through the specific means of criminal law, they would trigger a *de facto* reaction of those offended and they would lead to permanent conflicts, such that social life […] would be impossible. This is why these values, sheltered by the Criminal Code, have gained constitutional status, human dignity being enshrined in the Constitution, Art. 1 (3), as a *supreme value*."[49] Thirdly, the Romanian constitutional judges observed, an argument regarding tort liability was inapposite, since it did not appease the victim of the crime:

> [R]ecourse to civil redress, grounded on the provisions of Art. 998 of the Civil Code, does not constitute an adequate legal protection since dishonor is by nature irreparable and human dignity cannot be evaluated in money or compensated by material means.[50]

According to the third argument, since dishonor is by nature irreparable, money does not rectify damage to dignity, hence decriminalization would place the victim (who could not find adequate satisfaction) at a disadvantage.

From one standpoint or another, most of these notions can of course be perceived as interrelated. Even though the retributive theory of criminal law

---

[47] Decizia 62 din 18 ianuarie 2007 (M.Of. nr. 104/12 feb. 2007).

[48] Art. 1(3) reads: "Romania is a democratic and social state, governed by the rule of law, in which human dignity, the citizens' rights and freedoms, the free development of human personality, justice and political pluralism represent supreme values, in the spirit of the democratic traditions of the Romanian people and the ideals of the Revolution of December 1989, and shall be guaranteed."

[49] DCC 62/2007, *supra* note 47.

[50] *Id.*

is no longer in academic fashion, a plausible correlation can be made between human revenge instincts and the advent of modern criminal law. In this respect, the Romanian Constitutional Court would be in the select company of Oliver Wendell Holmes and Sir James Fitzjames Stephen.[51] It is also possible to identify theoretical parallels between the notion of human dignity, dignitary interests, and constitutional limitations on free speech.[52] Broad sociological-legal correlations between honor, honor-related satisfaction rituals, the rise of the notion of human dignity, and criminalized limits on speech have been observed.[53]

However, from a constitutional law standpoint, the entire panoply (personal dignity as a limitation on the fundamental right to free speech; human dignity as paramount constitutional value; the subjective reputational and dignitary interests of an individual; and the natural human desire for revenge) cannot be "sheltered by the Criminal Code" in the same way. Human dignity, "bricolated" from Article 1(1) the German Basic Law into the Romanian general principles provision, is legally absolute (*i.e.*, trumping other considerations and therefore precluding balancing) in its jurisdiction of origin or paramount in other importing jurisdictions only in the restricted sense of its original Kantian intellectual source. Namely, the legal order cannot instrumentalize individuals and treat them merely as objects.[54] The "dignity" as a justifiable limitation on speech is not, that is to say, as "absolute" as that "dignity" which we

[51] According to a famous statement by the latter, "the criminal law stands to the passion of revenge in much the same relation as marriage and sexual appetite." Quoted in O. W. Holmes, The Common Law 41 (1881).

[52] *See, e.g.*, W. Brugger, *The Treatment of Hate Speech in German Constitutional Law (I & II)*, 3 & 4 German Law Journal 12 &1 (2002-2003).

[53] *See* J. Q. Whitman, *Enforcing Civility and Respect: Three Societies*, 109 Yale L. J. 1279 (1999-2000) and *On Nazi "Honor" and the New European "Dignity"*, *in* C. Joerges & N. S. Ghaleigh (2003), Darker Legacies of Law in Europe: The Shadow of National Socialism and Fascism over Europe and Its Legal Traditions 243 (2003).

[54] The dignity clause of Art. 1(1) ("Human dignity shall be inviolable. To respect and protect it shall be the duty of all state authority.") does not contain any limitation clause. *See* definition of the "object-formula" BVerfGE 45, 187 (Lebenslange Freiheitsstrafe). *See also* the recent decision in BVerfGE 115, 118 (Luftsicherheitsgesetz) and comments on it and the dignity clause in O. Lepsius, *Human Dignity and the Downing of Aircraft: The German Federal Constitutional Court Strikes Down a Prominent Anti-terrorism Provision in the New Air-Transport Security Act*, 7 German Law Journal 761 (2006) and M. Ladiges, *Comment – Oliver Lepsius's Human Dignity and the Downing of Aircraft: The German Federal Constitutional Court Strikes Down a Prominent Anti-terrorism Provision in the New Air-transport Security Act*, 8 German Law Journal 307 (2007). *See*, treatment of dignity as "imported" into EU law, Case C-36/02, Omega Spielhallen- und Automatenaufstellungs-GmbH v. Oberbürgermeisterin der Bundesstadt Bonn [2004] ECR I-9609, where the ECJ restricts its proportionality analysis to a consideration of legitimate aim, suitability, and necessity (i.e., without going into a balancing of dignity against fundamental freedom), apparently "internalizing" the degree of protection afforded human dignity in German constitutional law.

can find in Article 1 (3) of the Romanian Constitution, apparent homonymy notwithstanding. Likewise, as the reader may have already anticipated, the constitutional requirement of express statutory provision for press offenses is a long-fought desideratum of liberalism and a protection of freedom of press rather than – as the judges take it to be – a constitutional imperative of criminal repression. Finally, as the two dissenting judges also noted, should one treat the dignity or honor of the victim as a subjective matter (what constitutes satisfactory reparation to the victim of an insult), and starting from the constitutional premise that dignity cannot be evaluated in monetary terms, it is not apparent why criminal punishment would offer acceptable satisfaction.

Many Romanian jurists could reconcile the apparent tensions in the reasoning, by noting that the crucial passage of the majority decision was strikingly similar to a famous 50's "Guideline Decision" of the Supreme Tribunal of the People's Republic of Romania. That decision, well-known to the contemporary readers of more historically-inclined tort textbooks, instructed trial courts to no longer award pecuniary compensation for non-pecuniary damages, since such awards of "moral damages" were incompatible with socialist morality: "One cannot conceive the payment of a sum of money as equivalent to human suffering. The compensation for injuries of an immaterial nature is adequately ensured through the imposition of punitive measures on the offender, by publishing the conviction decisions, and by all other means adequate to the way in which the moral damage was caused."[55]

Some could deem it constitutionally inappropriate that the Court paraphrases nowadays Stalinist-era jurisprudence. Critics could however be appeased by the fact that the guideline decision of the Supreme Tribunal was also a constitutional one, based on the horizontal (third-party) effect of the honor-related clause of Article 15 in the 1952 Constitution of the People's Republic of Romanian,[56] a public norm which at that time permeated private civil law relations still governed by the bourgeois order of the 1864 Civil Code. Human dignity, a true universal, is accordingly assured nowadays a treatment of constitutional continuity, spanning over three constitutions (1952, 1965, 1991), one constitutional amendment (2003), and at least three major system transformations (state socialism, post-communism, and European, respectively).[57]

[55] Decizia de Îndrumare nr. VII a Tribunalului Suprem al Republicii Populare România, Culegere de decizii (Vol. I) 25-26 (1952-1954).

[56] Art. 15 read: "In the People's Republic of Romania work is a duty and a matter of honor for any capable citizen, according to the principle 'who does not work, does not eat.' In the People's Republic of Romania the principle 'from each according to his ability, to each according to his need' is ever broader realized."

[57] It is not my intention to imply that, since part of a Communist-era judgment from the 1950's is paraphrased in a 2007 decision, the judges would be crypto-Marxists. The justices are no more inclined towards Marxian legal theories than they are liberally – or indeed theoretically – inclined towards any comprehensive worldview of constitutional interpretation. The permeation

4.2. Public Dignity – The Protective Dimensions

Constitutions can be very versatile documents. If human dignity has, in contemporary Romanian constitutional law, vindictive-retributive implications in need to be sheltered by the Criminal Code, public dignity is a paramount constitutional value that needs to be, inasmuch as possible, sheltered from it.

The fight against corruption has always been a pillar of the accession process and continues to be the most important benchmark of the Cooperation and Verification Mechanism. Certainly, corruption as such may be a nebulous, perhaps legally intractable socio-cultural and historical phenomenon. Framing the issue as fighting ministerial corruption however brings the matter into clearer focus and within manageable legal scope. The relevant constitutional provision, Article 109, is also rather comprehensible:

> (2) Only the Chamber of Deputies, the Senate and the President of Romania have the right to demand that legal proceedings be taken against members of the Government for acts committed during the course of exercising their official duties. If such legal proceedings have been requested, the President of Romania may decree that they be suspended from office. The commencement of criminal proceedings against a member of the Government entails his suspension from office. The case shall be within the competence of the High Court of Cassation and Justice.
>
> (3) Cases of liability, and penalties applicable to members of the Government shall be regulated by a law on ministerial responsibility.[58]

The Law on Ministerial Responsibility, in its original 1999 form,[59] provided that the same degree of protection in regard of lifting procedural immunity before commencing criminal investigations would apply to actual and former ministers with respect to prosecution for crimes committed in office. This caused a measure of consternation: a 2004 stand-by agreement with the IMF, GRECO recommendations, and the 2004 Country Report of the Commission all required the lifting of former ministers' immunity from criminal prosecution.[60] Belatedly, in 2005, an Emergency Ordinance was passed, amending the law, so that former members of Government would be stripped of this procedural

of Marxian theory was purely lexical and superficial in Romanian legal education. This passage is only an indicator of "bricolated" constitutional interpretation and of the possible sources of bricolage (a mixture mostly of rudimentary textualism and various interspersed idiosyncrasies, prejudices, and stereotypes surfacing randomly).

[58] Official translation of the Constitution which can be accessed on the website of the Chamber of Deputies: http://www.cdep.ro/pls/dic/site.page?den=act2_2&par1=3#t3c3s0a109.

[59] L. nr. 115 din 28 iunie 1999 privind responsabilitatea ministerială (M.Of. nr. 300/28 iunie 1999; amended, republished, M. Of. nr. 334/20 mai 2002; M.Of. 200/23 mar. 2007).

[60] *See* 2004 Regular Report on Romania's progress towards accession (COM (2004) 657 final) at 22-23, *available at* http://ec.europa.eu/enlargement/archives/pdf/key_documents/2004/rr_ro_2004_en.pdf.

immunity and subject to the general rules of criminal procedure. Charges were subsequently brought against a number of former ministers.

An exception of unconstitutionality raised in the course of an ensuing criminal trial reached the Court in July 2007, the petitioner arguing, among others, that restriction of the procedural immunity to incumbent ministers discriminated against former members of the government and infringed on the constitutional requirement of non-retroactivity, the right to equality before the law, and the right to a fair trial. The Court agreed on all three counts. The skeptical observer could point out that only substantive changes in the definition of a crime or in the penalty provision must not retroactivate. This is arguably one of the specific corollaries of the *nulla poena sine lege* principle that "no conduct shall be held criminal unless it is clearly specified in the behavior-circumstance element of a penal statute."[61] The Court anticipated such fastidious reservations observing that:

> Given the finality of such procedure, namely to protect the ministerial mandate exercised by Members of Government, and consequently to shelter the public interest, it must be considered as the more favorable to the accused, in the meaning of Art. 15 (2) of the Constitution, and thus in derogation from general law.[62]

Thus, a procedural exception designed to protect the mandate, by ensuring that acting ministers are not maliciously harassed in the exercise of their in office by politically-motivated, vexatious prosecutions, is transformed into a substantive criminal procedure guarantee ostensibly aimed at equity in individual cases. Our skeptic may have also inquired into the precise meaning of equality in this setting. Equality, this most arcane of constitutional quandaries, does in the abstract mean treating likes alike. But how are former ministers alike present ministers, in terms of the application of onerous procedural immunities, exceptions from the general criminal due process guarantees? Since special procedural protections of the mandate, deriving from separation of powers considerations, are not a personal privilege attached to a title, extending them to former officeholders appears, contrariwise, to be a privilege. To be stripped of a privilege is arguably not discrimination but rather the purest form of equality, which subjects all citizens indiscriminately to the equal application of the Criminal Procedure Code. Nonetheless, in the Court's interpretation, it is the ministerial mandate itself that renders them objectively equal and elevates all ministers equally above "the arbitrary criterion … of the moment of commencing criminal investigations."[63] It would be therefore, the Court followed, also an infringement of the right to a fair trial not give all ministers, past and present, the benefit of the same procedural guarantees.

[61] J. Hall, *Nulla Poena Sine Lege*, 47 Yale L. J. 166 (1937-1938).

[62] Decizia nr. 665 din 5 iulie 2007 (M.Of. nr. 547 din 10.08.2007).

[63] *Id.*

Our skeptic would now seek in vain, with the help of his narrow earthly dichotomies, to pin down the true nature of ministerial responsibility. Ministerial responsibility in Romanian constitutional law has acquired a dual nature, which transcends trivial theoretical hairsplitting and legalistic-doctrinaire minutiae. While it is simultaneously substantive and procedural, a criminal procedural guarantee and a protection of the mandate, an individual, personal, subjective right and a collective, impersonal, objective protection, it evades preexisting taxonomies. Public dignity, the dignity of office, for the fortunate few who partook of it, accompanies them indefinitely thereafter, like a higher, collective self.[64]

The second constitutional question pondered on by the Court concerned determining which institution could lift the immunity and trigger prosecution. Constitutionally, the matter seemed prima facie rather uncontroversial: the President, the Chamber of Deputies, or the Senate could each exercise this right. The Law on Ministerial Responsibility established a procedural framework. In its original form, the law provided that the President would decide, following a request to authorize prosecution by the Prime Minister, the Prosecutor General of the Prosecutor's Office attached to the High Court of Cassation and Justice, or the Head Prosecutor of the National Anticorruption Directorate. The President would make a final decision based on the recommendation of a special commission attached to the Presidential Administration. The final decision to authorize commencement of criminal investigations would be forwarded to the Minister of Justice. Where the minister was also a Member of Parliament, the request would be forwarded to the respective House. Each House could also authorize or request prosecution (either based on the presidential request or independently, of its own motion), deciding in Committee of the Whole, following a judicialized procedure (summons, hearing, etc.). The parliamentary debates would be based on the report of a standing or special inquiry committee of the respective House.[65]

In mid-January 2008, the Minister of Justice received authorizations from the President regarding commencement of prosecutions in the case of

[64] *See generally* E. Kantorowicz, The King's Two Bodies: A Study in Mediaeval Political Theology (1957).

[65] The law was amended by an emergency ordinance in 2007 to "judicialize" the procedure of the presidential advisory committee (requiring that its members be judges and follow a quasi-judicial procedure). Following an "exception of unconstitutionality" raised by the Ombudsman, the Constitutional Court declared both the amendment and the initial presidential committee procedure unconstitutional, on rule of law (judicialization of these procedures would create a pretrial, indeed pre-prosecution, presumption of guilt) and separation of powers considerations (unconstitutional condition to the presidential prerogative and encroachment on the independence and impartiality of the judiciary). *See* Decizia Nr. 1133 din 27 noiembrie 2007 (M.Of. nr 851/12 noiembrie 2007). Since this decision is unproblematic and since its overall argument is tangential to the issues discussed here, these developments are in no need of commenting further.

seven current or former ministers. The two Houses of Parliament and the High Council of the Magistracy immediately petitioned the Constitutional Court, asking that the initial requests for prosecution and all the case files be forwarded to Parliament for prior approval. The petitioners pointed out that four of the respective former and current ministers were at the time also Members of Parliament. As Article 109(2) gives all three institutions the right to authorize commencement of criminal investigations, this could only mean, the petitioners argued, that they should act in tandem or that there should be an order of preference with respect to former or current Ministers who are also MPs, such as the law had initially established.

A majority of the Court agreed, noting that Article 109(2) does not provide a clear rule but rather is "a synthetic formula" which provides "a procedural norm of constitutional principle value"[66] in need to be 'optimized' in terms of other constitutional principles and values.[67] The problem had to be analyzed therefore in the broader context of balance of powers . The Court observed that the first section of Article 109 concerns political collective responsibility of the Government as such, whereas the other two sections deal with individual criminal responsibility of the ministers. This textual proximity could not be coincidental. Indeed, the Court noticed, whereas the President appoints a new Government, the Government has to obtain a vote of confidence in Parliament before investiture.

Analogously, in the case of criminal prosecution for malfeasance in office, a balance between the branches of power should be established. The enumeration in Article 109 instituted therefore neither an alternative, nor a priority or a cumulative competence. This could, said the Court, be perceived clearly by observing the specific use of the conjunction "and":

> As regards the use of the conjunction 'and,' in the text of Article 109 (2) it signifies the end of an enumeration, which confers on all three authorities an independent attribution. The constitutional text excludes both an alternative competence of these three public authorities, and a cumulative competence thereof.[68]

The truth could only lie in the proverbial middle and, as the Court further observed, the Constitution institutes no incompatibility between a ministerial appointment and MP elective status. This could only mean that the Prosecutor General of the Prosecutor's Office attached to the High Court of Cassation and

[66] Decizia nr. 270 din 10 martie 2008 (M. Of. 290/15 aprilie 2008) [emphasis in original].

[67] This is perhaps an unusual procedural gloss on Alexyan theory. *See* R. Alexy, A Theory of Constitutional Rights (2002), arguing that the constitutional necessity to balance arises from the fact that, unlike rule-norms, that "can be fulfilled or not" (i.e., the application of one to a given factual situation excludes the application of another), constitutional rights provisions are principle-norms, imposing on the judge an optimization requirement in cases of collision and, consequently, the recourse to the balancing methodology.

[68] DCC 270/2008, *supra* note 66.

Justice would need to ask the President to authorize the prosecution of current or former ministers who are not at the time of the request MPs, the Senate in the case of Senator (former or current) members of Government, the Chamber of Deputies in the case of Deputies, respectively. *Suum cuique tribuere*, each is given his own, as the old adage goes.

5. Borderline European Constitutionalism: Substantive, Formal, and Reflexive Elements

The judges of the Romanian Constitutional Court are not to be excessively blamed, though their newfound activism and syncopated reasoning might disturb the esthetic sensitivities of a few more demanding observers.

At the beginning of the past decade, when the new constitution was being assembled together from momentary compromises and hastily translated pieces of foreign texts, the justices and their generational colleagues in the constitutional drafting committee may have pondered over the overall meaning of the resulting puzzle. No one had been educated on such matters for more than fifty years. They may have secretly hoped that, in time, the deeper sense of those new and unfamiliar expressions would be revealed to them: "separation of powers"; "judicial independence"; "accountability"; "equality"; "dignity." What could these exotic phrases possibly mean? For all the talk around such matters, surely the words had great significance. Deeper levels of meaning and subtle historical and philosophical understandings (which one could only acquire with much effort and time) must have lain underneath.

Many years after, along with the long-awaited occasion to join Europe, the opportunity and obligation to learn presented itself. Everyone was now to be educated on the correct meaning of rule of law, democracy, and respect for human rights, as part of a mandatory intensive lecture in constitutionalism, with many midterms and a severe final examination. After graduation, teacher and pupil would be equal in knowledge.

As the course wore on, it became however clearer that the lecturer knew little more than the pupils and, when a certificate of completion was granted, the judges and their colleagues drew the new lesson to its ultimate conclusion. There was little more to constitutionalism than a text, and an open-ended text full of vague terms at that, to be interpreted freely, as the case and the place may be. They were equal purveyors of world constitutionalism and, from now on, they needn't take their lessons from someone or somewhere else. Their only guiding light would be now the text and perhaps a general sense of justice (and opportunity).

Now that the justices and their peers are all members of a larger graduate seminar in European constitutionalism, it can be hoped that in time they and their counterparts will acquire a measure of reflexive ability of dealing with and accommodating difference; probably a few asperities will be tactically smoothed over. But what the larger audience will learn from the seminar proceedings can from now on only be presumed.